W9-AAV-474

PRAISE FOR
GAME CHANGER

"I've interviewed many entrepreneurs over the years, and Rob Angel's journey is among the most compelling. *Game Changer* not only tells the incredible story of how Pictionary came to be, but shows us all that with impassioned perseverance, we can achieve whatever we put our minds to."

—JJ RAMBERG, former host of MSNBC's *Your Business*, and co-founder of Goodpods

"Rob exemplifies the courage, determination, and focus it takes to win big at business and life while never wavering in his love of the game. Rob's *Game Changer* serves as a guidepost for anyone who wants to know what it takes to be the best."

—WARREN MOON, Hall of Fame quarterback

"This book is a rare example in which philosophy meets actionable steps. I highly recommend it."

—DR. GREG REID, author of *Wealth Made Easy*

"I have such fond memories of playing Pictionary with friends and family that as I read *Game Changer*, I felt like I was right there with Rob, rooting for him as he sketched out every step of how his iconic game came to be. If you love Pictionary, you'll fall in love with the story—and the man—behind it."

—JOSIE BISSETT, actress and author of award-winning *Tickle Monster* and *Boogie Monster*

"When Pictionary launched, toy sales were driven by TV and PR. Rob Angel took a different path. He tirelessly led in-store game demonstrations and engaged directly with consumers. Rob's grassroots approach led to Pictionary becoming one of the hottest board games the toy industry had ever seen. Read this book and learn what it takes for a novice to become legendary."

—JIM SILVER, CEO and editor in chief of TTPM (Toys, Tots, Pets & More)

"Many of the most successful brands are born out of a genuine desire to create joy for others. Rob Angel has done just that with Pictionary for tens of millions of people worldwide. *Game Changer* is a pure joy to read."

—FRANK SHANKWITZ, creator and
co-founder of Make-A-Wish Foundation

"As the creator of Pictionary, Rob Angel's unbelievable life story has impacted millions of people worldwide. *Game Changer* offers a rare look into the creation of a cultural phenomenon and serves as an encouraging blueprint for entrepreneurs. I couldn't put this book down."

—DAVE MELTZER, author of *Game-Time*
Decision Making: High-Scoring Business Strategies
from the Biggest Names in Sports

"Pictionary is much more than a game. It's a report card on the power of communication, creativity, and playful interaction. A must-read for every entrepreneur who wants to turn a simple idea into a multimillion-dollar enterprise—and who is crazy enough to believe he or she can change the world!"

—DAN CLARK, author of *The Art of Significance*

"*Game Changer* is the perfect title for this book, as it is just that. A powerful and riveting read, Rob Angel's story is not only inspiring, but it shows how taking that first step really matters in changing your prosperity course and, very possibly, impacting the rest of the world. Rob did it, and you can too."

—DAVID CORBIN, *Wall Street Journal* bestselling
author of *Preventing BrandSlaughter* and *Illuminate:*
Harnessing the Positive Power of Negative Thinking

GAME
CHANGER

www.amplifypublishing.com

Game Changer: The Story of Pictionary and How I Turned a Simple Idea into the Bestselling Board Game in the World

For more information, please contact:
Amplify Publishing, an imprint of Mascot Books
620 Herndon Parkway #320
Herndon, VA 20170
info@mascotbooks.com

Library of Congress Control Number: 2020901848

CPSIA Code: PRV0320A
ISBN-13: 978-1-64307-497-9

Printed in the United States

To Sam and Ben, who
give me so much to be
grateful for.

GAME CHANGER

THE STORY OF PICTIONARY AND HOW I TURNED
A SIMPLE IDEA INTO THE BESTSELLING
BOARD GAME IN THE WORLD

ROB ANGEL
CREATOR OF
PICTIONARY®

AUTHOR'S NOTE

A few of the personal scenes in this book have been adjusted to accommodate the effect of the passage of time on the clarity of memories. Additionally, the sequence of a couple of events have been slightly shuffled for a more seamless story flow. Otherwise, what you are about to read is a true story.

CONTENTS

PART III: END GAME

FIRST, A WORD

Not every great business or invention starts with a big dream. Mine didn't.

I'm the creator of Pictionary, the bestselling board game in the world that sprang from a simple idea.

After graduating college in 1982 with a business degree, I had no grand plan. No wide-eyed vision of my future. And I certainly wasn't a genius; I'd barely graduated. I was just a normal, everyday guy waiting tables, making two bucks an hour, plus tips.

I was in my early twenties and wasn't passionate about anything—yet. I walked through life saying "YES" to adventures and opportunities as often as I could. Grabbing one of those opportunities changed the trajectory of my life.

My roommates and I played a simple drawing game we called "charades on paper." We stayed up until all hours of the night sketching words for each other to guess while laughing hysterically. It was the most fun part of my day.

Eventually, I moved to Seattle, hoping the big city would inspire my career destiny. But as the weeks and months went by, I was still waiting tables, missing those game nights and connecting with my friends.

And that's when it hit me. *Maybe the career I'd been waiting for was right there in front of me. Maybe, I could turn our game night activity into a real board game.*

In that moment, a rush came over me like nothing I'd ever experienced; I knew instantly that I had found my something to believe in.

But the whole idea was nearly derailed. It didn't take long for self-doubt to set in. I panicked. *Who am I to create a board game? I am just a waiter.* I knew nothing about the toy and game industry and had no idea where to begin. It took some time, but eventually, I shook off my fears and took the easiest first step I could think of.

I grabbed a pen, a pad of paper, and opened my old, worn-out *Merriam Webster* pocket dictionary. Scanning the first page, I wrote down the first word I thought would be perfect to draw. And, there it was. "Aardvark."

By writing down that one simple word, my big dream had begun.

"Finding my aardvark" ignited my passion for developing the game that would change my life, and the lives of countless others. Nothing could stop me from making Pictionary a reality, not even my very real limitations of money, talent, and skill.

I was on my way and, almost immediately, the people I needed to handle what I couldn't do on my own presented themselves. A fellow waiter, Gary Everson, was the first to join me on the adventure, designing the game board, game pieces, and packaging. Next, a friend of a friend, Terry Langston, came on board to manage the business and operations. I did what I excelled at: sales and marketing.

We quickly learned, however, how little we knew. And it was a lot. There was no manual on how to do any of this, no internet to consult. So, we made up our own manual, completing one task at a time, putting one foot in front of the other. Our North Star was trusting our guts and instincts, then letting the chips fall where they may.

With a $35,000 investment, we assembled the first 1,000 games by hand in my tiny apartment. After a year of development, Terry, Gary and I launched Pictionary on June 1, 1985 at the restaurant where I was still waiting tables.

From that moment on, I barely caught my breath. I'd sell games out of my car. I'd convince stores that didn't carry games to sell *our* game. I did game demonstrations hundreds of times, and was on my feet for hours every day. I did whatever it took to succeed.

As we moved forward on a path none of us had ventured on before, we met generous mentors who guided us through a maze of obstacles. Overcoming each challenge made every small victory that much more rewarding. Our love for Pictionary, our vision of the future, and the bond we created with each other grew stronger and stronger.

IN JUNE 2001, SEVENTEEN YEARS after I'd "found my aardvark," we sold Pictionary to Mattel, the toy giant. During the seventeen years Gary, Terry, and I owned and nurtured Pictionary's growth, we sold an astounding 38,000,000 games across 60 countries in 45 languages. For most of those years, no other board game sold more than Pictionary. And we did it all with just two employees.

I call it my seventeen-year start-up.

In that span of time, we produced two TV shows and brought an additional 10 versions to market, including Pictionary Jr., Second Edition, *The Simpsons,* and *Austin Powers.* Sitcoms, including *Friends* and *Facts of Life,* featured Pictionary. And who can forget the Pictionary scene in *When Harry Met Sally?* Mini-games were co-branded with household names like Post Alpha-Bits cereal and Kraft Macaroni and Cheese. My personal favorite tie-in was when Pictionary was displayed on a champagne bottle in France—got to love that!

The list goes on and on.

MY PICTIONARY DREAM BEGAN WITH the simple intention of creating a game so entertaining and engaging that people would love playing it with their family and friends as much as I loved to. I wanted to share that experience with the world.

And speaking of experiences, in this book I share all the hard-won life and business lessons I've learned along my remarkable journey with Pictionary. I share all the victories and failures, ups and downs, and everything in between, so that one day you too can "find your aardvark."

This is not a "How-to" book. It's a "You can, too" book. If there's anything creating Pictionary has taught me, it's that if you're willing to take even a small step toward your potential, you'll open your life up to infinite possibilities. One in which a waiter from Spokane, Washington, can turn his ordinary life into an extraordinary one.

I grabbed an opportunity the universe threw my way and turned it into something that changed the world.

Let me draw you a picture . . .

PART I
DRAWING THE FUTURE

BEFORE PICTIONARY

On what otherwise would have been a typical day in February 1978, my fate changed.

I was a sophomore at Western Washington University College of Business and Economics. Jimmy Carter was our president; the Bee Gees' soundtrack to *Saturday Night Fever* was topping the Billboard charts; *Happy Days*, *Three's Company*, and *Charlie's Angels* were TV hits; and Marlena Evans and Don Craig were finally engaged.

If you're unfamiliar with the latter names, they were characters on *Days of Our Lives,* my favorite NBC soap opera. I was so obsessed with the show that I'd often choose to stay in my dorm and watch it instead of going to class. These were days before VCRs, let alone DVRs, so how could I go to class without knowing if Marlena and Don would put off the wedding of the century yet again?

Unfortunately, *Days of Our Lives** wasn't my only college-days diversion. There were girls and beer, too. I was either going to class hungover and not paying attention or skipping it altogether.

---

* Years later, on a flight from North Carolina to Seattle, I sat in first class next to none other than Drake Hogestyn, the star of *Days of Our Lives* who played John Black. Still a fan of the show, I was wildly excited to talk with him and get the inside scoop on future plotlines. He chuckled and thanked me when I told him about my obsession with the show, but he did not take responsibility for my poor grades.

And so, on this otherwise typical day, I was not entirely surprised to receive notice from the WWU administration that I was being placed on academic probation. One more quarter of my nonsense and I'd be sent packing.

In my room later that night, I was trying to figure out how to tell my parents about my probation, when the phone rang. My now very atypically bad day was about to get much worse.

My father was calling with his own bad news.

"I was fired today, Robbie," Dad said matter-of-factly.

"*What?*" I managed to say after a moment to let the shock wear off.

It felt like the rug had been pulled out from under me, let alone from under my dad. *How could it be?* I thought. My father had a really important job as president of Alaska Steel & Supply, a pretty big company that even as a small child I knew was a big deal. *He* was a big deal.

Through a fog, I heard Dad say something about a strong difference of opinion with the owner of the company . . . something about the direction of the business.

"I don't understand," I said. "Eight years with the company and just like that, it's over? That's it?"

"Yes, Robbie," my father responded coolly. "That's it. I was summarily let go."

I was still in a haze of disbelief when I heard my father say something about my college tuition fees.

"Starting next year, I'll no longer be able to pay your tuition and expenses," he said. "You'll have to pay your own way if you want to continue at WWU."

My stomach fell. How was I supposed to get my grades back up *and* pay for school?

But in that moment, paying tuition wasn't what was most unsettling. My worldview, as I knew it, had changed. My dad, whom I idealized, was no longer employed.

And I was on my own. With no net.

I felt very far from my cozy childhood.

BORN IN VANCOUVER, BRITISH COLUMBIA, I was the third child of Beryl and Don Angel and the younger brother of sister Leslie and brother Harvey. As a toddler, we moved to Kimberley, British Columbia, and moved again when I was five across the American border to Spokane, Washington, where our baby sister, Jackie, was born a year later.

Our family of six settled into a split-level house on a suburban cul-de-sac, in a safe, family-friendly neighborhood. My brother, Harvey, and I joined the close-knit group of twenty-five neighborhood kids who'd gather in each other's homes on the weekends and play board games like Clue, Monopoly, and Risk—the game I dominated.

In the summer, we'd ride bikes and play outdoor games like kick the can and capture the flag. Even our parents got involved in the fun. Our annual Fourth of July "Kids vs. Parents" baseball game was a highlight. The grownups always won—because they always cheated—and we let them.

Growing up in this loving, nurturing environment gave me a strong sense of friendship, connection, and belonging. The carefree joy of playing and having fun with friends and family left an indelible mark—one that years later would open me up to the idea that inspired Pictionary.

AFTER A FEW YEARS IN Spokane, my father's sales prowess led him to a senior management position at Alaska Steel & Supply, an impressive operation. Alaska owned the largest scrap metal yard in town, a huge fabric store, and a monstrous hardware store.

One summer, my dad needed thousands of metal screws manually removed from some funky electronic equipment. He recruited me and two other kids from the neighborhood for the task, warning us that it would be a tedious, backbreaking job that needed to be completed over the next couple of days.

I was up for the task; this was my chance to impress my father. If I did, I might have the opportunity to get hired to work at Alaska that summer, full time. This job was coveted, and I'd have to earn a spot just like anybody else.

Over the next two incredibly hot eight-hour days, I worked my ass off, unscrewing most of the screws myself. The project manager, who had no idea I was Don Angel's son, took notice of how hard I worked and reported to my father about the kid with grit, tenaciousness, and eagerness to work hard. The manager also told him that if it were *his* decision, he'd hire me right then and there.

I got the full-time job.

From eighth grade through high school, I'd spend my summer breaks doing odd jobs at Alaska, from stocking shelves to cutting bolts of fabric. My favorite job was helping customers on the floor, doing my best to emulate my dad's sales charm.

I noticed the respect the employees showed my father. He looked impressive behind his desk. It made me proud to be his son. It also gave me the motivation to want to follow in his footsteps and someday be the big boss, too.

For now, though, earning a paycheck every summer gave me a sense of accomplishment and independence. I felt empowered by no longer being beholden to my parents to pay for the things I wanted, like a new, cooler, faster bike. This early life lesson of working hard to earn my freedom was one that I'd embrace throughout my life.

EXCEPT, THAT IS, UNTIL I got to WWU and quickly became distracted by a different kind of freedom: college life. I fell into it easily. Because my parents were paying my tuition and room and board and giving me a stipend, I had lost my motivation to earn my own money and get good grades. I was lazy. Now, with one phone call, I was on the edge of losing the college education I'd been taking for granted just hours earlier.

The moment I hung up the phone with my father, something inside me switched back on.

His firing made me resolve to never work for "the man." *I* would be the man and in charge of my own destiny. I'd never be beholden to a boss who had total and somewhat arbitrary sway over my future. To avoid this fate, I'd need to create a better, more dedicated, more determined, and more responsible version of myself. I had been coasting through college life—drinking beer, dating, and watching TV—while I could have been, *should* have been, working my ass off.

My father's news pushed me back on this path. It was time for nineteen-year-old Rob Angel to grow up and take responsibility for himself. I was determined to not let anything get in my way.

First, I'd need a job. The only one available midsemester was scooping ice cream at SAGA, the school cafeteria. Like my summer jobs at Alaska Steel, I saw the short-term gig as a potential long-term job if I applied myself. I grabbed it. There I was the following Saturday night, scooping ice cream for my fellow students in my red-and-white-striped women's smock with boob-darts jutting out. I was the first male to have the job.

I took the jabs like a man.

"What's your bra size, Rob?" the guys would jeer. Or, "Hey, Shirley, can I have another scoop?" But I'd just keep scooping. The job paid the bills—or at least some of them. I took a second job waiting tables at a local restaurant. On summer break, I waited tables and added a back-busting stint at a moving company. And when fall rolled around, I put my lady-apron back on and scooped up as much ice cream, and cash, as I could. I was tireless—and extremely tired. But I kept going, determined to graduate.

I took all the entrepreneurial classes I could. They generally didn't have yes-or-no answers to the questions. Nothing was black or white, and this creativity resonated with me.

I finally got my shit together academically, and my grades improved. I was making ends meet. Life was pretty good.

Unfortunately, though, by the final quarter of my senior year, my fifth year, I ran out of cash. Tuition had climbed dramatically from the $170 my parents paid for my first quarter at Western. I was so close to the end, and the last thing I wanted was to quit school and work full time.

Mom and Dad still weren't in a position to help, though they really wanted to.

Cap in hand, I approached my uncle Jerome and aunt Anne, who owned a successful chain of fabric stores across Canada called Fanny's Fabric, for a $2,000 loan. They agreed with generous terms. There would be no monthly set amount due or set time limit to repay the loan, and I wouldn't have to start payments until nine months after I graduated. I was very appreciative of the assistance.

Thanks to that bridge loan, on June 12, 1981, my twenty-third birthday, I graduated from Western Washington University with a bachelor's degree in business administration—if only by a hair with a 2.9 GPA. Still, there I stood in front of my mom and dad, now in my cap and gown, proud of myself for finishing the job I had started.

I was elated. Exhausted. Thrilled. Scared. And *ready.*

I could only hope the world was ready for me.

WANNA PLAY A GAME?

I moved back home to Spokane, and moved in with my best high school buddies, Sean Curran, Bart Cloninger, and Rob McWilliams. (Since Rob and I share a name, I'll call him "McWilliams" going forward. He was also one of the kids from the old neighborhood growing up.) Our rental house was in a rough section of the city, but we weren't worried. It was cheap, and we were having fun.

While it felt great to put college behind me and be back with my friends, I had no clue what to do with my shiny new business degree I had worked so hard to achieve. I had no earth-shattering plan or unique vision for my future—yet. For now, life was simple, and that's the way I wanted it. I was content to revel in my hard-won freedom and take it one day at a time.

As it would turn out, it was exactly that spirit of openness—a willingness to embrace whatever life had to offer—that ultimately paved the way to my future.

I took a job waiting tables at Rocking Horse Saloon, a local restaurant whose claim to fame was that their waiters poured honey onto customers' biscuits from atop a ten-foot ladder. I was quite good at it and making some pretty decent tips. I started knocking out the debt I owed Uncle Jerome as soon as possible—while still saving enough money for a five-month backpacking tour of Europe. I loved Jerome and wanted to earn his respect, but it was also important to me that I be a man of my word. I dutifully dropped his check in the mail every month—whatever I could afford. Sometimes it'd be as little as five dollars. And some months, when I was bereft of funds getting ready for my trip, I'd send Jerome a note that simply read: "Hey, Unc. Can't afford anything this month. Will catch up. Hope you're having a great day, Robbie." He didn't care what I paid. It was important to him (and me) that I acknowledged the debt, and my notes were enough to let him know I was on it. I never missed a monthly payment or note.

McWilliams, Sean, and Bart also worked at restaurants around town, waiting tables or bartending. When we got home from our shifts, we'd crack a beer, or three, and shoot the breeze, gabbing about the women we were dating (or wanted to be dating), sports, and life as we knew it at our tender age of twenty-three. But one night, when we ran out of things to catch up on, McWilliams said, to no one in particular: "Hey, you wanna play a game?"

I'm sure we looked confused. "On who?" Sean quipped.

"What kind?" I asked, fondly remembering the games McWilliams and I played as kids in the neighborhood. So, hell yeah, I was open to trying a new game.

"Best way to describe it is 'charades on paper,'" McWilliams said. "My college buddies and I played it all the time at Washington State University. Two players to a team. One teammate sketches a random word to his or her teammate, while the other player does the same to his teammate. The sketchers can't speak while they draw. The first person to guess the word from the sketch wins a round for their team."

I got the concept immediately; its simplicity was brilliant.

Looking back on that night, not one of us sitting at our Salvation Army kitchen table was thinking about anything that remotely resembled a commercial idea for the *next big game*. Especially not me.

We scrounged up a couple of pencils and notepads and teamed up: McWilliams and Sean; Bart and me. And we got to playing.

McWilliams wrote "Alpine" and secretly showed it to me so Bart and Sean couldn't see it.

I looked at him, thinking, *How do I . . . ? Never mind. I'll figure it out.*

McWilliams shouted, "Go!" and the two of us began drawing furiously.

I started by sketching the pointy top of what I thought an alpine mountain range looked like.

"Triangle!" Bart shouted.

I made a *grrrr* noise in my throat and kept drawing, adding more lines to resemble snow.

McWilliams was sketching a downhill skier. As Sean watched him, the fingers of his right hand tapped rapidly on the tabletop while his left knee bobbed up and down so fast it was a blur.

Sean: "Chopsticks!"

McWilliams and I said nothing and kept sketching.

Bart: "Geometry!"

We kept sketching, faster now.

Sean: "Snow!"

The game was getting more tense and louder, a lot louder. As Bart and Sean felt they were getting closer to the answer, they started to scream.

"Alpine!" Bart yelled like the house was on fire.

"Yes!" I yelled back, high-fiving my teammate while we both laughed hysterically at my awful sketch. Not that mine was any better than McWilliams's. His sucked, too. And soon we were all laughing uncontrollably.

"Let's keep going," I said, once I caught my breath.

This time, we flipped sketchers, and since Bart guessed the word, he got to pick the next one. Taking a minute to think, he finally wrote something down, showed it to Sean, and the madness resumed.

"Airplane!" I bellowed. "No—*bird!*"

"Penguin!" McWilliams screamed at Sean's pitiful sketch.

Sean slapped McWilliams on the back and yelled, "*Yes!*" and tore off another sheet from the tablet.

Bart groaned. "Come on, Angel. How come you didn't get that?"

"Because you suck at drawing!" I howled, my sides hurting from all the laughter.

The frenzy continued late into the night as the four of us played hardcore "charades on paper." There was no scorekeeping. No winning team. We just had a blast guessing words and laughter was the reward.

Our game nights grew in size with more and more friends joining us, huddled around our little table. We played almost every night, and the games got even louder and crazier, with all of us yelling our guesses at the same time—sometimes until three or four in the morning. We became game-night junkies.

ONE GAME NIGHT, WITH MY friends laughing and playing in friendly competition, I was reminded of the togetherness and neighborhood fun I experienced as a kid playing board games with my friends. It felt like home, and it was a wonderfully warm feeling

And then, I had an epiphany.

"Hey guys, this would make a cool board game," I mused out loud. My idea fell on deaf ears.

"Come on, Angel, your turn to draw."

The next day, I was still glowing from the experience of the previous night and began to wonder what it was about the game that got us so amped up and laughing like maniacs. *Why did it keep us coming back for more?* I noodled on this question for days.

Then it hit me: *The words!* Every one of us guessed differently, and we all sketched differently, but the one common denominator was the words. The words were the engine that drove our game.

Whenever we couldn't immediately come up with a suitable word, we'd get mildly frustrated and eventually bored. Attention waned. Interest faded.

Each new round we needed to identify a drawable word quickly so that we could get right to sketching and keep the game in motion. I realized we were going to need a better source for the words than the ones that came flying out of our mouths. One night, as I lay in bed unable to sleep, trying to figure out a solution, I rolled onto my side and there it was, right before my nose, literally. On my nightstand was the faded red $2.85 paperback *Webster's Collegiate Dictionary* with worn edges that I had used throughout college.

Pay dirt! In fact, later I would realize I'd hit the mother lode.

The solution was simple: now, whenever we needed a fresh word, we could open my tattered *Webster's* to a random page, point to a word, show the other team's artiste, and yell, "*Go!*"

The following night, we gave it a try. It worked much faster, and the quality of words were better. But, even with the dictionary, it would sometimes take a few extra seconds to open the dictionary to a few random pages and scan for a drawable word. But at least we knew we were getting closer with a larger supply of words than before.

One night, as I was flipping one too many pages, Sean snatched the dictionary out of my hand. "Gimme that damn thing!"

As he was looking, he started reading out loud the definitions of obscure words.

"What are you doing?" Bart complained, anxious to get back to the action.

"It's an old game I used to play at home called 'Fictionary,'" he told us.

I'm sure you can guess what came next.

"Hey! Why don't we call the game 'Pictionary'?" Sean said.

Pictures + Dictionary = Pictionary.

My buddies and I looked at each other and smiled, knowing Sean had named the game.

We took it for a test-drive.

"Yo! Wanna play Pictionary?" Or, "Hey, come over and play Pictionary with us." Or, "Sean was a machine at Pictionary last night!" This was all so much easier than, "Would you like to play that game where we draw pictures and the other person tries to guess them . . . you know, it's sorta like charades on paper."

Yeah, *Pictionary* was spot on!

The name made the game feel tangible, and suddenly I had a gnawing sense that it might be worth spending some serious time developing it into a real board game. If I really wanted to turn our friendly game nights into something hundreds, even thousands, of people could play, I'd need a better solution to the word problem than a dog-eared *Webster's*.

But before Pictionary was going to become anything of value to anyone, I had to figure out how to come up with enough easy-to-sketch words like *alligator* and *zebra* so the game wouldn't be too difficult to play, but also not too simplistic that it'd get boring after a couple of rounds. Plus, the words couldn't be so challenging and obscure that players would get frustrated and quit just as they were getting started.

Animals were one of our ongoing go-to type of words. They were always good for a laugh.

"You're saying that's a *rabbit?!* Are you nuts? See those two humps there, Rembrandt—that's a *camel!*"

"No. They're *rabbit ears*, not *humps*, ya moron!"

"Oh . . . I thought it was Dolly Parton."

And so forth.

But you can only draw so many critters before getting bored. If the game was to have any value, commercial value that is, it would be in the words.

The words powered the drawings, the drawings powered the guessing, the guessing powered the fun, and the fun enriched the friendship and camaraderie—and all of that created memories. And that's exactly what Pictionary was all about to me. Not the winning or losing, but the memories I was creating with my friends. And man, we were building plenty of memories with those wild nights!

Now that our game had a name, and I understood that words were the key driver, I was inspired to figure out how to structure it into a real board game.

I grabbed a pen and yellow legal tablet and started jotting down ideas. They weren't all good. For example, an early iteration was to make the game half Pictionary and half traditional charades. We'd never played charades, so this was odd, but I was looking for something different. But the game didn't need to be "different." I quickly dismissed the idea and others that made the game play complex. To make Pictionary work commercially, it would need to be simple and straightforward.

I wanted to recreate the freewheeling energy we had playing at the house, but I knew for it to catch on, there'd need to be a way to crown a winner. After all, people are ultimately competitive, and besides, all board games of the day had a winner and a loser. On the other hand, it had to stay a team game.

I didn't spend a lot of time on the rules at that point. The word list was the most immediate nut I had to crack.

The challenge was how would the words be *delivered* to the players? How would I get them into an actual game? I thought of tear sheets. *Nah, won't work. The sheets will get lost and make a big mess, like ripping pages out of a dictionary.* I thought of printing words in little flip books. *Nope. They'll wear out by the fifth flip-through.* I even thought about adding a paperback dictionary to the game but dismissed the idea for the obvious reasons. An alternative was to print a special Pictionary dictionary with words that were appropriate for the game. But how much would *that* cost? And how much time would players take thumbing through it, looking for the ultimate word? It all seemed totally impractical. Until I could figure that piece out, I felt stuck.

I WASN'T DONE WITH PICTIONARY. I just felt I needed to walk away and not try so hard to find the perfect solution. I believed the solution would come to me when I was open and ready to receive it. I stashed all my game notes in a cardboard box, stored it in my closet, and soon after, left on my five-month backpacking trip through Europe.

It was May 1982. I was twenty-three and had never hitchhiked. I had never even backpacked before. But there I was, heading off on my grand adventure. Let's just say I wasn't the most well-prepared traveler. I didn't even know how to set up the tent I borrowed from a friend.

But my European adventure taught me a lasting life lesson. I was discovering how to navigate unfamiliar environments, adapt to new circumstances, and take things as they came, minute by minute. I had no survival manual; it felt like it was me against the world. I went to whatever city or town the driver who picked me up was headed to and treasured and embraced the mystery of not knowing the destination. I was surrendering day by day and loved it. I was *free!* Just me and my thumb catching a ride, meeting new and interesting people along the way. The more uncomfortable the situation, the more alive I felt.

The trip energized my spirit and lit a fire in me. By the time I returned, I knew I could do anything I set my mind to. *Anything!* And there were big things ahead of me that would require—no, *demand*—I adapt to every situation. I'd have to go with the flow of life.

This was the genesis of the philosophy that would permeate and dictate the journey of my life. I didn't know how to articulate it then, but I would later come to call it living a life of being "OPEN."

When I arrived back in Spokane that fall, I had to find work. Buoyed by my exhilarating experience, I wanted to try my hand at something new rather than go back to waiting tables. I was willing to try anything.

First, I tried selling vacuum cleaners door to door. Well, I sucked at that. I only lasted a day. The high-pressure sales tactics weren't for me.

Next up: real estate. For a year, I toiled at a career I didn't love. I managed to sell four houses, but my heart just wasn't in it.

Then, I had a go hawking this weird new thing called "cable TV" door to door. But I soon tired of knocking on strangers' doors in the cold Spokane winter to convince people to sign up and pay for something they already had: three free perfectly fine network TV channels.

None of these jobs, or others I considered, resonated. I needed to do something that *mattered to me*. Something I *cared* about. Something I *loved*.

Like calzones.

Pete's Pizza, "The Calzone King," was a fixture in Spokane. The joint near Gonzaga University was super popular, and the calzones were, hands down, the best in town. I couldn't calculate how many hundreds of dollars I'd handed over to Pete's. I decided it was finally time to put that hard-earned college degree to use. With only confidence to my name, I would approach the owner and namesake, Pete Baranco, to buy a franchise. I would own my own business and not be beholden to someone else's whim like my dad had been.

I visualized opening Pete's stores near college campuses across the nation, one after the other. I was going to turn Pete's into a behemoth and make millions. No experience? Ha! I wasn't about to let the fact that I'd never run a business, much less a pizza franchise, stop me. Oh yeah, and the fact that Pete's wasn't a franchised operation wasn't going to stop me, either.

I approached Pete at the restaurant one night with only the unwavering belief in myself and this crazy idea. Pete was a portly man of sixty, with a thick Italian accent and a heart of gold. I didn't have a business plan, and I had no money to invest, but I offered him $50,000 for the franchise rights. It felt like a number he couldn't refuse. I had absolutely no clue where I would get the money, but I wasn't going to let a silly detail like financing get in the way of my great idea.

Pete took to the idea immediately.

"You're the right kid for the job," he said, beaming, as he slapped me on the back. Then he became serious for moment, frowned, and said, "But the Mrs. . . . *she's* the one in charge." He'd said that last part with what I detected as a slight twinge of fear.

The next day, Pete and I sat next to each other on a living room couch across from his wife, like two schoolboys who'd been summoned to the principal's office. We explained my proposal and waited anxiously for her response. I couldn't tell if she liked the idea or not from her blank expression.

After an interminable pause, she shook her head and flatly said, "No."

Pete and I sat there, stunned, hoping for something more. A clarification. Maybe an addendum, like *Not now. Maybe later.* We sat in silence, barely breathing, waiting for what felt like an hour for an explanation.

"I want to save it for the children," she finally said.

Pete looked confused. "But the kids don't want to be in the family business," he countered. "We've asked them a dozen times, and their answer is always no."

But Mrs. Pete's Pizza wasn't budging. And just as fast as it came, my dream to become the world's next Calzone King was dashed.

But damn it, at least I had given it a shot; at least I'd done that. Apparently, the universe had other plans for me—or so I hoped.[*]

What was clear from this experience was I'd given my all to Spokane. It was time to seek my fortune elsewhere.

It was February 1984. I crammed my twenty-five-year-old self and everything I owned into my 1976 four-door white Mercury Monarch and hit the highway with only $300 in cash in my pocket. It was all I had left to my name after paying Uncle Jerome back in full.[†] My destination was the big city: Seattle.

As I drove down the I-90, Prince's "Let's Go Crazy" was blasting on the radio, and I was determined to *get through this thing called life.*

---

[*]   In 1991, Pete sold Pete's Pizza. My high school buddy Sean Curran and I approached the new owner for the franchise I had been denied five years earlier. We opened two successful stores in Seattle. I was finally The Calzone King.

[†]   It felt great sending off that last payment to my uncle. I had a sense of accomplishment that would stick with me. I'd had the integrity to live up to my commitments, and I'd showed it not only to Jerome but to myself.

IN (TRIVIAL) PURSUIT
OF GREATNESS

When I got to Seattle, I moved into the last available bedroom in a house with three friends from high school: Lynn and Tom Mounsey and Laura Shlicker. I had to find work to pay my share of the rent and fell back on my old standby: waiting tables. For the first few months, I strung together part-time work at three restaurants, even bussing tables for the first time. I needed the money, and the free meals during my shifts were a much-welcomed added bonus.

I eventually landed a job at Lake Union Café, a fine-dining restaurant where real tip money could be made. I was able to quit the other three gigs and take the night shift, full time.

Meanwhile, while unpacking at my new home, I came across all my old yellow notepads with all the rules and regulations for Pictionary that I'd jotted down two years earlier. I leafed through them, smiling and reminiscing about all the late-night fun I had playing with my roommates in Spokane.

But then I remembered what had stumped me about formulating it all into a proper, playable board game. *The darn word list! How do I get them physically into a game? How can I put a word list in the game in a way that feels intuitive, natural, and fun for the players?*

I tossed the notepads aside in frustration and continued unpacking. But now, Pictionary was top of mind again.

IN MARCH, I RECEIVED A surprise package from my mom. I took it into the den and sat on the couch next to Tom, who was watching *Alice* on TV.

Inside was navy-blue box that looked like a classy coffee-table book. The words "Trivial Pursuit" were emblazoned across the top in cursive metallic gold lettering. Lynn and Laura walked in as I read Mom's note:

Hi Robbie, (Mom always called me Robbie) *I had fun playing this game and thought you'd like it, too. It was invented here in Canada. Love, Mom.*

I removed the cellophane wrap and lifted the lid off the box, which gave off that wonderful new-product smell (really, a glue-and-plastic smell.) *What distinctive packaging,* I thought. *Beautiful, elegant, solid.* Trivial Pursuit looked and felt like no other game I'd seen—or played.

"Hey, Angel, want to play?" Lynn said, moving toward our new foosball table.

"Huh?" I said, distracted by the box. "Oh. No thanks. Maybe later."

Lynn and Laura began spinning rods and smacking the balls. On TV, Flo was asking someone or another to *kiss her grits.* And I was enraptured by the box in my lap.

I opened the gameboard, noticing that it unfolded into a square shape, unlike the gameboards I was familiar with that folded in half. The game pieces were brightly colored pie wedges that nuzzled perfectly into empty slots of the bigger circular pieces. I assumed they were the pawns. Finally, I slowly opened a smaller box filled with cards. I pulled out the first; it had six questions printed on it.

As I stared at the card, I could feel my heart rate speed up a bit. A foosball landed in my lap, and I barely noticed it, flicking it back to Lynn. The voices at Mel's Diner faded into the background. I was experiencing one of those otherworldly moments when the universe suddenly focuses a laser beam on a holy grail. *My holy grail! I'd print the Pictionary words on cards!*

"That's it!" I yelled, shocking my roommates.

"What's it?" Lynn and Laura said in unison, stopping their game to look at me.

"What?"

"You just yelled, 'That's it!'" Tom said, noticing the bewildered look on my face.

My head was spinning. I looked from Tom to Laura to Lynn and back down at the game in my lap. I looked back at Tom again to see if he was seeing what I saw. Nope. Blank stare.

"This is my *future!*" I said, holding up the game card. "Oh my God, guys—this is *it!*"

After two long years, the missing link that had been bugging me, taunting me, laughing at me was right there in my hand.

Son of a bitch!

I had always known that the answer would come to me someday; I just didn't know the when or where. I had to be present, open, and aware enough when it arrived. And here it was: the answer in the form of these stunningly simple, printed cards.

If they could work for Trivial Pursuit, they would work in Pictionary. It was a discovery so overpowering that I had no choice now but to take action.

THE NEXT MORNING, I WOKE up eager to get started. I could already see Pictionary on a store shelf. It was easy for me to visualize it sitting right there next to Trivial Pursuit.

But it didn't take long for my brain to start messing with me, and I began to overthink things. I started imagining all of the steps needed to make Pictionary a reality. I'd need to write a business plan, initiate market strategies, secure financing, find partners and suppliers . . . there were a million potential production and distribution issues.

So . . . many . . . steps.

It was all too much to process. I became anxious and overwhelmed. I was so frozen with fear that I was unable to take even one small step forward. And if even if I could, I didn't have the faintest clue what that first step should be.

Then, to make matters worse, self-doubt crept in and took a stranglehold on me and wouldn't let go. *I'm just a waiter. I can't do this. Even though I have a college degree, I'm not smart enough. This is way too far out of my comfort zone.*

This was the damn self-sabotaging box I'd put myself in. I was so far inside my head I couldn't find a way out. I was letting my future slip away.

I couldn't sleep. I could barely eat. I was losing focus at work.

I had to get back on track.

I had to slow my roll. I had to stop over-thinking and quit looking at the big picture. I needed to put myself in a "time-out."*

So, I went for walks. Hung out with friends. Played foosball with Lynn, Laura, and Tom. I did *anything* but think of Pictionary.

After a few days, I felt calmer and more centered. Rather than let myself slip back into the rabbit hole, I asked myself one simple question: What is the easiest first step I can take to get started and move forward? What can I wrap my head around and not spin out again?

The answer came to me in this moment of clarity: I'd begin with the words.

---

* I use the practice of taking a self-imposed time-out still to this day when I feel like things aren't going right—or aren't going anywhere at all. I take them when I'm overwhelmed and bombarded by too much input. The practice, as an active meditation, centers me and helps clear my head of all the noise and clutter rattling around in my brain so I can focus on the task at hand.

FINDING MY AARDVARK

Now that I had clearly identified my first task, I stopped stressing. I put my head down and got to it.

Everything I needed was right there in the house. I grabbed my trusty $2.85 *Webster's Ninth Collegiate Dictionary* (yes, the same one I'd used to play with the guys in Spokane), a yellow legal pad, and a pen, and I plopped down on a wobbly green plastic chair in the backyard of the rental house. I took a deep breath and opened the dictionary to the letter *A* with my pen poised to write the first drawable word I'd come across. And there it was.

Aardvark.

My first word.

I stared at it. *Aardvark.*

Just like the moment I saw that first Trivial Pursuit card, my heart raced a bit, and a cold sweat dampened my brow.

I wrote "aardvark" down on my notepad.

I stared at it. With aardvark, I had begun. This first small step changed my life; my big dream would start with one simple word.

In that one glorious moment, I was no longer a waiter. I was a game inventor.

Okay, let's do another.

I wrote down "abacus."

Holy shit, now there are two words written on the page.

I kept going. I wrote down another word. And another word. And another. And I had thousands more to go.

This may seem overly dramatic. It was just a word. But I cannot stress enough how important these first few words were to me. They represented the moment of creation—the Big Bang, if you will—of something entirely new, an idea that didn't exist before, except in my head.

That was my first small victory to embrace, to relish—not the creation of the game, but the completion of my first task. The game had sprung from the realm of the imaginary into the physical world. As Dr. Frankenstein said after he zapped his monster with a thousand volts: "It's alive!"

Soon I was flying, enthused by the task of writing down silly, beautiful words. As I read and wrote, it became obvious that not all words could be included. I settled on two criteria for a word to make the list:

I had to know what the word meant. Pictionary had to be accessible to everyone, no matter level of education. I assumed that if I knew the meaning of the word, everyone else probably did, too.

The word had to conjure an image in my mind. It didn't matter if it was abstract or concrete; it had to be something I could immediately visualize.

My roommates would occasionally peer at me through the kitchen window as I sat in the backyard, yellow notepad on my lap, face buried in my decrepit dictionary, muttering to myself as I played with the words. I knew what they were thinking: *There's crazy ol' Rob, talking to himself again.* I didn't care; I was determined, steady, focused.

I spent the next three months filling six yellow legal pads with words. I divided the pages into four columns and filled the pages, from top to bottom, with words—from aardvark to zygote. By the time I was done, my thoroughly abused dictionary had given me all it could. It was spent, and so was I.

To my immeasurable satisfaction, I had amassed 5,018 words. It was the perfect number because I'd been aiming to meet the 6,000 questions in Trivial Pursuit, which I'd set as a benchmark.

Step one: *completed!* I couldn't stop grinning.

Meanwhile, I was already well into step two. While creating the word list, I also organized my first playtest. When we played in Spokane, it was a looser, informal activity. Now, I was making it a structured board game with rules and winning and losing teams. Would it be as entertaining to others as it had been for me, McWilliams, Sean, and Bart? Or was it just all the beers we consumed that made it fun? I had to find out.

I drove 120 miles up to Vancouver to use my mom, my older sister Leslie, and her friend Linda as my guinea pigs. Even though I'd chosen the least frightening way to test Pictionary—with my family—I was still nervous. What if they didn't love it as much as I did? If not, I'd have to go back to waiting tables—and back to the drawing board . . . literally.

My approach to introducing my family to the game was to make playing as simple as possible. I just wanted them to draw and guess until a winner was declared.

I brought with me my word list and a rudimentary gameboard. I'm no visual artist—by a long shot. My first "gameboard" looked pretty childish: a piece of white foam core about two feet square where I wrote the words "Start" at the top and "Finish" at the bottom and drew fifteen horizontal lines in between. There were two columns, one for each team. When a team guessed a word correctly, I'd check off a line in that team's column. The first team to guess fifteen words right was the winner. Easy.

I crafted a small blue plastic folder that held a game card with two words on each card. One card would slip into a slot in the holder, and the player sketching would rip a Velcro tab aside to reveal the word and then secretly show it to the other artist.

My anxiety level increased as we picked teams. My sister Leslie and her friend Linda were Team A. Mom and I were Team B. After a quick run-through of my simple rules—and I mean *simple*—we got started.

I sat tight as Leslie picked the first word and then showed it to me: monkey.

Leslie and I began scribbling. At first, Linda and Mom just sort of stared at our sketches. Nothing. No guessing. Silence. (*We should have played a practice round*, I told myself.) Then, suddenly, startling me, Linda and Mom were screaming!

Oh. They'd been waiting for Leslie and me to finish our sketches before guessing.

"Cat!"

"Dog!"

"Pony!"

"Fox!"

When Mom yelled "Bigfoot!" we all roared.

Finally, Linda nailed it: "Monkey!"

Mom and I slouched in exaggerated agony over losing the first round.

Leslie proudly, and gloating a bit, checked Team A's first line.

In round two, to my tremendous relief, we were once again laughing and screaming. After each correct guess, my playtesters couldn't wait to get to the next word. Me too. I was so lost in the excitement and the magic of the moment, I'd forgotten that the whole purpose of being there was research and development. This gave me all the validation I needed.

Most important, Mom and I won!

I WAS MOVING FORWARD, BUT first, I had some business to clear up. I wanted to let my old pals McWilliams, Bart, and Sean know of my intention to work on the game as a business venture. I also wanted to make sure none of them were pursuing the concept. While none of us owned the idea, and there was no legal reason to inform them of my plans, we were friends, and I felt it was the right thing to do. I wanted to be transparent so they wouldn't think I was going behind their backs.

I had some angst making the calls. What if one of them *was* working on a similar concept? What would I do then? There were four of us in that house in Spokane, and any one of us could have run with the idea.

I picked up the phone and called each one of them and asked: "Do you have any plans to develop the old charades-on-paper game we used to play? I'm thinking about creating a board game based on it."

McWilliams: "I'm not. Go for it, Rob."

Sean: "Not on my radar, Rob. Not a problem."

Bart: "Not me. Good luck with that, Angel."

I placed the phone back in its cradle and let out a huge sigh of relief. There was no interest on their part whatsoever. At that moment, I took ownership of Pictionary.*

---

* People ask me if we're all still friends after thirty-five years—and the answer is absolutely, yes.

THE DREAM TEAM UNITES

As excited as I was to get started on developing Pictionary, I knew I couldn't do it alone. Notwithstanding my business administration degree, my passions and strengths lay in my focused vision for Pictionary, product development, marketing, and sales. So, I'd need to find someone to handle the operations side of the business, including accounting, logistics and to make sure everything ran smoothly. Then, given how crappy my Pictionary prototype had been, it was clear I needed to find a talented graphic artist to make my vision for Pictionary come to life. I knew that design and packaging was one of the keys to creating a successful consumer product. And consumers had to *love* Pictionary.

Finding the right people to fit my requirements was on my mind as I absentmindedly tied my black waiter's apron on and slid an order pad into my back pocket to start my night shift at Lake Union Café. As I approached my first table, I heard laughter coming from a four-top over in the front. It wasn't surprising to see Gary Everson, a tall, lanky fellow waiter, being playful with his customers. Gary had an endearing goofiness and charming eye-to-the-sky positivity about him that customers gravitated to. Even as most of us would be drained by the time we'd turn our last table for the night, Gary still had enough energy to fill the room. This was pretty remarkable since his shift followed his day job as a graphic artist for the Alaska Airlines in-flight magazine.

And that's when it dawned on me. *Maybe Gary is the right guy.*

During a break on our next night shift together, I chatted with Gary, something I hadn't done much of before. I wanted to feel him out, see if he might be a good fit, and gauge his interest in getting involved.

I knew Gary was six years older than me, but that was about it. I learned he had a degree in graphics and design from Wayne State University. When I asked him how he liked his job at Alaska Airlines, he told me he enjoyed the creative process at the magazine.

"At Alaska, I'm in charge of layout and even have some input on the editorial content," he told me, rather excitedly.

Gary's upbeat, take-charge attitude resonated with me.

Before leaving the restaurant after our shift, I briefed Gary on my Pictionary project and told him about the playtest success with my family. I kept it loose when talking about my plans going forward, speaking theoretically to see where his head was at.

At this point in the evolution of Pictionary, I was simply focused on creating a game that people would love playing as much as I did, that would be as entertaining as it was with my old friends. This was my sole intention. I didn't have grand plans to take on the game industry and sell millions of games. That would come later. For now, this was what drove me.

Gary liked the idea that Pictionary brought people together and told me how his experience could help. He impressed me with his knowledge of printing and production, as well as his philosophy and solid expertise on product design.

Over the next few days, I mulled over the idea of making Gary an offer. He was a kindred spirit, and I liked the thought of helping a fellow wage slave. But it was more than that. Something told me he was the right guy. Instincts, I guess. I couldn't put my finger on it, but I knew the next time I was to see Gary, my plan was to approach him about joining me.

I didn't want to reveal too much until we negotiated a deal. Best laid plans. When he walked into our break room, I couldn't help myself and blurted out, "Gary, I want you to design Pictionary!"

Gary looked surprised, then grinned widely and said, "That's exactly what I was hoping you'd say. This is the coolest thing I think I've ever had the chance to work on. What do you need to me do?"

"I need you work on the game design, including the components, color scheme, lettering, and graphics. And, when the time comes, I'll need you to help me with production."

I offered Gary his choice between a piece of the business or $2,000. Just like the cash offer I'd made to Pete Baranco for a Pete's Pizza franchise, I didn't have the money. I'd deal with this detail later.

Gary liked the options and said, "I'll get back to you."

A few days later, Gary approached me. "I'll take a piece of the company."

"That's awesome," I said.

I was relieved, and not only because I didn't have the two grand. Gary's decision meant he believed in Pictionary and me. And it was liberating. Now I had a partner to help shoulder the load, a collaborator—somebody to bounce ideas off.

GARY WANTED TO GET A sense of what the game was all about, the essence of it, before he started conceptualizing his designs. He started participating in playtests, helping me develop the rules, and before too long was spending a lot of his free time supporting me in the development process. I welcomed the help.

I was boiling over with energy and more eager than ever to keep pushing forward.

With Gary on board, I needed one more partner—someone with the skills to manage the business and operation side of the venture. And I had just the guy in mind for the position—my good friend Walt Westfall.

Walt was a manager at a local data-processing company. He was smart, articulate, skilled with a spreadsheet, and organized. Equally important, he was trustworthy. I didn't have to spend much time convincing Gary, whom I hadn't known very long, to join me. Surely Walt would be a slam dunk.

I was right. After our initial discussions, he could see I was on to something and immediately joined. I was really stoked that he got right to work before we even broached an offer. We met a few times to discuss potential business models and other ideas to move Pictionary forward.

I thought we were on the right track. Then, just that fast, Walt abruptly quit.

"I've been premature in agreeing to come on board," he explained. "I accepted a new position, a promotion actually, with my current company. I'm getting married soon and I need a steady income."

I wasn't angry or even upset with Walt. How could I be? After all, I couldn't offer him a salary, and he had his life and priorities. But that meant I was back to my search. *Oh well, just keep going with the flow,* I reminded myself, again and again. *The right person will turn up.*

And soon, that person did. Being a good friend, Walt organized a playtest in a setting where Gary and I could try out a new set of rules we'd been developing.

Walt and his roommate, Vic Marshal, invited one of their friends, Terry Langston.

He's a little mild mannered and shy . . . a bit too buttoned up, I thought, and I figured he'd be a bust as a player. But then I thought, *What the hell! Let's see if Pictionary can wake up an introvert like this Terry guy!*

I teamed up with Terry and learned something about him during the first round. He could draw okay, but he really struggled with a pretty bad stutter. He couldn't pronounce the letters *h* or *m*, so when the word was something like mouse or harp, it took a while, a long while, to come out with his guess. And as the game went on, he would sometimes only get in one or two guesses before the other team nailed the word, or the one-minute time limit—a new rule we were testing—expired. Sure, it didn't help that my sketching stunk.

Nevertheless, I loved being his teammate. I was witnessing one of the most beautiful things about Pictionary. Even though Terry and I got our asses kicked, we still had a blast playing. We were laughing and teasing each other like teenagers over our constantly goofing up. It was the *playing* that was the fun part of the game, not the winning. It was the journey, not the destination.

I saw how Pictionary eliminated social barriers and judgment. And something else, something more ethereal, was happening. Terry and I were really connecting, interacting as if we'd known each other for years.

When we took a break between games, Terry told me the Pictionary game night was just what he needed to lift his spirits. He had recently been let go from his job as a comptroller for a large local import/export business where he oversaw financial reporting, payroll, and operations. I gave him a pat on the shoulder and told him I was happy he came and how he'd been one of my favorite teammates of all time. And I meant it.

Terry impressed me. Here was a guy whose stutter hindered his ability to play a game that required quick communication—but it didn't hinder him from having a good time or even from trying.

Going over his skill set as he described it, it hit me. Had I just found the guy to replace Walt?

I waited until we packed up for the night to take Terry aside. I came right out with it.

"Listen, I'm looking for a partner: someone to run the business and operations side of Pictionary," I said. "Would you be interested in discussing it?"

Without batting an eye, Terry said yes.

We met a couple of weeks later at a local restaurant. I arrived first, found a two-top, and waited for Terry. And waited. A half hour went by, and I was pissed. *Maybe I haven't found my guy. Screw him. On to the next*, I thought. If this had been a date, I'd have assumed I was being stood up and left.

And I was about to do just that when Terry finally arrived, drenched in sweat, and plopped down across from me.

"I'm sorry, Rob. I was so eager for this meeting that I got a speeding ticket on my way here," Terry said, holding up the ticket as proof. "I don't know what it means, but it *has* to mean something."

How could I be upset with a guy who wanted to get started so badly that he got a speeding ticket? I could see myself doing the same thing and forgave him immediately.

We continued with some idle chitchat so Terry could collect himself. The waitress brought over a beer, which Terry polished off. He put the glass down, and without losing a beat, grabbed a napkin, took a pen out of his pocket, and began scribbling notes. It was time to get down to business.

"It's simple," he said while quickly drawing out his notes like it was a game of Pictionary. "We make games. We sell games. That's the broad strokes, of course, but we do it like this," he said, while illustrating his strategy on the fly.

Running out of napkins, Terry grabbed the damp one from under my beer and carried on with bullet-point tasks for each of us. There was a gleam in his eye, and I could feel in my bones how energized he was about the plan, the game, the idea. He was vibrating on a higher level. Terry was no doubt the most analytical guy I'd had ever met. He'd only heard a smidgen of any real information about Pictionary, had only played it once, yet here he was, analyzing data, calculating risk and reward, and was not stuttering.

Terry's comptroller experience meant he could deftly manage the business and operations side of our venture. More importantly, my instincts were shouting oh so very clearly: *This is the guy!* This is *my* guy.

Even though I had just met Terry a couple of weeks earlier, I felt compelled to listen to the overwhelming positive feeling in my gut. I offered Terry the job right then and there.

Terry didn't have to think about it, either. He felt the energy too and immediately proffered his hand to shake on it.

Awesome!

"By the way," I said with a big smile, "why did you agree to meet me?"

"Because I seriously hate games," Terry said, catching me by surprise. "But I had a such a great time playing with you and figured if *I* could be won over and have so much fun, anyone could."

Terry continued. "Ever since I was fired from my job, I vowed not to let anyone else be in charge of my life or career. I won't be beholden to a large corporation for my success or even my failure. I see the potential in Pictionary, and I want to take the shot with you and Gary. With my stutter, I have always worked in the background, but I feel I'm meant for bigger things. This is my bigger thing."

There *it* was: the reason why Terry resonated so strongly with me. I got it in a flash. We were of the same mindset from the beginning. I had vowed never to be in that position when my dad got fired, and Terry was living it now. It would become our unbreakable bond and a driving force in our lives.

It gave me goose bumps.

After Terry left, I lingered for a few minutes, marveling at the fortuitousness of events that were transpiring. I knew the only way such a diverse group as Terry, Gary, and me could come together so seamlessly was that the universe had conspired, or should I say *inspired*, to connect us. None of us knew what the future would hold—and it didn't matter. As it would turn out, we were the perfect triumvirate to take Pictionary to heights we hadn't yet even dreamed of.

And at that moment, Rob Angel, Gary Everson, and Terry Langston became a little independent board game company called Angel Games, Inc.

WE COULDN'T AFFORD TO SET up a legal entity, or even draw up a partnership agreement, so we agreed verbally on the percentage of ownership Gary and Terry would each receive. I had faith in my new partners that they would stay the course and see this project to the end, whatever that would look like and however long it would take. In turn, they trusted me to be a man of my word and give them their shares as promised when we did eventually incorporate.

We all operated on the principal of mutual trust and respect and got to work.*

WE WERE LIVING THE START-UP dream, or nightmare, depending on the day. My cramped apartment at 569 Lee Street on Queen Anne Hill—all nine hundred square feet of it—became Pictionary headquarters. My apartment didn't have many windows, only a sliding glass door that overlooked the street that didn't let in much light on the infrequent occasions the sun deigned to shine upon Seattle. The décor included a musty forest-green seventies-style shag carpet, rusty appliances from the sixties, an ancient dresser, and in the middle of the living room, a twelve-dollar desk from Goodwill that butted up against the fake-wood paneled wall.

On that wall, I taped and tacked things that inspired me every day. It was my ever-expanding vision board. Among the photos and clippings was an article from *Playboy* magazine that listed unconventional jobs and how much you could potentially earn from them. I had highlighted one that caught my eye: *Marketing a new game or pet rock: unlimited!* (See, I did read *Playboy* for the articles.) My hope was that someday the wall would be filled with articles praising Pictionary.

Adding to my beautiful mess were Gary's markers and drawing materials found here and there, empty pizza boxes and Rainier beer bottles left over from long workdays and nights. My apartment looked more like a war zone than a place to run a business.

It was perfect!

Our roles and responsibilities were *technically* defined. Gary would

---

* Indeed, in the months and years ahead, we each followed through with the promises we made to one another.

handle graphics and box and board design. Terry would be in charge of accounting, financials, and operations, with the added responsibility of making sure we stayed on task and on track. This would be crucial. I would focus on consumer experience, sales, and marketing.

That was the plan, anyway. As with every start-up, we all pitched in as needed. Anything that needed doing, we as a team made sure it got done. Our roles melded and shifted from the very beginning. No one worked in a bubble; every big decision was a group discussion.

After all, there was no manual for producing, selling, and marketing a board game. For better or for worse, we had no experience, so we made up our own manual, taking one small step in front of the other, one day at a time, one task at a time. Treading forward, we went with our instincts and gut feelings.

Still, we were confident, for the most part anyway, that we had what it took to move from the conceptual stage to product development. Now, the "game" could really begin.

ADVENTURE CAPITAL

Terry and I may have left his brilliant quick-fire cocktail napkin business plan at the restaurant, but the gist of it remained perfectly clear: make games; sell games.

Terry, Gary, and I sat around my kitchen table to discuss the challenge at hand, which was deciding how many games to produce for our initial run. Fortunately, I had a clue to get us started. I knew three buddies in Portland, Oregon, who'd produced a board game that sold seven hundred units in the first year. Seven hundred sounded achievable to us, but we decided to be a little more audacious and set our sights on producing and selling one thousand games.

"Good," Terry said as he wrote "1,000 games" in his ledger. "Now we need to calculate how much capital we'll need to raise to produce one thousand games."

Our extensive playtesting had given us a sense of the game components, but we had no hard data on the production cost of each item, let alone on a finished game. Pricing out our production costs was challenging because it's not like we could just source estimates on the internet, which didn't yet exist. We also had no idea how to project sales and marketing costs with any kind of accuracy. We were flying blind across the board (pun intended).

"We'll need to make a few guesses," Terry said with authority as he wrote.

"I think we just need to dive in and make some estimates," Gary added. "I have knowledge about publishing and printing costs from my work at the Alaska Air magazine, so let's start there."

Gary listed all the game components, estimated costs for each, and came to a per unit cost of roughly twenty dollars. Terry added estimates of legal and accounting costs. I added a small budget for marketing and advertising.

I handed Terry my Texas Instruments calculator from my high school days that had somehow managed to follow me wherever I went. After a few taps on the buttons, Terry held up the calculator to reveal the tally: $31,000—a shitload of money in the mid-1980s, at least to us. Accounting for inflation, $31,000 in 1984 would be about $77,000 today.

We were low-key confident that our calculations were at least in the ballpark and agreed to seek an initial investment of $35,000, which would get us our one thousand games, a small marketing budget, and some left over for contingencies. Who were we kidding? The entire business at this point was a contingency. There was no talk of salaries; every dollar would be invested directly into Pictionary.

"Okay," Terry said, circling in red the "$35,000" he had written down at the top of his page. "Now, where are going to get that kind of money?"

Gary was still working for the magazine while waiting tables. I was waiting tables, and Terry had a new nine-to-five job as a financial controller at a medical device company. We'd be lucky to net thirty-five grand after tax, *combined*. Maybe.

The only way to fund our venture was through the traditional "friends and family" route.

The three of us made a list of names of potential investors. On that list was my uncle Jerome. Possibly saving us the long and arduous task of piecing together funding from multiple sources, I suggested,

"Let's start with him. He's the one person I know who has the financial wherewithal to invest the full amount."

I had enough faith in Pictionary and us to believe my uncle was a viable option. If he said no, we'd get busy working through our list of other potential investors.

Working with Terry's Lotus 1-2-3 program on his IBM PC, we put together what we hoped was a compelling business plan. It had the requisite short- and long-term projections, expenditures, production costs, and so on, but our main focus was on producing and selling one thousand games.

A few weeks later, we were ready make the call.

"Hi, Uncle Jerome." I said a little too enthusiastically when he picked up the phone, trying to hide my nerves. I was eager to get to the point. "I won't take much of your time. I just want to ask if you'd be willing to meet with me and my business partner, Terry Langston, to discuss a business venture."

I held my breath.

"Robbie, you paid back your student loan," my uncle said after a thoughtful pause. "And you've proven to me that you're a *mensch*, a man of your word. So, yes, I'll take the meeting. In fact, Auntie Anne and I will be on a business trip in Vancouver next week. You can make your pitch at our hotel."

Terry, Gary and I busied ourselves over the week, fine-tuning the proposal. All three of us were a bundle of nerves, understanding the enormity of the ask.

Gary wished us luck as Terry and I drove off to Vancouver. Once there, we cruised up and down a side street looking for the cheap, fleabag hotel we'd reserved. We finally found it after realizing the light bulb over the front sign had long ago burned out. After checking in, we walked into a room with 1960s décor that reeked of cleaning solution. We were relieved the hotel had a bar, and Terry and I ordered beers to calm our nerves. *Yeah, good luck with that.* We sat there rehearsing the pitch over and over, imagining how the meeting would go—and, in my head, how they'd just throw the money at us.

"Only thirty-five thousand? No, no, no, Robbie," I imagined my uncle saying. "You're probably going to need fifty grand. I'll put a cashier's check in the mail first thing Monday."

Next thing we knew, the bartender announced last call. *Crap!* It was one thirty in the freaking morning! We'd been talking nonstop, so intensely discussing the proposal that we had lost all track of time and were completely hammered. I don't remember getting into bed, but all too soon the alarm clock was screaming: *8:00 a.m.! Get the hell up!* This was it. Our day of reckoning had arrived. The biggest meeting of our lives and I was stupidly hung the hell over.

I threw up a little as I looked around for coffee, even though I knew all the coffee in the world wasn't going to bail me out of this stupor. We both shook off our regret, showered, dressed, and slowly made our way into the car to get to our meeting.

With foggy heads, Terry and I found ourselves sitting on a couch opposite Jerome and Anne in their plush hotel suite at the Four Seasons. *So, this is how the other half lives*, I noted to myself.

Like a man possessed, I passionately launched into our pitch, explaining Pictionary: how it was played, how excited the three partners were for its potential, and how great the playtests had gone. Then, I passed the torch to Terry, who went over the numbers and laid out our plan for how we'd manufacture our first one thousand games. Despite throbbing hangover headaches, Terry and I were putting on one helluva show. We even played a few rounds with our potential investors so they could get a taste of our excitement.

Shit. Of all the people who had played Pictionary, Jerome was the *only* one who didn't have fun. He didn't seem to get it. With every round he seemed less and less engaged.

Was I doing something wrong? Was I not explaining the game well? Was it him? Was it me?

Was it over?

Jerome asked for a few minutes to discuss our proposal with Anne. Terry and I looked at each other with panic as they stepped into the bedroom and closed the door.

Disappointed in my performance, at this point, I was just hoping that being their nephew would get them to say yes. And in a way it did.

When the bedroom door finally opened, my heart raced as I braced for bad news. Poker-faced, my aunt and uncle sat down across from us and, without pause, Uncle Jerome said, "Robbie, to be honest with you, we don't understand the game, but Anne and I agree, your excitement and enthusiasm sold us. We may not get what you're trying to do here, but we believe in you. And so, we believe in Pictionary. Anne and I have agreed to invest the full thirty-five thousand."

I thought I was going to pass out. Terry and I threw quick glances at each other to confirm we'd both heard the same thing.

"Wow," I said. "Thank you!"

"We will give you the first installment now and the rest later," Jerome said.

Smiling, we all stood up and shook hands. Then, I gave my uncle a hug and whispered in his ear, "I appreciate you having faith in me. I won't let you down."*

Terry and I walked on air back to the car. We couldn't stop high-fiving each other. The elation of what had just transpired pole vaulted us out of the fog of our hangovers.

"We did it, Terry," I said, stopping for a second to acknowledge the moment before we got to the car. "We're on our way!"

"Yeah, Rob!" he said. "Hey, let me see the check. I have to see this thing."

"The check?" My jaw dropped. "I thought you had it."

Shit!

---

* For Jerome's investment, he negotiated a hefty equity position in the company. He told me years later that he went into the bedroom with Auntie Anne to do the math on how much he could write off on his taxes. While supportive, he never expected to see his money again.

We were so excited that we had walked out of the hotel without getting the first $5,000 installment. We played rock-paper-scissors to see who was going to go back and retrieve the check. I lost.

When I arrived at the suite, there was Jerome, waving the check in the air with a big smirk on his face. I'm sure I blushed like a fool, but so what? Pictionary now had enough fuel in the tank to get the engine running.

When Terry and I arrived back in Seattle and gave Gary the news, the energy in my apartment was electric.

While I knew there was a long and complex road ahead, and it was going to be bumpy, I never doubted the three of us were in it together. For the long haul.

WE GOT DOWN TO BUSINESS and quickly fell into a rather free-flowing business culture. Terry, Gary, and I were learning how each of us operated, and what made us tick.

From the start, there was never any judgment of the ideas and thoughts we shared. We never felt like we had to hold anything back; no idea was too off the wall or out of bounds. If Gary or Terry had an idea at ten o'clock at night, and my line was busy, they'd come pounding on my door, and we'd stay up till all hours fleshing out whatever the big idea was. I loved it.

The crazy hours, the talking, the shooting the shit, the spit balling, the brainstorming . . . this was the heart of our working relationship.

We developed mutual respect and a genuine friendship built on the foundation of our shared mission. The bond that was forming was real—through trial and error, fire and fury, pain and accomplishment.

Years later, Terry would so eloquently describe our dynamic: "I think a vital core to our business was our loyalty to each other, allowing each of us our own voice while still being loyal to our brand. One of the reasons it worked is that we accepted each other for what we were, and more importantly, what we weren't. We just moved on and went with it from there."

PLAYING THE GAME

With financing secured, the next task was to finalize the game play experience, word list, and rules.

I knew the word list was critical to the success of Pictionary, if not the most critical element. Having developed the original list, and having studied the entire dictionary, word by word, I had the most intimate knowledge and unique sense of which words worked and which didn't, so I felt I was best suited for the job. No matter how much we contributed to each other's roles and responsibilities, the word list—*every* word list—to be included in any game was my sole purview. I demanded it and was unwilling to concede ownership. While I would always consider Terry's and Gary's suggestions, ultimately, the final word list was *my* decision.

Rather than trying to devise random categories and then force the words to fit into them, I'd let the words dictate the categories. I took my list of 5,018 words into my private solitude, as I had when I first created the list in my backyard, and scanned it over and over, looking for commonalities.

The process was like solving a Rubik's Cube, turning my massive pages of words up, down, and around, trying to crack the code and see words in a clear pattern. I was getting cross-eyed as all the words and letters began to jumble together. But eventually patterns *did* reveal themselves, forming five distinct groups:

1. *Person/Place/Animal*: or related characteristics
2. *Object*: Nouns. Things that can be touched or seen
3. *Action*: Verbs. Things that can be performed
4. *Difficult*: Challenging words
5. *All Play*: This can be any type of word. All teams play the same word at the same time

I was diligent in making sure every word was put in the correct category. I smiled to myself as I put my old buddy "aardvark" in the Person/Place/Animal category, happy that my first Pictionary word now had a home. But even after reviewing the list ten times to catch any mistakes, there was one word I failed to give a proper home. Somehow, I put the word "blonde" in the Action category. (I wonder what I was thinking.)

The All Play category had its genesis in my fond memories of the crazy times McWilliams, Bart, Sean, and I shared in Spokane when we were sketching and yelling at the same time. I decided that while the category was one-fifth of all the words, it added so much fun that I wanted All Play to play an even larger role in the game. I added an arrow next to all the words I felt would be the most exciting for teams to play simultaneously. In the end, I designated 55 percent of the words as All Play.

THE GREAT THING ABOUT THE words is that there are endless ways to sketch and guess them. And drawing talent isn't necessary to win a game. In fact, being artistic is sometimes a hindrance because artists tend to be too exacting in their drawings and take too long to get started. The key strategy to up the chances at winning is to immediately get pencil to paper and begin drawing the second the timer starts. Drawing simple stick figures is more likely to help a player win than artistic talent is.

Pictionary is not only inclusive no matter one's artistic ability, but also no matter one's age and knowledge level. A grandma can team up with her teenage grandson, and a college grad can pair up with a high school dropout, and either could win.

For me, with my short attention span, I always enjoyed the instant gratification aspect. Each round proved to be a mini-game within the larger game, with a rush of emotions across the board, from anticipation to frustration to excitement—to elation or faux despair, depending on the result.

Still, Pictionary is as a competitive game, and many people enjoy gloating over a hard-fought victory. When we brought Pictionary to market, it was one of the few games where the board really wasn't vital to the enjoyment of playing. The players' attention isn't on looking down at the board, it's about looking up at the sketches and at each other.

Time and again, one thing proved to be true: winning or losing is completely irrelevant to whether one had a great time playing. Interacting, connecting and bonding with family, friends, even co-workers was the real joy.

Bottom line: from the start, Pictionary was easy to learn, simple to play, and guaranteed good, clean fun for *everyone*. And there was an additional benefit. There was tremendous play value because even if a player saw the same word in a future game, especially if they were playing with a new partner, it'd be like an entirely new word because *everyone* sketched and guessed differently. With Trivial Pursuit, when you heard a question once, you knew the answer, and so the next time you got the same question, the game lost its challenge.

Based on this, Terry, Gary, and I agreed that 2,500 words, 500 in each category, was enough to have significant play value. We settled on fifty-five for the number of squares on the game board. This was the optimal number to hold the game to around forty-five minutes—a decent amount of time to keep players engaged.

We imposed a one-minute time limit on each turn, adding urgency (and frustration) to each sketch. And we mandated no verbal communication, no letters or numbers, and no number symbol—now more commonly called a hashtag. No letters and numbers were obvious, but we felt the # would make too many words easy to guess. Other symbols like $, %, and & were allowed, but in retrospect I probably wouldn't allow those now for the same reason as the hashtag.

THE OBJECT OF THE GAME was this: teams of two to four players had to guess enough words correctly to advance to the final square on the board. To move forward, teammates would have to guess the word chosen on a card containing the five categories. Whatever square their marker was on would dictate what word to draw.

That was it, really: pretty simple and straightforward. The game's simplicity, I feel, was one of Pictionary's absolute strengths and one of the driving reasons for its ultimate success. People could open the game on Christmas morning and, within two minutes, read the rules and start playing and having fun. It was similar to the clarity of Terry's original business plan on the bar napkins: sketch words, guess words. And, because of its simplicity, people often made up their own rules, giving it even more play value.

We did over fifty playtests to fine-tune Pictionary into a coherent and solid board game experience. Because when it was all said and done, it came down to one simple question: Would the public's play experience be positive enough for them to want to play over and over again? We had to get it right.*

HOW THESE PARAMETERS WOULD TRANSLATE into the all-important packaging and board design would fall to Gary. The only requirement was that

---

* We thought with all the playtesting and player input, we had the rules nailed. Not quite. Over time, as we received player feedback, we adjusted and refined the rules to reflect their comments, if they made sense. We were flexible. Some of my jokester friends would even call in the middle of the night with rule questions. We updated the rules four times over the years.

Pictionary look sleek, classy, and upscale to appeal to the adult market. Also, it had to look cool and attractive so they wouldn't toss it in a closet, out of sight. We wanted people to display Pictionary on their coffee table, like any other home décor, so hopefully it'd be kept in plain view.

We wouldn't follow the mainstream board game style, which often included cheesy images of kids or families fake laughing on the back of the box. We were going after the upscale adult market, and our packaging had to reflect that Pictionary was created for them.

GARY COULDN'T WAIT TO GET started. Unlike his job at Alaska Airlines where his graphic design work was more structured and constrained, designing Pictionary was where his creative juices could really fly.

He went to Goodwill to pick up a pile of board games for inspiration: Risk, Monopoly, Trivial Pursuit, The Game of Life, to name a few. He studied them closely, from the game boxes, to how the components were organized, to the look and feel of the game components themselves. Gary considered the way games navigated players around the board, how the rules were communicated, and the big question: how to make it all work together in a glorious masterpiece of design.

After a few weeks of wading through all the questions, Gary announced he was ready and couldn't wait to show Terry and me his creation. I, on the other hand, was terrified, excited, nervous, and confident all at the same time. Gary was the design expert, and I trusted him to be brilliant, so I had sky-high expectations.

Maybe too high.

Terry was already at my apartment when Gary arrived carrying a brown paper grocery bag with both hands, like a precious cake.

Terry and I sat up, in rapt suspense, as Gary tenderly laid his creation on the table. Our eyes were glued to the bag as Gary slowly pulled out a nondescript box with *PICTIONARY* handwritten in capital letters across the top.

Okay, it's fine, but nothing special, I thought, a little crestfallen. I reminded myself that the real star of this big reveal was the board design and figured that's where he had spent most of his time and effort.

Gary pulled out the board and proudly unfolded it to reveal a design that wasn't as much "striking" as it was "shocking."

Are you shitting me!

It was an unmitigated disaster. It was a mishmash of tiny florescent inverted triangles, all pointing toward the center of . . . well, I wasn't sure what, really. I couldn't tell if there were fifty-five squares or two hundred, if that's what you'd even call them. They weren't big enough to place even the tiniest markers. I had no clue where the Start and Finish squares were. The colors Gary chose apparently had no clue where they were supposed to be, either; they floated around in no particular order or pattern. The damn thing didn't remotely resemble anything we could use. Or fix.

How could it be that Gary had so completely and utterly missed the mark? Had I missed the mark on Gary?

I was incredibly disappointed. And I was speechless, partly so I wouldn't blow up at Gary. We respected each other enough by this point that we could be—in fact would have to be—open and honest.

I looked at Gary and in a measured voice said, "I don't know, Gary. I don't like it. It's not what we expected."

Terry added, "Yeah, Gary. I'm not sure what you had in mind, but it's not something we can use."

As uncomfortable as it was at the time, in light of what was to come, it was an important lesson for me: I was learning to stop attaching my emotions to the outcome. Gary had worked hard and tried—and simply missed. It wasn't the end of the world, even if in the first few seconds it felt like it. And to be fair, this was his first attempt.

I went to the kitchen and grabbed three cold beers from the fridge and handed one to each of my partners. Gary looked sullen.

"Sorry, buddy. I know you worked hard on this," I said.

"Nah, Rob. I get it, and I'm sorry it's not what you and Terry were expecting. I just wanted to create something completely unique from anything else out there, and I can see how I went a little too far," Gary said, waving his beer bottle over the mess laying on the table. "Man, now that I look at it, looks like I went *a lot* too far!" Gary laughed, and Terry and I joined him.

I hated the design on the board, true, but the real pisser for me was Gary used that unimaginative, twofold board design that was the norm for board games like Monopoly and Clue.

We wanted to differentiate Pictionary from other games in the market, so every element of Pictionary needed to be unique. Our packaging and gameboard—even the way it unfolded—had to reflect that we were not just a better mousetrap, but also a different kind of mousetrap altogether. If the Pictionary gameboard unfolded like the same old, same old, Pictionary would also look the same—old and tired, that is—before players sketched their first word. Gary literally had to think "out of the box."

As Marshall McLuhan said, "The medium is the message," and we had one chance to get the message—and thereby the medium—right.

WE WERE A COUPLE BEERS in, riffing on ways to improve Gary's design, but were getting nowhere. I felt myself becoming drained, mentally and physically. I put myself in one of my time-outs, and without saying a word, I picked up my beer and walked over to my desk and plunked down. I closed my eyes and took some deep breaths, then opened my eyes and sat there, quietly.

The guys were so involved in debate I don't think they even noticed I'd left the conversation.

I looked for something to distract me and picked up a blank sheet of notebook paper that was lying on the corner of my desk. I absent-mindedly started playing with it, folding it this way and that, studying the shapes that were forming from different angles, moving my thoughts from one side of my brain to the other, giving it a different perspective on things, and admiring my origami-like creation.

Then, without any intention on my part, the paper randomly folded into thirds in my hands. As I looked at it, something told me to stop and pay attention to what was right in front of me. *Wait a second . . . What?!* My head jolted back. *Did I just come up with our board design?*

"Gary! Terry! Come here!" I yelled with a level of fervor even I hadn't expected.

I didn't say anything and just handed Gary my folded creation. He raised an eyebrow and brought it closer to eye level to inspect it more closely. He turned it over, unfolded it, folded it back again, and repeated the unfolding and folding process several times.

"It's going to require a rectangular box," Gary said, still considering the folded paper in his hands. Then he added, "It's unique, I can tell you that. There's definitely nothing like it out there." Gary looked at me and smiled. "Which is exactly what we want! It's great, Rob."

And with that, the distinctive, trifold Pictionary gameboard was born, and along with it, the unique long rectangular Pictionary box it would eventually nest in. Gary literally had to design the box to fit the board.

WHILE GARY WAS WORKING ON the prototype, he'd discovered that most board games had a catchy little tagline, a subtitle of sorts, and we'd need one for Pictionary. And not just any tagline. Ours would have to be succinct, clever, and memorable—and as with everything to do with the game, we wouldn't stop until we got it right.

Gary put together a list of taglines he'd come across in his research to help us spark ideas. Some of the better examples that inspired us are memorable to this day: "The Ultimate Trivia Challenge" (Trivial Pursuit); "The Game That Ties You Up in Knots" (Twister); "The Game of Strategic Conquest" (Risk).

After coming up blank independently, Terry, Gary, and I put our heads together one afternoon to brainstorm ideas. The only guideline was that Pictionary would be described as *The Game of . . .* something.

One of us said, "The game of drawing."

"The game of words?"

"Game of guessing!"

"The game of Terry!" Terry proposed.

Nice try.

Nothing clicked.

"There's something in the word 'drawing' . . ." Gary said in thought.

Terry and I knew Gary was on the right track and began throwing out ideas around the theme. But nothing resonated.

Gary seemed to have tuned us out, lost in thought.

Then, suddenly, a Cheshire Cat-like grin flashed across Gary's face. He stood up, shoved his right hand in his pocket, paused for dramatic effect . . . then shot out his hand, holding a pencil like an Old West gunslinger, whipping his six-shooter out of the holster.

"The game of quick draw!" he announced triumphantly.

"Damn, that's clever!" I yelled. I jumped up and gave Gary a big hug. "That's it! You did it. You nailed it!"

Gary's tagline combined the concept of drawing with guessing in limited time. That was it. *PICTIONARY: The Game of Quick Draw.*

PUTTING THE PIECES
TOGETHER

A few weeks later, Gary was ready to show Terry and me his revised gameboard and packaging ideas.

"I think you will both like it," he said confidently as he came through my apartment door.

I had a sense of déjà vu as Gary set his brown paper grocery bag on the table. The difference now was I had *no* expectations about what I was about to see.

Still, *Oh shit, here we go again,* crept in. *Please get it right.* My heart couldn't take a second failure.

As Gary began to pull the box out of his bag, my heart was racing. Slowly, but surely, out came a long, rectangular box, just like we'd agreed on.

Phew. Okay. So far, so good.

Then I examined the box design and it was, well, perfect. Absolutely perfect. It was a beautiful deep, rich blue. Across the top in a light pinkish hue was the word PICTIONARY in all capital letters. And in smaller type, below that: "The Game of Quick Draw." It was sleek, classy, and upscale, just like we envisioned. And I imagined everyone would be happy to display this handsome looking game on their coffee table, maybe sitting on top of their backgammon set or next to their chess board. Only cooler.

"Gary, you nailed it!" I applauded.

"I love the blue!" Terry added.

Relieved at our response, Gary went on to explain some of the details. "I love the blue, too, Terry. I wanted to balance the classic with modern here. To give the rich blue a modern, younger twist, I decided on salmon as the complimentary color. It's really the color of the moment, and the combo of the blue and pinkish appeals to both men and women." Terry and I nodded.

Gary went on. "The font is Goudy Old Style," adding, "and in all-caps, it makes a strong, classic statement to compliment the playful 'The Game of Quick Draw' tagline."

I nodded again, pretending I'd heard the term "font" before that very moment, let alone "Goudy Old Style."*

Gary's board design was equally spot on. Unlike his first muddled version, this iteration was open, inviting, and much easier to navigate. Each of the fifty-five squares were actually square with a clear path from Start to Finish. Gary's new design made the game look simple to play—and that was the beauty of it.

As for the game cards, each listed five words representing each of the five categories. The categories were color coded to match squares on the board. And like the board, each card had a letter indicating a category. For example, P was yellow and represented Person/ Place/ Animal. Gary designed it so that there would no confusion for the players about which word to sketch.

Gary had a wonderfully creative idea for the markers, more commonly known as pawns. He hit on the idea of using cubes—basically dice without the pips. And like dice, they were solid and heavy and a distinctive point of difference from the competition, which generally used clunky, cheap-looking plastic pieces as markers.

---

* This would be among the many lessons I'd learn from Gary. I didn't know what the terms font, pica, or even typeface meant until I met him. Soon, these words and many other design and production terms would become part of my lexicon.

The interior of the Pictionary box was even better. Gary engineered it so that every component had its place. There were two small boxes on either end: one was for the five hundred game cards; the other held four category cards, the markers, the timer, and the die. On a cardboard platform between them sat four yellow pencils that were shrink-wrapped to four four-by-six-inch pads of paper. The board lay perfectly over everything, and the rule sheet sat on top of the board so it wouldn't crease.

He made a list of every specification for every detailed aspect of the game, so when it was time for production, we would be prepared and leave no room for interpretation.

Given his limited, or nonexistent, background in games, Gary was really quite clever in his design. The look *and* feel of the game were critical to Pictionary's success, including how it presented itself on the shelf, what consumers felt when they opened the box for the first time, and if they had an emotional connection to the overall packaging. All of these things were critical to piecing together the Pictionary puzzle. Gary's brilliant handiwork gave us a fighting chance.

WITH OUR NONEXISTENT LIST OF contacts in the manufacturing industry, we didn't know of any company that could produce and deliver a finished game. Our challenge was to find suppliers for each of the nine individual components that comprised Pictionary.

To begin our search, we used the internet of its day: the Yellow Pages. This was a large, thick yellow book that was delivered every year to your front door. It weighed at least fifteen pounds, I swear. Younger readers can google that piece of history.

First up, the game's board, paper and cardboard pieces would have to be printed, cut, and assembled. I opened the phone book to "printers," scanned the long list, picked up the phone, and set up a meeting at a local coffee shop with the salesman from one company. They had the biggest ad, so I naively thought they would be the best fit. Gary naturally led the meeting, explaining our printing needs. But five minutes in, the salesman put down his pencil and said, "Is this a joke? What could you kids need with so much printing?"

"I think we are being very specific about our needs," Gary responded firmly.

Unconvinced, the sales rep picked up his notepad and briefcase and left. Apparently, the meeting was adjourned.

We were confused. Here we were, being direct and detailed with our requirements, and we were still summarily dismissed. From now on, no more coffeeshop-meetings. We needed to be taken seriously. We would go to their office (since we didn't really have one) and meet with them face to face, on their turf. I would lay out our plans for the business, and then Gary would list our needs in detail. This got their attention—and the results we were looking for.

When we left our third meeting, Gary told me he was confident we'd found the right printer.

One hurdle jumped . . . but there were still a few hundred more technical and creative hurdles to go. And many minefields lay between them all.

Our unique trifold gameboard required more technical prowess than we'd envisioned and was turning out to be a big headache. The board required a different manufacturing process than our printer could provide. It needed a specific tool to make the two cuts needed to create the trifold. He tried relentlessly to talk us out of our unique board design. "We can easily do a two- or four-fold board," he said. "We have the tools for those and can turn them around in no time."

But we were adamant: "We will not compromise our vision!" We would keep looking for someone able to produce it to our unwavering specifications.

Meanwhile, a second unanticipated problem related to the gameboard popped up. The sheet with all the game graphics on it called the "field" would need to be glued to the top of the bare boards. Our printer couldn't guarantee that they could apply the glue evenly enough for the field to adhere properly to the board and refused to even try. We had hit another wall.

It occurred to me to call our fellow game inventor friends in Oregon since they'd been through this before. Unfortunately, they didn't know a printer that could help but offered to set us up with a great connection who possibly could.

"You need to meet our friend Keith Corner," they said. "He'll hook you up."

Keith was a Seattle inventor of three successful card games. At the time, the Seattle toy and game community was made up of a small, eclectic group of people who were all supportive of each other and more than happy to help. We found Keith resourceful, engaging and well-versed in the ins-and-outs of the game business. We invited him to meet us at a popular hangout called Harry's Bar on Capitol Hill.

Keith was in his early fifties and mild mannered, but he possessed such an intensity that when he spoke, we shut up and listened.

In Keith we found the first person who really understood what we were trying to accomplish—someone who'd been there before and understood the resistance we were pushing against. We thanked him profusely, expressing our gratitude that he'd take his time to help complete strangers.

We knew we'd met our first mentor and were eager to glean all we could from him. We got down to business.

Keith asked the first question: "You guys talk to the people over at Ralph's Toys yet?"

"Uh . . . what's Ralph's Toys?" I replied sheepishly, sensing this was something I should already know.

Keith allowed a *silly boy!* smile. "Only the premier independent toy and games store in Seattle."

That summed up how much I *didn't* know. There I was, making my move into the game business with no clue about Ralph's Toys. It made me wonder: *What else don't I know?* But that didn't matter right now; I had to stay focused on my mentor.

We told Keith about our challenge finding a board manufacturer. His first assist was to refer us to his card printer in Los Angeles. He was confident they could take care of our problem.

We were quick to learn a valuable lesson in our first meeting with Keith. We realized we were in the presence of an experienced mentor. We paid close attention and followed his advice. It's one thing to listen, but without taking action, it meant nothing. Keith asked nothing from us for his time and his wisdom, except that we buy lunch. Thankfully he didn't ask for a piece of the business.

First thing the next day we contacted Keith's printer. They didn't see any issue with our production requirement and said they could get the job done to our specification. *Man, what a relief!*

Our challenges didn't end there, of course.

The back of a game box usually includes an enticing description of the game play, a picture of what's inside, the age of players, legal notices, and so on. This information is the hook that excites the customer enough to buy the game when they pick it up at the store. Based on the quotes we were getting from printers, Gary knew it would be more than we expected (and could afford) to print anything on the back of the box. He came up with a clever solution. He suggested we use a tear sheet instead—a black-and-white handout with all the relevant information printed on a separate sheet of glossy paper—and shrink-wrap the sheet on the bottom of the box, face out.* That idea probably saved us around seventeen cents per game, a substantial savings at the time.

Gary employed that same level of creative thinking to our box wrap—the printed sheet that's glued to the top of the cardboard box with the Pictionary name on it. There'd be a portion of paper trimmed off and thrown out. Instead of letting that paper go to waste, Gary designed a bumper sticker to be printed on the offcut. Since it didn't add to the overall cost, we agreed it was a genius idea.

---

* These sheets would also serve as handouts to those buyers we didn't want to leave a sample game with.

Over and over again, we learned that working with limited resources fostered our creativity and innovation. We had a finite amount of capital, and we had to make every cent count. All those little ideas, workarounds, and solutions were adding up to big savings.

With the printing head-scratchers behind us, it was a relief to deal with some no-brainer manufacturing issues. One of the easiest pieces to acquire were the pencils. We were producing a thousand games with four pencils each. I visited the local craft store and made their day by buying *four thousand pencils* in one fell swoop. The check-out girl thought I was crazy . . . she wasn't too far off.

"They're for a new game I've invented. It's called Pictionary. Be on the lookout for it," I said, beaming.

"Uh-huh," she replied without making eye contact.

"Just you wait and see," I called over my shoulder, awkwardly lugging two armfuls of boxes out of the store and running to my car in the crisp Seattle rain.

When I got back to my apartment, I piled those boxes of yellow #2 pencils on my desk. *Holy moly, I just bought four thousand pencils*, I thought. Pencils might not seem like a cause for high excitement, and they only cost us a grand total of $200, but they were physical evidence that the game was coming together. Now, we had something tangible, sitting right there on my desk in front of me, staring at me every day. It felt great to finally have a production piece go smoothly.

I was beginning to think we were on a streak of good luck when, after a relentless search, Gary's clever markers turned up at a small manufacturer in Oregon. We immediately placed an order. Another milestone achieved. That is, until I almost missed the delivery.

We couldn't afford a storage facility, so all the game components were being delivered to my apartment. On the expected delivery day, I didn't hear the knock on my door. By chance, I happened to look out the sliding glass door just in time to see the UPS driver putting a large box—*my* large box—back into his truck.

He drove off.

Shit!

I knew Gary would be royally pissed if I didn't get those cubes. I grabbed the keys to my Monarch, raced out of the apartment, and like Steve McQueen in *Bullitt*, I went tearing down the street, threading my way through traffic, hot on the heels of the UPS truck.

When I caught up to him, I skidded to a halt in front of the truck, Starsky and Hutch style, leapt out of my car, and said to the startled driver, "I'll take my package now." A bit shaken, he fetched it out of the back and handed it over.

Next came the timers. During playtesting, we found that 90 percent of all words were guessed within sixty seconds of pencil hitting paper. If we allowed players to sketch for longer, they got exasperated, or worse, the game bogged down, creating frustration and boredom. To keep things cooking, we needed to find a one-minute timer. *This'll be a slam dunk,* I thought. I was so wrong.

I searched for weeks and weeks. Three-minute hourglass timers with sand were easy, but a *one*-minute version didn't seem to exist. We didn't want to use mechanical timers for fear they'd break too easily. I looked up and down the aisles at cooking stores. Zero. I tore through every shelf at knickknack shops. Zip. The big-box stores. Zilch. I bought other games that used timers. All of *those* were three minutes.

I was stumped but not deterred.

Then one day, serendipity intervened. I was driving home when I noticed a hardware store tucked away on a side street near my apartment. I'd never seen it before. *What the heck?* I thought, and pulled over, went inside, and walked the aisles.

Well, I'll be damned! There, hanging from a hook on the back wall next to potholders and flyswatters, was my ever-elusive one-minute hourglass timer!

It was imported by a company based in Teaneck, New Jersey. I gave them a call, and the sales guy said, "We order the timers from Taiwan. How many do you need?"

Worried I was asking for too many, I hesitantly said, "Uh . . . can I get . . . one thousand?"

He snorted. "Minimum order's *five* thousand, son. Will take two months to ship."

What the hell would I do with four thousand extra timers?

Screw it. "I'll take *six* thousand."

Being the optimist I am, my rationale was that with such a long lead time, if we needed more for a second run, we would have five thousand on hand. On the other hand, if Pictionary didn't pan out, we were going to be giving one-minute timers as birthday presents for years.

By April of 1985, I had been working on Pictionary for a year while waiting tables at Lake Union Café at night. That's it. That was my life. My friends who'd always counted on me for fun nights out after work would say, "We never see you, Angel!" And they were right. I knew I was missing out on a lot of great times. But I, fun-loving Rob, was so engaged, enthused, and excited with where Pictionary was going, I didn't care. I was a man on a mission.

HOUSE OF CARDS

Even with the hiccups, we felt great about our progress on production, and Terry and I called our mentor, Keith, to give him an update.

"Great news. Now, it's time to plan the launch," Keith said.

"Launch?" I replied. "I haven't really given it much thought."

"We've been pretty focused on development and production," Terry added as a save.

We understood that eventually we'd have to introduce Pictionary to the public, but that seemed a very long way off. Besides, we had no concept of what that would look like.

"You need to have a big party to send your baby off into the world," Keith explained. Now we were talking. Throwing a party is something I could wrap my head around. But then, bummer, reality set in.

"We don't have anything in the budget for it, Keith," I replied.

But I knew he was right. We had to figure out how to make it happen. And I had just the idea of where to start.

BJ Wakkuri was general manager at Lake Union Café, and I asked him if I could hold the launch party at the restaurant on a Saturday afternoon when the restaurant was closed. BJ surprised me by not only saying yes, but also by informing me that he wouldn't charge a rental fee and by offering to let the staff help—off the clock, of course. He also said we could bring in our own food to serve to our guests.[*] It was a gracious and much-appreciated offer—not to mention how well it fit within our nonexistent budget.

All said and done, we were all in for $147. That was pretty much the money Gary had saved us on the bottom box wrap.

A COUPLE OF WEEKS BEFORE our planned launch date of June 1, 1985, we were feeling great. Things were coming together, and we had a strong sense everything was moving forward as planned. Eight of the nine game components were ready to be assembled into completed games. The markers and die were in the corner by the bathroom. Four thousand pencils were in boxes sitting neatly on my desk. The game boards from the supplier in Los Angeles were stacked in the kitchen by the stove. Cases of one-minute timers lined the hall between the living room and the bathroom. I couldn't even go to take a piss without tripping over a component. Thankfully, we had the bulky game boxes drop-shipped directly to the company that would assemble the finished product.

All we were missing were the game cards. We were producing one thousand games; each game would contain five hundred individual cards. The printer's job was to print those half-a-million cards and collate (sort) them so we would receive one thousand bundles of five hundred cards. Then, all we had left to do was simply place each of the collated bundles into the card boxes. It would only take us a couple of hours, and we'd be ready to take everything to be assembled and shrink-wrapped.

I called the printer to confirm delivery and the quoted price of $3,850.

"It's all good," he assured me. "Everything is right on schedule."

We felt comfortable with this guarantee, and with nervous excitement, we mailed out the launch party invitations.

Then, just a few days later, my phone rang. It was the printer.

---

[*] The staff was a little short-handed as one of the sous chefs had recently quit to find his aardvark in LA as a musician. He found it. He joined a little a little rock band called Guns N' Roses.

"I had to recalculate the invoice." He sounded tense. "I've got your new quote here."

"What do you mean *new* quote? We are expecting delivery this week."

"Yeah, made a slight miscalculation," he replied, hesitantly.

I felt a spike of adrenaline rip through my system as I waited for him to explain. Somehow I didn't think he was going to offer a me price reduction.

"Turns out the job is just much bigger and more labor-intensive than we thought. Way beyond what I envisioned."

Calm, Rob; remain calm.

"What are you talking about?" I said evenly, though my blood pressure was definitely on the rise. "The job was already bid, agreed, and signed!"

"Well, it's just gonna take a little longer than we thought."

"How much longer?"

There was silence on the line for a moment and a shuffling of paper. "Maybe three more weeks?"

"Are you *kidding me*?!" I screamed into the receiver. "We had a *deal*!" So much for calm.

"It's the collating; that's the problem," he hastened to say. "Without that step, we could get the cards to you in five days—"

"I've sent out the invitations to the launch party! It's all set—I can't just *uninvite everyone.*"

"Yeah, sorry about that—oh, and the price will be a little higher."

I was squeezing the receiver so hard I thought it might explode. "How *much* higher?"

He lowered his voice. "Twice as much."

"Double? Are you *insane*?"

He quickly said, "Listen, we're printing a thousand games at five hundred game cards per. That's half a mill—"

"I can do math," I said sarcastically. "You knew this going in."

"Yeah, but after we print it all, then we have to collate the—"

"I know the game! *I invented it!*"

I banged the Trimline phone against the wall and yelled "Asshole," abruptly ending the conversation.

My old friend Sean Curran, who had happened to stop by to say hi, tried to calm me down. "Easy, Rob. You'll just have to collate the cards yourself," he said matter-of-factly.

I was still so pissed off I couldn't even laugh at that one. "Half-a-million game cards! By hand! Just the three of us? That's an impossible task," I lamented.

"Four," said Sean. "I'll help."

When I broke the news to Terry and Gary, they were as pissed as me. But what other choice did we have but to complete the job ourselves if we wanted to hold firm on our launch date?

Five days later, fifteen boxes arrived at my already-too-cramped apartment containing the half-million *uncollated* cards. Whatever floor space was left had now vanished. We had a scant eight days before the launch. Terry, Gary, and I moved all of my furniture and game components into my bedroom and kitchen to make room for a production line. It all fit; fortunately, I didn't own much stuff.

We rented five eight-foot folding tables and placed them in the apartment in a maze formation. I called the closest Nordstrom and asked, "Got any empty shoeboxes you can spare?" They were happy to unload 170. We lined them up, side by side. (Little did we know our paths would cross with Nordstrom's in the most spectacular way in only a few short months.)

At the head of the first table, we stacked the cards. The idea was to fill each Nordstrom shoebox with one of each of the five hundred different cards—word card #1 through #500—making sure not to duplicate any. We would then place each completed stack into the card box. We'd repeat the entire process five times to finish off all one thousand games.

We had no idea if there was enough time to complete the seemingly impossible job of having the games assembled, shrink-wrapped, and ready in time for launch. What choice did we have? It was one of those moments where we threw up our hands and said, *To hell with it, we've got to get it done. Let's get to it.*

I put a note up at the restaurant asking coworkers to come help, with beer and pizza as payment. Even an hour or two would be appreciated. I also called a few friends for the favor. Gratefully, many showed up, including Norma, Victoria, Lori, and even Walt and his lovely bride, Doreen.

We got started, and in no time, we were in the flow of it, in assembly-line rhythm, shouting out the shoe brand names on the boxes to help keep our places.

"Adidas!"

"Birkenstock!"

"Nike!"

"F-F, uh, Frig, um, Ferag—" I stuttered trying to pronounce the name on the box with a brand I didn't recognize. "What the hell kinda shoe is this?!"

"Ferragamo, a high-end Italian brand," Terry said with no discernable stutter. Everyone caught it, and we all cracked up, including Terry.

This monotonous job went on for days. If Terry, Gary, me, and even Sean weren't at our paying jobs, we were sorting cards. I saw cards in my sleep, falling into shoeboxes like Tetris blocks. It was nauseating, mind numbing, grueling. Our 170-box assembly line went eighteen hours a day at a relentless pace.

We were three days into our task when I abruptly stopped in the middle of filling a shoebox. Gary bumped into me as I blinked my eyes and said, "Does anybody but me realize we can just put the cards directly into the card boxes and skip the shoebox step?"

A collective groan issued from the room. "Why the hell didn't we think of this before?" Gary said.

Since the card boxes took up less space, we could fit 250 on the table. Once we shifted, things went faster and more efficiently.

After six days and sleepless nights, we put the final card into the last box.

The experience might not seem like anything more than a giant pain in the ass, but there was an everlasting silver lining. This was when Terry, Gary, and I bonded like never before, getting to know each other on a deeper level. It's easy to operate when things are going well. But the real mettle of a person and team is tested when a challenge rears its ugly head. We worked together, in tight quarters, in sync as a cohesive group, shoulder to shoulder, for hours on end, to overcome our common adversary and reach our common goal.

We rose up to this beast together, and it had a lasting positive effect on our working relationship, which would come in handy as we dealt with the even greater challenges ahead.

With just two days to spare before the launch, we were ready for the final phase: the game assembly and shrink-wrapping. This would take place at Northwest Center Industry, a rehabilitation center Keith had referred us to.

Workers assembled every box by hand, putting all of the parts— timers, die, markers, pencils, pads of paper, card boxes, gameboard, and tear sheet—into each Pictionary box before running each one through the shrink-wrap machine, sealing them safely with protective plastic film.

Watching our beautiful boxes emerge from the machine all shiny and new filled me with feelings of hope and promise. After fourteen months of imagining and planning and collaborating and calculating and designing and printing and collating and sweating and working ourselves to the bone, they had arrived.

I cradled the first Pictionary game box in my arms like a newborn baby. I was a very proud father!

JUST BEFORE THE LAUNCH PARTY, a friend called to say he couldn't make it and asked where he could buy a game. We'd been so focused on producing our first run and organizing a successful public launch that I hadn't given a moment's thought to presenting Pictionary to retailers.

I had to find a retailer willing to stock Pictionary, and quick. Keith told me the University Book Store on the University of Washington campus liked supporting local inventors.

Even though we were knee deep in collating, I was able to secure an appointment to see the buyer the day before the launch.

This moved forward a question we had been discussing without conclusion: What would we set as the wholesale price for Pictionary?

We had the cost of the pencils and die, etc., but other invoices from other vendors had been trickling in for weeks and now sat in a pile on Terry's desk. We hadn't had any time or felt the urgency to calculate what each game would cost us to produce. *Now* there was plenty of urgency. We had to all take a break from collating to answer this burning question.

We didn't have to be swimming in profit but didn't want to be under water either.

As Terry added up the invoices, I said, "Look, guys, I think we have to set the price at what the market will bear. It's our most logical option. We all agree that Trivial Pursuit will be our main competition, which retails for thirty dollars. Keith says most retailers use a common industry-wide calculation called "keystoning"—stores double the wholesale price to set the retail price." (Deep discounting wasn't the norm; almost everyone sold at full markup.)

Agreement—or was it resignation—all around.

We turned our attention to Terry, who was staring at his spreadsheet, tapping the keys on his calculator, then retapping, and doing it again. Finally, he let out a deep sigh. "Guys, I've got some bad news. There's no room for profit here. Our *hard cost* is twenty-two dollars per unit."

"Damn! That's a seven-dollar *loss* on each game sold," Gary said, wincing.

Terry rubbed salt in the wound. "That doesn't include the hundreds of hours we've put in so far."

"If we use keystoning just to break even," I added, doing the math in my head, "a twenty-two-dollar wholesale price would make the retail price, shit, forty-four dollars."

We knew that could never happen—not with Trivial Pursuit retailing at thirty dollars. With a fourteen-dollar price difference, we'd be lucky to sell even one Pictionary.

My sales call was the next day. We had to make a decision.

"We have to assume that we can make up our loss with higher production volumes, and economies of scale will eventually get the unit cost down to a profitable level "Terry said

With the painful knowledge that we were losing seven dollars a game, we matched Trivial Pursuit's fifteen-dollar wholesale price.

It was a completely unsustainable business model.

I DIDN'T SLEEP WELL THE night before my appointment at the University Bookstore. I was nervous, to say the least. I had never made a true sales call before. Selling vacuum cleaners or suggesting the Lake Union Café "fish of the day" was not the same as selling to a buyer at a store. Pictionary was *my* creation, and if I didn't represent it well—or worse, if I did, and it was still rejected—I would take it personally.

That morning, I psyched myself up by visualizing walking into the bigwig buyer's spacious office. They would be sitting in a classy leather chair facing a large wooden desk loaded with toys and games. I'd confidently give my perfectly rehearsed sales pitch, and the response would be: "What? You only have a thousand games in stock? I'll take them all, right now! How soon can I get some more? A *lot* more!"

It didn't quite happen that way.

My first Pictionary sales call was Thursday, May 30, 1985, a strangely hot eighty-degree spring day in Seattle. I picked out my wool blazer, wool slacks, and a gaudy striped tie—a selection made easy due to the fact this was the only "business" attire I owned. I could have used a pair of those Ferragamo shoes right about now.

When I arrived I was sweating profusely from both the heat and nerves.

I checked myself in the rearview mirror and wiped my brow with my jacket sleeve. I hopped out of the car with all the confidence I could muster and headed for the building. Ten feet from the door, I froze. *Shit!* I'd left my sample game and brand-new official Angel Games, Inc., order sheet, which Terry had prepared for me the night before, in the car.

By the time I was back at my car, I could feel the sweat on my back. I patted my pockets for the car keys—*What the . . . ?*

The keys were in the car.

Still in the ignition.

And the car was still running.

Way to go, dumbass!

I was so nervous that I'd forgotten to turn off the damn car. I had three options: laugh, cry, or smash a window.

Several amused college kids stopped to watch me, no doubt entertained by this old man (twenty-six years old) in his wool suit, running around his car, frantically yanking on each of the four door handles like an inept car thief. I was about to go with option three, when *click!* A supposedly locked back door of the Monarch mercifully popped open. I thanked God (and the Ford Motor Company) for the crappiness of the Mercury and wondered how many months I'd been parking my car on the street assuming it was actually locked.

With the order form and Pictionary game box in a vice grip under my arm, I collected myself and ran/walked quickly back to the store, now fifteen minutes late, and soaked through with sweat. I paused at the door, stood up straight, threw my shoulders back, put a smile on my face, and filled myself with positive energy. *Now,* I was ready.

"I have an appointment with the toy and game buyer," I said to the young woman at the front counter, who could not have been less enthused by my presence if she tried.

"She's standing right there," she said, bending her head toward a woman standing two feet away in a white blouse, black pants, and a pair of reading glasses hanging from a chain around her neck. She looked at me, looked at her watch, and looked back at me like a hall monitor catching a student late for class.

"Let's go over to the perfume counter," she said as she led me down an aisle filled with Father's Day gifts like mugs, picture frames, and University of Washington purple-and-gold baseball caps.

Perfume counter? Father's Day gift items?

As I obediently followed, I had two thoughts. First, I was intrigued by the idea of a bookstore selling a variety of products other than books and bookmarked this discovery for my Pictionary sales strategy.

My second thought was wondering if the buyer chose to relocate the presentation to the perfume area because my body odor was too pungent for an enclosed office.

"Unusual product for a bookstore," the buyer said without any irony in her voice as we passed a display of University of Washington purple-and-gold teddy bears.

Unusual place to do a sales presentation. I didn't want to do a presentation out in the open where everyone could see me. I was nervous enough as it was. "I look forward to showing you why I think it's a perfect fit for your store," I said.

The buyer said nothing as we approached the counter and motioned for me to set up the game next to a display of Revlon's Charlie and Love's Baby Soft. A couple of college girls were spray testing a bottle of something so overpowering, I felt faint. I reminded myself to stay focused, cleared my throat, and launched into my well-rehearsed presentation.

"Pictionary is produced right here in Seattle," I said, leading with Keith's hot tip of the buyer's affinity for local products. I proudly held up the Pictionary game box in my left hand, waving over it with my right, just like a *Price Is Right* showcase model. "And just look at the beautiful box. But it's what's inside that will . . ."

"How much?" the buyer said, cutting me off.

How much? I was just getting started! I was a little disappointed that

I wasn't getting to finish my first pitch, not to mention impressing her with the quality of the game.

"Uh, fifteen dollars. Wholesale. Each. But they come in packs of six. So that's—"

"I'll take six," the buyer said.

"You *wha*—you will? Thank you. Excellent. Yes, thank you. You will enjoy them. Err, your customers will love the game," I said, my heart pounding with excitement.

Holy crap! I just made my first sale—in under ten seconds! Now what do I do? Oh yeah . . . write up the order, dummy.

I pulled Terry's order sheet out of my bag and stood there, pen poised above the sheet, unable to move. *Shit! I didn't go over the form with Terry.* It was my first sale and I had no idea how to write up an order.

Sensing my confusion, the buyer softened with a smile. She gently, and without judgment, took my pen and the sheet from my hands, pulled her glasses up from her chain, and onto her face, inspected the form and without hesitation, scribbled down some figures.

"Shipping allowance?" the buyer asked without looking up.

What the hell is a shipping allowance?

Before I could say I would be delivering them from the trunk of my Mercury, she said, "It's usually a dollar a game."

"That's right—that's *exactly* what our shipping allowance is," I said to her as she looked up, catching my poker face.

"Perfect," she said, jotting that down. "Advertising allowance?"

Oh geez, here we go again.

I sensed that by now the buyer knew I was a rookie. "What's standard?" I asked.

"Three percent."

"Yes, good. That's it. Three percent."

I had no idea what an advertising allowance was, but I felt the buyer was taking me under her wing, and I weirdly trusted her. I would figure out what an advertising allowance was later.

She handed me the order sheet and with a smile said, "Okay. Deliver the games tomorrow."

That's all it takes to sell the game? I could do this all day long!

As I walked back to my car, a big smile came over my face. I had done it. I'd made my first sale! The enormity, the bigger picture of what just happened, began to wash over me, over all of me. This wasn't just the sale of six games; it started a shift in my attitude. My mindset and heart-set were taking me in a completely new direction.

Until now, my partners and I were solely focused on the tasks of designing, testing, and producing one thousand games. We were taking it one foot in front of the other. But these were defined tasks. Now, with this sale, I was in new territory. *Where would my next sales call be? How would I market Pictionary? How do I get Seattle to know about Pictionary?* I had questions with no obvious answers. And I utterly and completely loved it.

Thinking, plotting, strategizing, and doing was my new mindset. *I was stepping into the unknown.* In this galvanizing moment, I was no longer just an inventor. For the first time, I felt like an entrepreneur.

Damn, it was empowering.

READY FOR LAUNCH

Saturday, June 1, 1985, the day all our hard work would culminate with the launch of Pictionary: The Game of Quick Draw, had finally arrived. I was a ball of nervous energy. We all were.

Unlike the prototype we'd been testing until now, our guests would be playing a *real* live game of Pictionary. It was like Pinocchio becoming a real live boy. Not only were we hoping our guests would love *playing* our game, we also needed to see if they would *buy*—at $30 no less. After all, for only $2.50, you could buy a movie ticket to *Back to the Future, St. Elmo's Fire,* or *The Goonies.*

The launch party would be a wedding of sorts. Terry, Gary, and I were getting married to Pictionary and publicly declaring our love and devotion. In the weeks leading up to the event, we mailed the invitations and made innumerable phone calls. Our families, friends, and everybody we'd ever met in Seattle, even strangers we met on the street, were invited to witness the happy occasion.

A little overzealous perhaps, but we were intoxicated by the product we created and wanted to share it with anyone and everyone. Besides, we had a thousand games (minus the six I sold to the University Book Store) to unload.

The morning of the launch, we three rookie entrepreneurs made last-minute preparations at Lake Union Café. An air of excitement pervaded the room. We had designed a classy game, and this was a classy venue. White tablecloths elegantly draped long tables in the center of the dining area. A Pictionary game sat on each one, deep blue and shiny in its shrink-wrap, like blocks of pure sapphire.

Gary, Terry, and I were grooms on the verge of a nervous breakdown. We had no idea how people were going to react to our new union. *Would they stand up in objection? What if they hated our beautiful bride?* We had managed every aspect of the relationship with Pictionary, but now it was in the hands of the consumer. We had faith that we'd done the best job we could, and it was time to let her fly . . . or fall.

One by one, our guests began to arrive, including my ever-supportive mom. As they entered the restaurant, Terry and I thanked them for coming, and Gary seated them. As soon as the first eight people were seated, creating two teams of four players, I gave them a quick rundown of the rules and stepped away.

"This is it," I whispered to Gary and Terry.

I looked back over to the first group to see how they were doing. *Did they get it? Did they need more explanation of how to play the game?*

I let out the breath I'd been holding and smiled. They had dived right in. They were drawing, guessing, and *hysterically* laughing. All decorum was lost as they yelled out their guesses—louder and louder as the fun and hilarity of playing Pictionary completely captivated them! And their laughter was contagious. It made *me* laugh hysterically.

Gary set up the next couple tables of players as the room got more and more boisterous. Everyone was loving playing.

Okay, looks like we were over *that* hurdle. But would they open their wallets after the game was over? That was the still the thirty-dollar question.

Terry sat at a front counter with a stack of hot-off-the-press Pictionary boxes and a metal cash box, in hopes of a table rush. I stood nearby with my optimistic silver metallic pen to autograph purchased games. And Gary worked the floor, keeping the action going, seating new arrivals at player tables, flitting from one to the next—the Pictionary concierge of Lake Union Café.

When the first team finished playing, they sauntered over to Terry and inquired, "How much?"

"Thirty dollars," Terry said. They didn't blink. They didn't hesitate. Wallets came out, cash gladly thrown down. Then, they held out their box for my signature like I was some kind of celebrity. And, I kinda felt like one.

The enthusiasm kept up throughout the day, as happy players congratulated us on our accomplishment and then purchased games. Terry stashed their cash, and I flourished my silver pen, scribbling a signature that looked more like a Pictionary drawing than my name. As the day wore on, the three of us would catch each other's eye and nod. A little smirk, really. We had succeeded in accomplishing our goal; we'd created a game that people loved playing as much as we did. None of our guests wanted to leave, not even those who'd already purchased a game.

Near the end of the day, I was finally starting to relax. I was buoyed by the thought that we might sell enough games for me to get a dog and buy a new car. Talk about a motivation to keep pressing ahead.

By the end of the day, we sold forty-two games for a grand total of $1,260—a four-figure confirmation that our many months of hard work were valued. And just as I was about to pat myself on the back, BJ, the restaurant manager, leaned in and asked, "Where was the press?"

"The *who*?" I got a sinking feeling in my stomach as he went on.

"The media. You know, the news people? How else is the rest of Seattle supposed to hear about Pictionary?" he said.

Now that BJ pointed it out, *of course*, I should have invited the media. I didn't beat myself up over it. I didn't know what I didn't know. I was still learning.

I asked BJ for his advice on how to correct the situation, and first thing the next day, I went into repair mode. BJ referred me to the corporate headquarters of Red Robin, the regional gourmet hamburger chain that owned Lake Union Café. The PR people invited me in and generously explained how publicity works, including how to write and send a press release.

"The most important thing," the exec told me, "is to stress the 'local-boy-makes-good' angle. You're a Seattle kid. That's the spin you need to put on it. This angle will resonate with the Seattle media. They won't care about an inventor from, say, Chicago. But you being from here? They'll be curious to find out what you're all about."

I took the advice to heart and used the hook to my full advantage.

Our next move would be to give the media their own special experience with Pictionary. We called our first party the "soft launch," but the press event would be the *real* coming out party.

Two weeks later, we were back at Lake Union Café for our "Local Boy Makes Good" press event. Our friends happily agreed to come back and shill for us. Two of the biggest local TV stations informed us they'd come to the event to cover it. The third, KOMO, sent a nice letter saying they were too busy to attend (read: it isn't important enough to cover).

When the first television crew from KIRO arrived, I greeted the reporter and cameraman with as much bravado as I could muster up, which wasn't much. The thought of being interviewed on TV made me anxious. Like, really anxious.

The reporter waved me over to a side booth, where we could have a little privacy.

I took my seat in front of the reporter as his camera operator loomed behind him, balancing a VHS camera the size of a small refrigerator on his shoulder. I kept my eye on the rig, thinking, *If he drops that thing on me, I am goner.*

The reporter asked me the first question . . . and then I blanked the whole thing out as I stared hypnotized by the camera lens. My best recollection of that first interview went something like this:

REPORTER:	"Tell me, how did you invent this game?"
ME:	"Rob Angel."
REPORTER:	"No, not who, *how?*"
ME:	"Oh. Two years ago."
REPORTER:	"Okay then, tell me about your growing up in Spokane?"
ME:	"Right here in Seattle?"
REPORTER:	"Hmmm. All right then, the words. How did you come up with the words for this very unique game?"
ME:	"Yes, I did. Thank you."

By now it had become clear to the reporter that he was talking to a deer in headlights. "Okay," he said, showing mercy, "that's a wrap. Thanks so much, Rob."

I was still skittish at the start of the second interview with a reporter from KING 5 TV, but I could feel myself becoming more comfortable in front of the camera and tried to relax. This time, I nailed it. I think.

That night, Terry, Gary, and I sat down in front of the TV in Pictionary HQ nervously watching KING 5 TV, waiting for our story. All of us were wondering if I'd sound at least half bright, or if I'd come off as an oaf and be an embarrassment to my partners. Thank the powers that be, the interview played amazingly well. *Look at me—I'm actually comfortable*, I thought with amusement. I listened with interest in what that confident young man was saying, as if a stranger unto myself, for I had no recollection of anything I'd said.

By mid-June 1985, we had spent fourteen months putting the game together. Now, with a launch under our belts—two launches, actually— it was time for me to get out there and start selling.

But first, we had a couple of urgent legal matters to tend to.

THE NAME OF THE GAME

Terry knew a partner in a big Seattle law firm. We set up a meeting to secure patent protection and, most importantly, to protect the name Pictionary. We were assigned to Andy Bassetti, a junior associate. I guess our fledgling game business didn't warrant senior-partner status. Andy, who sported a big, bushy moustache, was a guy our age who had the same capacity for detail-oriented thinking as Terry. We liked him right away.

"The name 'Pictionary' is your most important asset," Andy explained, "but the challenge is that the prevailing wisdom at USPTO [United States Patent and Trademark Office] has determined that an *idea* cannot be patented. Generally speaking, only a product or a design can be patented. While Pictionary is a physical item, it's based on a process that primarily involves guessing and drawing—activities generally that cannot be patented."

I wondered what this would mean for the future of Pictionary. We'd worked so hard on developing, proving, and introducing it, and now we were hearing that our idea was at risk of being copied.

"It's difficult and very expensive to successfully challenge the USPTO if they deny a patent application," Andy explained. "However, you do need to trademark the name Pictionary to protect it from anyone else using it, or any name that sounds similar, in conjunction with another board game. Once your trademark is approved, it'll become your intellectual property—or IP, as it's commonly known. Finally, I highly recommend you file for copyright protection on the Pictionary game rules, word list, and other written materials so no one can use or copy those either."

We did as Andy advised. While our applications were working their way through the sluggish approval process, Andy quit Perkins Coie and opened his own office with some colleagues, including his good friend Rob McAulay. This presented us with a quandary: Stay with the top-tier law firm or go with Andy to his much smaller, unestablished firm? We liked Andy. He was reliable and responsible, and in the months we'd worked together, he proved we could trust his advice and counsel. We liked the idea of being the bigger fish in a smaller pond. We stuck with Andy.

There was an added bonus for me, personally: Andy's very attractive office manager, Renee. After meetings with Andy, I'd casually walk into her office to do a little old-fashioned flirting. It wasn't long before Terry and Gary started teasing me, calling Renee "Mrs. Angel." Andy joked that he couldn't kick me out because I was his client. Renee didn't seem to mind. I was smitten and had the sense she was too.

It had been a couple of months since our filings with the USPTO, and we were anxiously awaiting the official response. When it finally arrived, we were happy to learn we'd been granted our copyright for the word list and the game rules. We were stunned, however, when we were informed that the trademark for *our* name, Pictionary—the very thing we needed most—had been denied.

The trademark office had determined that the name was too similar to a registered trademark for an old parlor game called "Fictionary"— ironically, the very game that my housemate Sean had mentioned that sparked the name Pictionary. The USPTO said "Pictionary" would "cause confusion in the marketplace" and therefore would be in conflict with the Fictionary mark. The denial felt like a heavy steel door had slammed in our face.

There was no way we were going to accept this news without a fight. We'd gone too far down the road with "Pictionary," and changing our name now would mean changing all our graphics, promotional materials, sales sheets—*everything*. We'd pretty much be starting from scratch. I wasn't about to let that happen. Besides, the name Pictionary was perfect, and I was not going to just let it go.

The reality, however, was that we didn't have the funds, time, or patience for a protracted legal fight. Choosing not to follow Andy's well-thought-out legal advice, and with maybe a little naïveté on our part, we decided the best option was to pick up the phone and talk to the owner of the Fictionary mark directly. Go to the source, be up front and honest, and deal with the consequences. Besides, given our financial strength, or lack thereof, we had little choice.

With my heart beating through my shirt, I called the owner, ready with the script Terry and Andy had prepared: "Hi there," I said jovially when he picked the phone. "I'm Rob Angel, a new independent game developer from Seattle with a new board game called Pictionary. Despite the similarity in the nomenclature, my game doesn't compete with yours at all. Fictionary is based on bluffing; Pictionary is based on drawing. Nobody could or would ever confuse the two activities."

That was it. I shut my mouth. That was hard for me.

"Okay," he said. "So, how can I help you?"

"If you'd be willing to give us written permission to use the name Pictionary, it'd save us a king-size headache dealing with the USPTO."

No threats, no hint of reprisal or legal action. Just the facts. We went for the straightforward, no-bullshit approach and hoped he'd respect it.

A short, albeit agonizing, silence. Then: "I don't see a problem," he said. "I won't challenge your application." His only caveat was not to use the name Pictionary for a CD-ROM as he planned on developing one for Fictionary.

I held my hand over the phone and mouthed to Terry, "What's a CD-ROM?"

Terry shrugged his shoulders, mouthed back, "It's not important," and motioned for me to agree.

"Agreed," I told Mr. Fictionary. "We will not develop a Pictionary CD-ROM."

Andy drafted a release agreement and mailed it out that day.

Within a week, we received the signed release, and Terry literally ran the letter over to Andy's office before the Fictionary owner could change his mind. Andy expedited its delivery to the trademark office. And two months later, we were the proud owners of the "Pictionary" trademark!

Catastrophe averted.

SELL, PROMOTE,
REORDER, REPEAT

With my first retail sale at the University Book Store under my belt and the *two* game launches behind us, it was time for me to get out there and sell the remaining nine hundred–plus units of Pictionary.

By now, I'd familiarized myself with our order sheet and could fill it out with proficiency and speed. I learned industry terms I first heard at the University Book Store, like "shipping allowance." Ours was a dollar, courtesy of said buyer. It was the amount we would discount each game for shipping. Since I was, for now, delivering games from the Monarch, anything we charged over that went to our bottom line. Okay, truth be told, unless the buyer asked, I didn't volunteer the discount. Why give it away?

I learned that the "advertising allowance" is the discount given on wholesale price the retailer could use to spend on promoting and advertising Pictionary. If they didn't spend the money, the 3 percent would go straight to *their* bottom line. I made a note to keep up to speed on retailers' advertising efforts.

Keith gave us some great advice about reorders: "They're the holy grail. Like most products, you can sell anything to anybody once. But the reality is, if retailers don't reorder, it means consumers aren't buying. Also, if the product isn't on store shelves, potential customers can't buy the product even if they want it. And that means—"

"We have to let the retailers know when they're out of stock," I said, finishing his sentence.

He nodded. "That's part of it. The other part is that you have to create a demand for Pictionary and keep that demand stoked. You want the consumer to compel retailers to keep your game in stock or they will miss out on potential sales."

Keith's advice meant we had to not only sell Pictionary, we had to create buzz in order to keep it top of mind and create demand. Our promotional efforts would be just as important as my sales efforts.

Thanks to people like Keith, Andy, and even the buyer at the University Book Store, we were constantly learning on the job, gaining valuable experience, filling the voids and gaps in our knowledge base. But, ironically, it was our collective naiveté that became a major asset. We didn't know all the ins and outs of the toy and game industry, the politics of how things were "normally" done, or what the rules were. How could we break them if we didn't know they existed? (I forgot to ask.) Just like there was no written manual for producing a board game, there wasn't one for the sales and marketing of one, either. We'd be writing our own "how-to" manual.

WHEN IT CAME TO SALES, my philosophy boiled down to a pretty simple premise that I'd gleaned from my first sales call at the University Book Store: if a retailer sold *anything*, they should be selling Pictionary.

In those days, if you wanted to buy a board game, you were relegated to the few independent toy stores or to national retailers like Target, Kay Bee Toys, Walmart and the big kahuna, Toys "R" Us. We didn't have access to those big box outlets as they wouldn't accept product from independent game inventors, so by default, I was forced to get creative.

I walked up and down busy streets and randomly popped into stores to sell them on stocking Pictionary. *Any* store. *Every* store. Alternative distribution? We were the Lewis and Clark of board game sales. I was fearless.

I approached real estate companies with the pitch: "Why not have Pictionary strategically resting on a coffee table so when folks are strolling through the property they think 'family values'?" The local Century 21 office took six. That one felt great given my unsuccessful real estate career.

Craft stores: "You sell pencils and paper, right? That's what Pictionary's all about!"

Party stores: "Pictionary is the ultimate party game! No brainer."

Souvenir shops: "Why not mix in a few Pictionary games with your tourist items and knickknacks? At a hundred percent markup, you'll make a killing!"

A friend owned a clothing store. I *made* him take six.

I even managed to sell Pictionary into a local pharmacy. I don't remember my pitch, but it worked! It was all a bit seat of the pants at this point.

My strategy paid off. I sold six games into nontraditional outlets here and there, which enabled consumers *not* shopping for a game to discover Pictionary. It became an impulse purchase, even at thirty dollars. Pictionary was the only game all over town—literally.

My real ulterior motive, though: I wanted to reclaim my apartment.

The easiest sale? Good old Ralph's Toys.

But there was one surprising nut I couldn't crack.

Elliott Bay Books was *the* premier bookstore in town. They sold books with pictures and words. I expected the sale to be a slam dunk. But the buyer couldn't see the connection. "We sell books *only*," he said, wishing me good luck as he handed me back my sample.

We had a few nontraditional marketing strategies. We dubbed one "Demand and Supply." Gary would call local merchants and ask, "Say, do you carry this new game . . . it's called Pictionary?" They'd say they'd never heard of it. Next day, he'd call again with the same question, slightly different voice. Seeds were planted all over town, and Gary kept watering them with repeated calls. By the time I'd walk into the store, the sale was ripe for harvest.

"Hi there. I'm selling Pictionary. Who do I talk to?"

"Oh man, we've been hearing a lot about that game lately. Let's see what you've got!"

Gary told me he seeded the game at Metropolis, one of Seattle's newest high-end novelty stores in the trendy Capitol Hill. The area was known for enjoying a nice day of window shopping or having dinner and drinks at outdoor restaurants on warm summer nights. Dutifully, I went to Metropolis and, not surprisingly, I made the sale. On my way out, I noticed Harry's Bar was right next door. I had an idea.

A few days later, Terry, Gary, and I went to Harry's and grabbed the outdoor table nearest to the heaviest foot traffic—basically, right in the middle of the sidewalk. We ordered drinks, set up a game, and started playing—*loudly!* As people ambled by (and sometimes tripped over us), they'd ask, "What're you guys doing?"

"Ah, just playing this new cool game called Pictionary. Here, pull up a chair and join us."

And *presto!* A boisterous crowd gathered around, merrily playing along. I'd toss a thumb over my shoulder and pointedly mention, "You know, they sell Pictionary right next door at Metropolis." And, for good measure, I'd throw in, "I invented it."

Worked like a charm.

If they didn't bite on buying one, we'd hand them a Pictionary game card. Our thinking was, they'd get home, find the card in their pocket, and remember the spontaneous fun they'd experienced and buy a game later. Or at least it would make a lasting physical impression on them.

We were high on the excitement and sales we created for Pictionary with this trendy crowd, but when we packed up for the night and left Harry's, our hearts dropped. The Pictionary cards we'd handed out were strewn all over the sidewalk. *Guess they didn't take them home.* Dejected, we scooped up the cards and headed right back into Harry's for another round—and to strategize.

When I returned to our table with the beers, I found Terry sitting deep in thought as he inspected a rejected card.

"Why don't we just give them a minigame? They wouldn't throw *that* away," Terry said.

"A *minigame?*" I looked at him askew and took away his beer.

"Nothing complicated—just a rule sheet, pad of paper, golf pencil, and a few cards." Terry said, taking back his beer. He waited for our response.

It took a couple seconds to register, but Gary and I soon saw the brilliance of his idea. I wholeheartedly agreed with his thinking. "And we'll give *those* away!"

Pretty damn clever.

We dubbed Terry's creation the "PicPack." It was a simple idea worth its weight in marketing gold. We handed out PicPacks all over town. The minigames enabled people to try the game with no financial risk. Moreover, they could play in the privacy of their own home, eliminating the debilitating fear of not being able to draw, which we knew held some people back from even trying to play.

This led to Pictionary going viral. Of all our marketing devices, sampling Pictionary with PicPacks was one of the most effective and most brilliant.

Damn if Terry wasn't revealing a real flair for ingenious, creative ideas. *He's not just a "numbers guy,"* I'd come to understand. *Terry is ready for bigger things.*

We sampled, sampled, sampled. People loved PicPacks. And no more cards littered the street. We had hundreds made. They were inexpensive to produce and afforded us the opportunity to promote the game anywhere: Inside a restaurant. In the lobby of a movie theater. I winged one like a frisbee into a convertible with the top down as it pulled to a stop sign. (I nearly got slugged for that one!) The minigames gave us a way to approach people and strike up a conversation with no possibility of rejection. How do you say no to "Here . . . it's free!"?

The biggest advantage of all that PicPacks helped us overcome was our number-one challenge with potential consumers: getting the pencil into their hands. The formula was simple: pencils in people's hands translated into potential Pictionary sales.

I often drove the two-plus hours north to visit my mother in Vancouver. One time I was stuck in a long line at the Canadian border. Glancing in the rearview mirror, I spotted a KOMO TV News van four cars back. KOMO was the one major local TV station that hadn't shown up to our launch party.

Seeing an opportunity, I jumped out of my car, hot-footed it to the van, handed the startled driver my business card, and tossed a couple of PicPacks through his passenger window. I quickly gave him my "local-guy-makes-good" pitch and ran back to my car.

Who knows what will come of it? I thought. *But, hell, I had to take a shot!*

A week later, I got a phone call from a TV producer asking me if I'd like to appear on KOMO's top-rated local talk show, *Town Meeting,* hosted by Ken Schram. *Are you kidding me? You bet I would!*

I was on the show with Victor Kiam, the guy you saw all over TV in those Remington commercials with his famous tagline: "I liked the shavers so much, I bought the company." It was pretty cool being on a TV show with such a famous guy. And this time I didn't freeze. I was becoming much more comfortable in my own skin in front of the camera and being interviewed by reporters. I was growing in confidence.

PicPacks weren't the only item working magic for the promotion of Pictionary. The bumper stickers Gary had created from recycling the over-trim of the Pictionary box wraps were also proving useful. I always had a fresh bumper sticker on my car.

One day, at a red light, I caught sight of a guy in my side-view mirror getting out of his car a couple vehicles behind and rushing toward me.

I was a little unnerved when he banged his palm on my window. He had a friendly but frantic smile on his face, so I tentatively rolled down my window a few inches.

"I saw your Pictionary bumper sticker," he said, "and thought maybe you'd know where I could buy a game."

I smiled, reached around to my back seat, where I always kept a couple of games in case I needed to dash into a random store to make a sales pitch (and twelve in the trunk if I made the sale), and passed one to him through my now wide-open window. "You came to the right car," I quipped, as he happily took the game from me, wide eyed. Smiling, I watched him run back to his car, carrying our blue game box overhead as I drove away.

Late one night, I was watching the *Tonight Show*. Johnny Carson was interviewing actor Ed Begley Jr. Ed talked about playing Trivial Pursuit with his friends, Geena Davis and Jeff Goldblum. Being the aggressive (i.e., shameless) promoter I was becoming, I thought to myself, "He needs to be talking about Pictionary!" and snapped off the TV.

After some digging, I found an address for Begley and sent him a letter and two games, encouraging him try it and get in touch with me. A few weeks later, it blew my mind when I received a handwritten note from him (which I still have to this day).

Dear Robert,

Sorry it took so long to play your great game. Jeff Goldblum and Geena Davis finally got me to play (Jeff started me on Trivial Pursuit as well). The best game I have ever played. Send me a dozen for my friends and family.

Thank you for both games you sent.
Ed Begley Jr.

Pictionary was definitely going places.

And it was taking me with it.

ON A RARE NIGHT OFF, I was getting ready for a date with a woman named Lesley when the phone rang. I hesitated to answer but picked it up in case Lesley was calling to say she was running late. It wasn't her. It was a storeowner in Tacoma, thirty miles south of Seattle. "I want twenty-four games," he said with a level of urgency in his voice that both excited me and made me realize I might be the one who'd be late for my date.

Before I could even grab an order pad to jot down the information, he said: "I'll be in Seattle soon. Can I pick them up around seven?"

Crap! At seven o'clock, I'd be knocking on Lesley's front door. But saying no to the storeowner wasn't even an option. Not with $360 on the line.

Do I call and tell her I can't make it, or tell her I'll be late?

Thinking fast, I gave the storeowner Lesley's address, described my car, and said, "Meet me at this address at exactly ten till seven."

I arrived at Lesley's house at 6:50 p.m., but, darn it, the storeowner was late. At 7:00 p.m., I knocked. Lesley invited me inside. "I just need a couple more minutes to get ready," she said as she walked back to her bedroom. And just as the door was closing behind me, I spotted a car pull up next to mine.

I called out as she walked out of sight. "I'm gonna run out to my car for a second. Be right back, okay?"

"Sure," she said.

I rocketed to my car as the buyer was getting out of his.

"Open your trunk!" I hollered.

"What?"

"Quick! The trunk!" I repeated as I grabbed four six-pack game cartons from my trunk.

I heaved them into his now-open trunk. "I'll invoice you later," I sort of screamed to the bewildered customer and dashed back into Lesley's house just in time for her to be coming out of her room. The entire clandestine operation had taken a mere ninety seconds.

KEEPING SALES LIMITED TO SEATTLE was by design. At this point, we had roughly two dozen outlets around town, all independently owned. I only sold to stores I could physically get to in my car. We needed to keep close tabs on our inventory. We started with one thousand games and needed to be aware of where each game in the sales chain was located: in our possession, in stores, or in consumers' homes.

For store checks, I'd walk into a store and eyeball the inventory on the shelves. If low, I'd track down the owner and, if they had more inventory in the back room, offer to help restock. If they were out of stock, I'd press for a reorder on the spot. (And you *know* I always had games in my car to sell them.) The effort was crucial to keeping Pictionary on the shelves and not gathering dust in the storeroom.

Store checks were also important for merchandizing. Where the game was placed on shelves was key. If I'd spot Pictionary on the bottom shelf of a display where nobody could see it, or on the top shelf where it couldn't be reached, I'd move into action. If Gary was with me, he'd be lookout while with blinding speed I rearranged the display, moving Pictionary to eye level, front and center. *Bye-bye, Trivial Pursuit. Enjoy your new home on the bottom shelf!*

Every one of the one thousand games was like gold to us. I was the only one allowed to remove the shrink-wrap and open a game, and that was strictly to do sales demos. They were so precious that when Gary asked me if he could have two games for his family, I replied: "I suggest Metropolis on Capitol Hill." He paid full retail just like everyone else. Gary had access to inventory and could've just taken the games. But we all understood the importance of each game. We needed the cash flow, and we needed the games in consumers' hands—and being played. (And of course, customer service being a priority, I called Metropolis shortly thereafter to see if they needed to place a reorder.)

By far, the most successful marketing tool we had was the "social media" of the day: word of mouth. Every person who played Pictionary became a Pictionary evangelist (what we might call the "influencers" of the day). When people played with family and friends, they were usually so taken with the experience, they'd run out and buy their own. Or when someone would come to their workplace bleary eyed from staying up late playing, they would tell their friends and coworkers about Pictionary.

Boom! More sales. And so on and so on.

The cycle was self-generating and self-perpetuating. People would tell their friends how much fun they had and invite them over, and the cycle would continue.

SLOWLY, I WAS MAKING HEADWAY with small, independent stores. I continued playing the "local inventor" card, which got me in the door. Next, I'd point out, "It only takes a ninety-dollar investment to get *in the game* of making money" (six games to a carton; fifteen dollars per game).*

And if that didn't seal the deal, and the buyer asked how we were going to get the games *off* their shelves, I offered to personally come and do in-store demonstrations.

I can still vividly remember how I energized and gung-ho I felt at my very first demonstration. It took place at Magic Mouse Toys, a specialty toy and game store in the Pioneer Square area of Seattle.

I walked in feeling a bit jumpy, having *no* idea what to expect. The store manager led me down a busy aisle, past parents buying Cabbage Patch Kids, Care Bears, and Glo Worms, then turned down another, past some kids reaching for Transformers and G.I. Joes. That's okay, I thought; Pictionary doesn't belong among these *toys*. The manager probably set me up in the board games section. But when he led me

---

* There was a practical reason for six games to a carton. The game weighed nearly five pounds. At almost 30 pounds to a carton, we couldn't add any more weight for fear of throwing out our backs delivering those babies.

down another aisle, past Monopoly, Risk, and Trivial Pursuit, and kept going, I nearly choked on my Life Savers.

I was taken to the lower level to a small table set up with a Pictionary game splayed out. The table was situated between the pool toys and stuffed animals—not exactly what you'd call a "prime location." But there I stood, determined to make it work. *This is even better than any of those other spots we passed,* I said to myself. *Sure, there are fewer customers here, but that also means it's easier for me to grab their attention.*

Within seconds, I found my chance. A young couple was walking by my table, barely noticing my presence.

"Hey!" I called out. "Want to try a fun game called Pictionary? C'mon—grab a pencil and draw."

They paused, gave each other a "why not?" shrug, and walked over. I hastily explained the rules, handed the woman a pencil and game card, and within two minutes, they were going bonkers!

But all the fun came to a screeching halt when they noticed the thirty-dollar price tag. They politely said no thanks and began to walk away.

I was crestfallen but snapped into action. *No! I won't just let them walk away!* I thought. I called after them.

"Look, if you buy a game, I'll autograph it!" I said, realizing I had neglected to tell them I created Pictionary.

The couple stopped in their tracks. Turns out, they were struck by the idea that they had been playing with the actual inventor and decided to purchase a game! *Nice!*

While the couple went to pay, I anxiously searched my pockets for the silver marker I was grateful I'd remembered to bring with me. When they returned, the woman held out the game for me to sign. Shaking like a leaf, I put my pen to the game box and scribbled *Robert S Angel* in metallic silver across the bottom left of the blue box—although, I'm sure my signature did not remotely resemble any discernible letters. The couple was a little giddy as they thanked me and walked toward the exit, seemingly forgetting what they originally came to buy.

It felt great! It was my first legitimate sale at retail—that is, to someone other than family and friends or the launch party guests. Then something hit me between the eyes: *Being the inventor has power, and I can use it to my advantage. Put me in front of a crowd of people, and I'll sell the shit out of it!* I'd discovered that being the inventor of Pictionary held cachet for consumers. I added this tidbit to our DIY sales and marketing manual.

I SOLD ONLY TWO GAMES in the five hours I was at Magic Mouse Toys, including the inaugural sale to the young couple. But I wasn't remotely disillusioned or tired from standing all day pitching to shoppers. I felt like I was on fire! These were two more games than we had sold at the beginning of the day.

It's funny, I remember the little numbers like these first two sales better than when some of the larger sales numbers started flowing in. These first sales were so important to me because I'd done this with my own two hands, with my stick-to-itiveness and guts. That was powerful.

THE NORDSTROM
BREAKTHROUGH

By the middle of July 1985, just six short weeks after we launched Pictionary, I was developing a newfound confidence in my sales and marketing abilities. We were making great progress, averaging fifty sales per week. All our hard work was slowly paying off. Sales were steady, reorders were coming in, and we were gaining real traction. Still, it was time consuming to sell and service each of the small independent stores who were ordering only six games at a time. There had to be a different avenue to sell larger quantities.

That's when it hit me: it takes the same effort to sell six games to an independent as it would to sell thirty-six or more to a buyer who oversaw several stores. I had been thinking too small. It was time to take the sales training wheels off and go play with the big boys.

My brother, Harvey, put me in touch with his friend Jack Minik. Jack was the vice president of footwear at Nordstrom.

"We don't have a game department," Jack said rather emphatically when I called to ask how I can get Pictionary into Nordstrom. "In fact, Nordstrom has never sold anything even remotely resembling a game."

Being a shoe guy, Jack didn't know what sort of angle it'd take to sell a game to Nordstrom's upscale clientele. Nevertheless, he suggested I call the accessories buyer, Linda Wright. He explained, "Her department has the most SKUs—stock keeping units—which means she has the most varied items for sale of all the departments. You know, jewelry, scarves, handbags, and the like"

I called Linda and left a message with her secretary.

Three days, nothing.

I called again, left another message.

Two days go by, more nothing.

Being the persistent (okay, *stubborn*) guy that I am, I called every two days over the next two weeks.

One day—there *is* a God—she picked up. "Accessories, Linda speaking." (Her secretary must've been on her break.)

I introduced myself, told her Jack suggested I call, and said I wanted to meet and talk about a product I thought Nordstrom should consider stocking.

Long, dead pause.

"Did you get my messages?" I asked.

"Sure, Ron," she said.

"Rob," I corrected.

"Why don't you come in and we'll talk?"

It was a smooth brush-off as she hustled me off the call under the pretext of taking another one. She probably finally agreed to a meeting just as a courtesy to Jack. Who cares? It was an invitation.

Foregoing my usual wool summer suit, I slid into a pair of jeans, put on a white button-down shirt, grabbed a sample game, and drove over to Nordstrom that afternoon.

I was escorted into Linda's office. She looked at me, then she looked at something on her desk. Up at me, down at her desk.

"You look like this kid," she said, pointing to what seemed like a newspaper.

I approached to see what she was looking at and saw my mug staring back at me. A day or two earlier, a news story about me and Piction-ary had run in the *Seattle Times*. Apparently, Linda hadn't made the connection between the guy who had left umpteen messages with her secretary and the guy in the story . . . till now.

"I was just reading about you," she said, finally connecting the dots.

I couldn't resist the pun and said, "Nice to know we're on the same page."

I looked at the article splayed out on her desk and could feel in my soul I was in the right place at the right time. Had we connected a week or two earlier, before the article came out, she clearly would not have been as interested in hearing what I had to sell her. And in this moment of serendipity, here we were.

I launched into my spiel, telling her how well we were doing at Metropolis and other nontraditional stores. I also told her how the women who shop for accessories are the exact demographic who were buying Pictionary like hot cakes all over the city. (I made that last part up on the fly.)

Despite the news article, I could tell Linda was skeptical. Nordstrom didn't sell anything even remotely resembling a simple-ass board game. Still, I got the sense she was stretching her imagination and all her marketing skills to envision how a board game would fit in at the tony Nordstrom department store.

Ten minutes in, she held up a hand to stop me and said, "I just don't think it's going to happen, Rob. I don't see our clients wanting to buy a board game when they are here looking for a piece of jewelry to go with the beautiful outfit they just bought. Sorry."

I damn well wasn't going to take no for an answer. Something deep inside me told me I *had* to nail this sale. There was something bigger here than just selling a few games.

I promised Linda the moon and stars—and everything in between.

"I will talk to everybody who works the floor and show them how to play Pictionary so they will be fully equipped to sell them."

She nodded halfheartedly like that wasn't a bad idea, but I could tell she still wasn't on board.

"And whatever you don't sell," I quickly added, "we'll take back. You're looking at a can't-possibly-lose situation."

She gave a meaningfully little nod. I sensed I was close to the threshold she needed to cross to give Pictionary a chance.

I kept at it. "I will *personally* hand deliver the games to each and every one of your stores."

Now she was looking right at me. I didn't let up.

"I'll do demonstrations to help your customers understand the game and move it off the shelf," I said, "and that translates to higher profits for you."

What every department store manager wants to hear.

I put everything on the table. Every possible thing I could offer was anted up and sitting in the pot. No matter what she decided, it was the very best sales pitch I could have given. I was proud of my performance.

I crossed my fingers, my arms, and my legs as she jotted something down.

"Okay, you sold me." She tapped her pen to the paper to make a period, or a decimal point, and said, "I'll take twelve games."

Twelve units. That's a good starting point.

"So, that's seventy-two games total for the six stores I manage. We'll see how those units sell and take it from there."

Twelve games per store! Now we're talking: $1,060 in revenue—in just one sale! This was, by far, the largest order to date. But more important, we had now cracked the best retailer in the city of Seattle, if not the country.

We didn't know it at the time, but this sale would be our big break.

But there was an unforeseen hiccup. Linda scheduled the games to be delivered mid-September, after the school year started. Back at Pictionary HQ, Terry and I did the math, and current sales projections combined with the Nordstrom sale indicated that we were likely to going to run out of our one thousand games around the time Linda wanted delivery. If we sold out of games before we were to ship the Nordstrom order, Linda might cancel the order entirely.

"I can't believe we're going to sell out of games by the end of the year!" I said, half incredulously and half bewildered.

Terry looked at me from his screen with a huge smile and then quickly got serious.

"We're beating our projections by a mile, which is incredible, yes, but since Nordstrom is the big fish, let's take seventy-two games out of inventory and put them aside until Linda's delivery date."

"That's still a couple of months away. We need to fill *current* orders to get Pictionary into the hands of consumers as quickly as possible to continue the momentum we are building," I said. "We can't hold back any stock to fill the Nordstrom order, no matter the risk of it being canceled if we can't deliver. Our future is now!"

Stopping deep in thought, Terry said, "Rob, we simply have to produce more games. We have no other choice."

Until that moment, we'd been comparing ourselves to my three friends in Portland who had sold seven hundred games. Now, we were on the verge of blowing past that auspicious number and within striking distance of our goal of one thousand.

Our "one-foot-in-front-of-the-other" business model was now obsolete, and we were in virgin territory. For the first time in our short history, we had to plan long term. It was time for us set our own goals and benchmarks.

WHAT WE KNEW FOR SURE was that we'd been operating in the red—a loss of $7 per game.

By economies of scale, we assumed a larger production run should result in a lower unit cost. (For us, it simply *had* to.) Another one thousand games wouldn't cut it, and we couldn't hand-assemble a larger quantity in my cracker-box apartment—that would kill us. No, what we needed was a manufacturer that was equipped to deliver a ready-to-sell completed game *and* at a price that would return a decent profit for Angel Games, Inc.

Terry, Gary, and I assessed that 10,000 games would fulfill our orders in hand and give us room to grow at a manageable pace given our company's small size. It was still just the three of us, and hiring employees was out of the question. We wanted to err on the side of caution and not overextend. Keeping control of inventory was still extremely important.

That said, not only had a few games made their way outside of Seattle, they'd begun to cross state lines. We were beginning to receive orders from outside the state of Washington. A little static on the line before I'd hear "Hello" was the telltale sign that the call was coming from a different area code. I developed a habit of waiting a beat when I picked up the phone to listen for the static, almost anticipating it. It was a thrill to get calls proving our game wasn't just a local hit. But it also meant we had to figure out how to efficiently service these out-of-state orders.

We went to our true-blue mentor, Keith Corner, and explained our production challenge.

"I HAVE A CONTACT AT Western Publishing," Keith said. "They're located in Racine, Wisconsin."

Western published the Little Golden Books children series we all grew up with and manufactured games for other companies across the nation. They had more than enough capacity to fulfill our needs.

Keith set up the call. Gary sent Western a game, along with detailed specs, right down to the typeface font (Goudy Old Style) and Pantone color number (14-1323) for the stylish salmon "Pictionary" name on our beautiful blue box.

When the bid finally arrived, we breathed a sigh of relief: *$8.60 per unit*! Music, and dollars, to our ears. This cut production costs more than 60 percent and would enable us to reap a gross profit of over six dollars per game!* And to boot, Western offered to switch out our standard #2 yellow pencils with blue pencils with erasers that matched the box. I thought this was a fantastic change, giving the game an even more polished look.

But the celebration was short lived. Ten thousand games would cost $86,000. We had nowhere near that kind of cash on hand.

Terry played wheeler dealer with Western. Somehow, he convinced them to let us pay $15,000 up front (this was *all* our available cash on hand, but Western didn't know that) and the balance when they started production.

We weren't yet sure how we'd pay the second installment of $71,000, but as Terry had begun to say in situations like these, "That's a production issue."†

Producing 10,000 games was a hefty gamble. No doubt about it. If we couldn't raise the extra capital in time, we'd be out our last $15,000 and dead in the water. We'd have no product to sell—and worse, no cash to continue operations.

We had just shy of sixty days to pull off a miracle.

---

* We also sold Western our 5,000 timers at cost to get them off our books and thankfully, out of my apartment. Sorry, no presents!

† That response would become one of our standard axioms that roughly translated to "Let's do what needs doing now to move us and the company forward and figure out the details later."

ON FIRE FOR PICTIONARY

I n July 1985, the heat was rising in Seattle, as was our blood pressure. We had to raise $100,000, and time was not our friend. This round of funding would cover the second installment of $71,000 owed to Western, allow for some marketing and promotions, enable us to pay a few bills that were past due, and maybe even provide us with enough left over for a very modest salary.

No bank had any interest in the "potential" of Pictionary. They couldn't wrap their heads around a *game*. To even consider a business loan, they demanded collateral if we defaulted. My $1,200 Mercury was clearly not going to suffice.

Our obvious first choice was to hit the road to Vancouver again and pay another visit to Uncle Jerome. If he refused to buy in, we'd be in deep shit with no money to buy a shovel. We would be forced to put our sales and marketing efforts on the back burner and spend all of our time focused on looking for alternate sources of financing.

This time around, we were the consummate professionals. No beer binges. No hanging out at the bar till last call. No triple espresso breakfast to counteract hangovers. Lesson learned. We came prepared with records of results to date and a well-thought-out business plan.

We gave Jerome our best pitch. We painted a picture of our growing business and a bright outlook for our future—which is precisely what we intended to create for Pictionary. We laid out a solid plan of action.

My uncle seemed impressed with our proposal and this time didn't go into the back bedroom to figure out his potential tax loss. He indicated he was inclined to make the investment. But I detected from something in the way he said it he had some reservations. In the end, he said, "I'll get back to you."

Terry and I drove home to Seattle, thoughtful and silent most of the way, our minds fixed on what was to become of Pictionary and a partnership we'd grown to love if Jerome said no.

Jerome's accountant was emphatically telling him not to make the investment. He felt that Jerome's original $35,000 to support his "starry-eyed" nephew's "little" venture was one thing, but it would be foolish to put another $100,000 into a startup that, according to the accountant, had no future.

Just like the banks, Uncle Jerome's accountant had no imagination. Even our robust sales projections and newfound business savvy hadn't swayed him. We could only hope it was enough to sway Jerome.

Three agonizing days later, Jerome picked up the phone and called.

"I told you in Vancouver I thought I could do the one hundred," he began in a flat voice.

My heart sank.

He continued, "But my accountant emphatically argued against it."

"I understand," I said, trying not to sound crushed.

He went on, "But I'm going against his advice."

My heart leapt back up into my chest.

"I've decided to loan you the money. Unlike the first time where we took an equity position, this transaction will be treated as a loan to be repaid. It will be collateralized by the games."

"Thank you for continuing to have faith in us," I sort of stammered as I hung up the phone.

In that moment, I was the happiest man on the planet. My uncle had enough belief in my creation that he saw it as an asset with enough value to mitigate his risk with a follow-up investment. Who am I kidding? That's just double talk for "he took a shot." Jerome wired the money—no checks to forget this time.

Western Publishing confirmed the games would be delivered in September, in time to fulfill the Nordstrom order. It was life-saving inventory for upstart Angel Games, Inc., and a giant step forward for Pictionary. But there was also serious risk. Despite our unwavering belief in the venture, there was no guarantee that 10,000 customers would snap up Pictionary. We couldn't shoulder the burgeoning costs for very long. I'd have to sell, sell, sell like never before.

With money in the bank (one that turned us down) and financial stress off our backs, we were men on fire.

For the rest of the busy and highly energized summer, Terry began putting inventory and financial control systems in place so we'd be prepared when the 10,000 games arrived. Gary and I had figured out where and how to play and promote the game in public to gain more attention and name visibility. I wrote press releases for the local media to inform them of our various events and invited TV and newspapers reporters to show up—which they did, periodically. And I did as many in-store demonstrations as I could. And of course, we continued to sell to new outlets. We were gaining recognition as three local hustlers who were starting to make some noise in the Seattle game business.

By September 1985, I was still working shifts at Lake Union Café, and Gary and Terry were working their day jobs. While I needed to pay my bills, it was a grind, and I longed for a sign from the universe that I could ease out of my waiter's job and focus solely on Pictionary. That sign would come soon, in quite a dramatic and terrifying way.

I had a real knack for making the house special "flaming coffee" at Lake Union Café. Dressed in my tuxedo, I'd position my cart in front of a customer's table, pour Bacardi 151 rum into a wine glass, light it on fire, and twirl it around as it flamed. Then, I sprinkled in a little cinnamon, which sparkled brightly in the fire, and then I would pour a shot of Cointreau liqueur to give the brew a nice glow. I'd top it all off with coffee and whipped cream, and voilà, a fun show for the customers. I was so good at lighting it up that I could make three at a time.

One night, the restaurant owner asked me to make some flaming coffees for him and a couple of his guests. I positioned my cart, set up three glasses, poured rum into each, swirled them to coat the glass and make the flame a tad more exciting to impress the boss. But during one of the swirls, a tiny portion of flaming rum sloshed out and onto the front of my shirt, eliciting a small gasp from the startled customers. I nonchalantly set the Cointreau bottle, now in my hand, on the cart, grabbed a napkin with my free hand, and dabbed out the small blaze. From 151 swizzle to flaming splash, it was over and snuffed out in three seconds, before it could catch the fabric of my shirt. Unfazed, I smiled at the guests, seamlessly picking up the bottle of Cointreau to continue my routine. The guests breathed a sigh of relief and relaxed as I tilted the Cointreau toward the still-flaming glasses of rum.

What I had failed to realize was that when I put the Cointreau bottle down to put myself out, it had caused vapors to form at the neck of the bottle, so when it touched the flame, it ignited. Fire, and alcohol, shot from the mouth of the bottle like a flamethrower, this time dousing my shirt in flaming liquor. The horrified guests shrieked and shoved back from the table.

"Oh my god!" I cried out and hurled the booze and glasses to the floor. I turned to the busboy tending the table and shrieked frantically, "Put me out! Put me out!"

The poor busboy, whose face was frozen in a mask of terror, tossed a napkin at me and bolted as flames enveloped me, the table, and the chair next to me. I grabbed two glasses of water from the table and went screaming like a banshee toward the back of the restaurant, dousing my head and face with water as I ran. I was convinced my hair was on fire and was imagining my face horribly disfigured.

By pure luck, neither happened. Thank goodness—but the sign was loud and clear. It was time to step into my future. That was the last time I'd ever make a flaming coffee. Or wait on a table.

I was twenty-six years old, and I quit the last "real job" I would ever have.

SHORTLY AFTER MY "FLAME OUT," Terry would have *his* day of reckoning.

One morning, after putting in another exhausting eighteen-hour workday between Pictionary and his day job as a financial comptroller at Spacelab, a local manufacturing business, Terry woke up in a cold sweat. His mind was racing with all he still had to get done for Pictionary. Something had to give.

A couple nights later, after a brainstorming session at my place, I dropped Terry off at his apartment. He got out of my car, turned back, stuck his head in the window, and without a flinch, said, "By the way, I put in my two-week notice today."

"You *what?*" I said.

My quitting my job was one thing. But now, two futures were on the line.

"I see the big picture here, Rob. I see the vision. I'm ready to go all in, too," Terry said. "Besides, I already quit! Let's make this happen!" he added, resolutely.

"No going back now," I said. We looked at each other, knowing it was the right decision.

He nodded. "Yep. No backup plan if we fail."

"We won't."

"We won't," Terry affirmed.

Terry and I were now both committed to Pictionary full time. We started collecting a monthly salary of $500, the meager sum we paid ourselves. I'd be eating ramen for most meals. Terry had credit cards. Gary had just been promoted to creative director at the magazine, with more responsibility and a higher salary. He couldn't live on $500, so he stayed at Alaska Airlines but continued working just as hard as ever on Pictionary during his off hours.

A FEW WEEKS LATER, WESTERN Publishing called to let us know one of us needed to come for a press check on the 10,000 games. Press checks would confirm that Western was printing the games to Gary's *exact* specifications, down to the most minute detail, including colors, card and board sizes, print, finishes, packaging, *everything*. Neither Western nor we could afford any mistakes. Normally, this would be Gary's role, but having just begun his new position, he couldn't take the time off.

My intense marketing and sales schedule made it impossible for me to fly to Wisconsin, so the job fell on Terry. Gary gave him detailed instructions on where to look for potential problems. He schooled Terry on how to look through a magnification loop to examine the printing for technical details, to check that the items that had to be glued down were done edge to edge in perfect alignment, to make sure there was no color bleeding in the printing—all the things Gary routinely did at his day job.

One of Terry's superpowers was his innate ability to take in information, analyze it, and assimilate it into whatever the task required. He could do or hear something once, and it instantly became part of his DNA. We sent him off with full confidence that he'd do a fantastic job representing our interests.

What could go wrong?

PART II
WINNING STREAK

IS IT PINK OR SALMON?

A wall of boxes stretched what seemed like the width of a football field and stacked up as high as the Empire State Building. All 10,000 games packed in 1,667 glorious cartons had arrived at the warehouse we'd rented. I took a few steps back, taking in the enormity of it all. I could hardly believe what I was looking at. *Ten thousand Pictionary games! Ten thousand!*

I couldn't wait to hold a shiny new game in my hands. I sliced open the plastic wrapping on one of the pallets with a pen knife and slowly pulled out a case. Gingerly I slit the tape along the top and sides so I wouldn't nick the contents. Didn't want to damage the goods. And with a sense of pride and awe, I methodically and carefully lifted out the first Pictionary box like it was being birthed out the womb.

I held the fruit of our creation—*my future!*—in my hands. Gazing at the perfect name, Pictionary, emblazoned gave me goosebumps. *What a beauty*, I thought, grinning ear-to-ear. *What a beautiful sight*. I turned the box over in my hands and . . .

"What the *fuck!*" I yelled, my voice echoing throughout the warehouse.

The back of the box was staring at me, blank and stark white.

There was no tear sheet—the one Gary had so ingeniously designed to be shrink-wrapped onto the bottom of the box. The *hook*. The *sell*. *Where the hell is it?*

I ran over to the storage facility office to call Gary.

"What's wrong with those idiots? We gave them specific instructions!" I fumed, trembling with anger.

"Describe what you see," Gary said.

"Nothing! I see nothing!"

"I have an idea," Gary said. "Open the box."

I tucked the receiver under my chin and quickly ripped the cellophane off the box, not giving a shit anymore if I damaged it. I threw the lid over my shoulder, and there, *inside,* was the tear sheet. *Where nobody could see it!*

"Those assholes put the tear sheets inside the goddamn box! Why would they do that? We're going to ship all ten thousand back, at their cost, and have them do it right!" I barked into Gary's ear.

I was so pissed. I wanted to hang up on Gary so I could call Western and rip them a new one.

"Rob, Rob," Gary implored, trying to calm me down. "Take a breath. We don't want to burn any bridges."

Burn any bridges? I was ready to go to Racine and burn the whole place down.

"Don't worry," Gary said, somehow unaffected by my angst or the catastrophe. "I'll call Western, and we'll figure out a course of action. These things happen. Hang tight."

I had to trust my partner. Still fuming, I went back to my apartment and opened a cold Rainier and waited for Gary's solution.

His idea really was the most expeditious fix, even though I wanted to stick Western with the job. We'd unwrap the ten thousand boxes here in Seattle and have Western reprint the 10,000 tear sheets. We'd leave the existing ones inside the box, eliminating the step of opening the boxes, and then "simply" re-shrink-wrap them with the tear sheet facing out as was called for.

THE REPRINTS ARRIVED A FEW days later, and we delivered them to Northwest Center Industries, the facility that had done such a great job on the assembly and shrink-wrapping of the original 1,000 games.

No sooner had they gotten started when it was Gary's turn to go apeshit: "For fuck's sake!" he said, holding the first Pictionary box off the assembly line like it was a dead rat. "They've screwed up the lettering! It's *white*, not *salmon*. I gave them *strict* instructions. How the *hell* could this have happened?"

"Gary," I said coolly, "we'll get the boxes reprinted. Whatever it takes. Don't worry."

"I want to know what the *hell* happened," he shouted, ignoring my words and searching furiously for a phone as the rehab center employees stood frozen, watching his meltdown.

Terry, who'd been uncharacteristically silent until now, finally spoke, albeit in an unintelligible soft voice.

"Uh, guys . . . I changed it. I was the one who changed the color."

A heavy silence descended, like the quiet just before the fury of an impending storm.

Gary quickly turned to face Terry. "You *what*?" he shouted. "Who the *hell* do you think you are, making a design change without consulting me? Do you know how much thought I put into the colors? Just picking that shade of salmon was hours of work so it wouldn't be too pink or too orange. And you just switched it to fucking white?"

Gary was so angry he was shaking.

I told the rehab center manager we had a "few things" to sort out. That was an understatement. "Wait for my call before continuing," I said as I grabbed a box and somehow managed to get Gary and Terry to come back to my apartment—in separate cars, of course.

Gary and Terry stood face to face, like two heavyweight prizefighters itching to go at each other.

"You went behind my back!" Gary fumed at Terry. "What the hell were you thinking?"

"I think the box looks better this way," Terry said. Gary took this as being dismissive of his work.

"Who told you to *think*? Your job was to *follow* my instructions!"

"White looks *better* than pink," Terry said, keeping his cool.

"It's not *pink*! For the hundredth time, it's *salmon*!"

"More people are going to like the white," Terry said bluntly. "It looks better. The name Pictionary pops—now you can actually *read it*."

"Screw you! *I'm* the one who decides what design the people are going to like—that's *my* area of expertise," Gary said, seething. "And this shit is not what I designed! I spent *hours* making sure I had the perfect package and you just, just—decide on *your own* to change it? You're an idiot, Terry. A damn idiot!"

"Take your ego out of this conversation and *look* at the damn box!" Terry said, his voice raising as he held up the game to Gary's face, then handed it to me. "You're acting like I hurt your feelings. This isn't about feelings. It's about what will resonate with consumers. I know you like your pink or salmon or whatever you call it, but most people don't share your aesthetic, no matter how much of a genius designer you are. This is about the consumer. It's about what's best for Pictionary—not what's best for you or your damn ego!"

Gary pressed his lips together and turned to me for support. I looked down at the white lettering against the blue box in my hand, then up at Gary.

"I agree with Terry's decision one hundred percent," I said. The salmon hadn't bothered me before, but now that Terry told his side of the story, I couldn't help but agree. The white lettering *did* make "Pictionary" pop, and in a sea of games on shelves, having a title that was simple, clean, and easy to read was visually very important.

I was about to give Gary my thoughts on why I was backing up Terry when he rolled his eyes, turned on his heels, and stormed out of the apartment. I didn't know if we'd just lost our designer, friend, and business partner.

Terry and I were stuck. We had a team of shrink-wrappers on hold. And Gary or no Gary, we had to keep the job moving. Were we going to wait for him? Move on without him?

Thankfully, we didn't have to make that decision. Thirty minutes later, there was a knock on my door. I opened it, and Gary walked inside with a businesslike demeanor.

I braced myself, expecting him to say he was resigning—and ask me for the $2,000 I'd promised him when he agreed to partner with me. Maybe he'd demand Terry pay to reprint the boxes with the "salmon" lettering out of his own pocket. I was ready for any number of bad outcomes.

But without saying a word, Gary went over to the suspect Pictionary box and stared at it while Terry and I stood side by side, frozen in anticipation. It was quite possibly the longest two minutes of my life.

Gary picked up the box and brought it closer to his eyes, then held it out at arm's length, studying it. He turned to face Terry and me. He'd made a decision. "You know what, Terry?" Gary said with an acquiescent half smile on his face. "You're right. The white does look better."

I nearly fainted. I could have hugged him! And hugged Terry, too, for that matter. In that one sentence, in that moment, Gary earned more of my respect than he had with all of his talent and technical expertise combined. He put his artistic ego aside for what he knew was best for Pictionary.

FROM THAT POINT FORWARD, GARY, Terry, and I resolved that any disagreement we had would never be personal or involve egos or feelings. Heated debates were reserved solely for what was best for our baby, Pictionary, and never our own self-interests.

It was a surprisingly positive conclusion to a stormy situation.

And the issue didn't linger as a wedge between us. No hard feelings. It was accepted as the new truth and was never brought up again.

I called the rehabilitation center and said one word: "Go."

Two days later, the re-shrink-wrapped games were ready. I had a sales call to make, so I asked Gary and Terry to take the games back to the warehouse and drop off several cases to my apartment that I could use for my sales calls. Even though the "salmon vs. white" issue had been sorted, I wanted to make sure that Gary and Terry could get back to where they were before the fight began. I was hoping that during the loading-unloading process they'd reconnect and any lingering tension between them would be resolved.

Oh, they reconnected all right.

After the appointment, I opened my apartment door to find hundreds of cases stacked floor-to-ceiling! My smart-ass partners had taken most of the cases to the warehouse, but realizing how much it cost to store them, decided to stuff as many cases as they could into my already-cramped apartment, leaving me with only a narrow passageway from the bathroom to the bedroom to the kitchen.

I couldn't help but laugh. They got me. I was back to where I was before I first set eyes on the 10,000 game boxes at the warehouse just days before: back in an apartment overrun with Pictionary.

I would have done the same thing.

In the end, we saved a lot of money. Now, making room to move around in my own home was a big motivator to get those games sold!

DEMONSTRATING MY SKILL

On the appointed day, I strolled into Nordstrom's flagship store in downtown Seattle to hand deliver to the first of six regional stores. As I passed the fancy dresses and expensive high heels in the women's shoe department, I felt as if I were treading on hallowed ground. *Crazy!* I thought, *I actually have a product at Nordstrom.*

I brought the twelve games to the accessories department, made sure they got onto the shelves, and talked with the staff just as I had promised Linda. I'd repeat this process at the other five area Nordstrom locations.

Later that week, appropriately decked out in my trusty wool blazer now that the September chill was in the air, I returned for Pictionary's big day—and mine. It was time to use my battle tested demonstration prowess to show Pictionary off to the well-heeled Nordstrom shoppers. Linda had set up a small, round table on the main floor, about five feet from the bottom of the escalator. Couldn't have asked for a better spot. I laid out my game and waited patiently for the hordes of Pictionary buyers to descend from above.

From my vantage point, the escalator looked a mile long. I watched with bated breath as my first prospect was lowered toward me.

I channeled P. T. Barnum. *"Step right up, ladies and gentlemen! Watch the man saw the lady in two, right here in our center ring!"*

"Want to try a new game?" I said as the shopper approached. "Come on, come on, let me show you. Let me show you how it works."

I'd done so many demos by now, I was assuming, maybe arrogantly, that people would see me smiling in front of a Pictionary game and start reaching for their wallets. But after a hard-fought four-hour day, I had sold only three games. My expectation of myself as Pictionary's premier promoter was rattled.

The biggest resistance people had was that, try as I might, I couldn't get Nordstrom customers to pick up that damn pencil. It was as if I was trying to hand them a red-hot poker.

I knew that people didn't think they could draw and were intimidated to even try, for fear of looking foolish in public. Shoppers were hounded by ego and self-judgment and would panic at the thought of having to sketch a picture with others watching. Yet the only way to fire up the engine that would produce the fun of the game (and subsequently produce a sale) was to get them to play, right there and then. I knew the problem existed, but in this store teeming with the well-to-do, the issue was severely amplified.

Gary, Terry, and I huddled to come up with a more effective way of demonstrating for these persnickety shoppers. I don't recall which one of us hit on the solution, but it was spot on given our dilemma: we needed to position Pictionary not as a *drawing* game, but as a *guessing* game. This adjustment in our strategy would prove to be pivotal in turning looky-loos into *buyers*.

At the next demo, I held up a drawing I'd scribbled on a pad. Instead of scaring them off by jabbing a pencil in their face, when the first shopper stepped off the escalator, I held up a rudimentary sketch of a nondescript animal and said, in a booming voice, "Hello there, miss. See if you can tell me what this is a drawing of?"

The woman looked at me, clearly thinking, *What the hell are you doing here, blocking my way?! I'm just here to buy a dress.*

Half looking at the picture, she said, "I dunno. A dog?"

"Wrong!" I declared, waving the paper in her face. "Try again!"

"Hmm . . . a mouse?"

"No, no, no! Try again! You're getting closer, though." No matter what her first couple of answers were, I was going to say, "Nope. Wrong!" Let her get invested with a couple of guesses, then throw the bone.

She scratched her head, then said with certainty, "A cat—it's a cat."

"Yes! How did you guess that so fast? Wow! Give me a high-five! Okay, now you draw something, and I'll guess. You're probably better than me at drawing. I can tell!"

When the apprehensive woman guessed the word correctly, she was proud of herself and more inclined to take up my challenge to draw. *Boom!* Mission accomplished. She started scribbling on the pad I'd shoved into her hand. She wasn't going to escape me. Even if I knew the word being sketched, I wouldn't say it at first. I wanted her to feel the excitement and tension for as long as possible before I gave her the victory and ego boost of me finally guessing the terrible drawing correctly. Inhibitions melted as my new best friend got more comfortable playing in plain view. Soon more people joined in and shouts of happy and engaged customers reverberated throughout the store. With this new sales tactic, I sold a very respectable nine games that day—the remainder of Linda's inventory. I secured my first Nordstrom reorder.

Two other department stores in Seattle, The Bon Marché and Frederick & Nelson, had been keeping an eye on the wild excitement over at Nordstrom. They didn't have game departments either but wanted in on the action, and the profits. They called *me* for an appointment. Oh, how things had changed. During the sales call, of course I told them I'd personally do demonstrations for their staff and customers. For them, it was like getting an unpaid employee. Done deal.

But *damn*—I should've done the math. The Bon Marché and F&N

each had three stores. Throw in Nordstrom's six, and I had committed to doing demos in twelve different locations—not to mention the independent stores where I'd agreed to do promotions as well.

By Thanksgiving, Linda was so pleased with Pictionary sales that she encouraged me to do demos whenever and wherever I wanted, especially as Christmas was just weeks away. And I took her up on it. I was happily bouncing around from Nordstrom to Nordstrom, slipping in some Bon Marché and F&N visits in between.

Even Terry and Gary got in on the demonstration action, picking up stores when their schedules permitted.

Sales, and our growing fan base, rose substantially in the lead-up to Christmas. Linda's numbers for the accessories department were through the roof, the best in years. Due to our growing success, Linda instituted a new policy. She gave her department managers at each store authority to write a purchase order at the end of the demonstration day to restock any sold inventory. It was instant reordering, something that had never been done.

It changed the course of our business.

I'd take the PO, run to my car, and get enough games to replace what I had sold that day and restock the shelves. As a result, Nordstrom *never* ran out of inventory. Equally important, they paid their invoices in twenty-nine days, like clockwork, contributing to us being cash-flow positive for the first time.

Linda's sales began attracting attention from other Nordstrom regional managers up and down the West Coast. They'd ask Linda, "How in the world are you doing this? What the hell is going on up in Seattle?"

"Pictionary," Linda said, adding, "the game sells itself."

Hey, Linda! It's me, down here at the bottom of the escalator every day!

While our philosophy had been to keep the game local, being in Nordstrom up and down the Pacific Coast was too tantalizing an opportunity to pass up. We agreed to ship to any of those stores, rolling the dice on our ability to maintain control of our growth and inventory.

And just like that we were no longer a Seattle company: we were a West Coast company.

WITH ORDERS FLOWING IN AND demand for live demonstrations growing exponentially, I was doing nothing but demos, day in and day out. It had almost become my full-time job. I would arrive at a Nordstrom when they opened at 9:30 a.m., and I'd demo at the bottom of the escalator till two o'clock, grab a quick bite on my way to The Bon Marché or Frederick & Nelson for three or four hours, grab another bite as I drove to a third store at six o'clock, and demo till closing time.

That was my life for the weeks between Thanksgiving and Christmas. And I still had to find time for marketing, writing press releases, and at some point, squeezing in some sleep.

Meanwhile, Gary and Terry were focused on the other parts of our burgeoning business. Gary was now going on a few sales calls, filling news orders, and doing store checks. Terry was focused on inventory control, invoicing, and customer service.

The pace was taking a toll on all of us, physically and emotionally.

MY ENERGY LEVEL AND ENTHUSIASM were beginning to bottom out. I was so worn down on some days that I simply could not face another demonstration. I was tired of arm-twisting strangers. My joy in the process had dwindled, and I began to question my passion for Pictionary. It was my job, and I was convinced it was my future, but some days dragging my ass out of bed was one hell of a bitch.

I discovered that passion alone wasn't enough to keep me going. What I needed was a change of mindset. During those days of flagging enthusiasm, I'd think about my *love* for my company, *love* of Pictionary, and *love and respect* for Gary and Terry. My attitude would quickly shift from my *passion* for creating Pictionary to my *love* of Pictionary.

It was like being the parent of a newborn screaming all night and day for my undivided attention. I was exhausted, but there was never any question of my devotion. These positive thoughts sustained and rejuvenated me and got me through some tough days.

Passion may have been what ignited my drive, but *love* was the fuel that kept my engine running.

ONE NIGHT, I CRINGED AS I looked around my apartment at the thousands of games still piled everywhere. We needed to find a way sell more games, and the sooner the better. As hard as we were hustling locally, selling Pictionary beyond the West Coast was our logical next step.

As fate would have it, a couple of days later, I thought the solution had arrived. The phone rang, as it had been doing quite often in those days, and Gary picked it up.

I smiled, imagining an order of 144 games.

Not quite.

When he hung up, Gary turned to Terry and me and asked: "How many games do we have left in inventory?"

Terry consulted his now-ever-present spreadsheet. "Around seven thousand. Why, Gary?"

"Kiss them goodbye!" he said. "JCPenney just ordered them all!"

Terry and I looked at Gary as he waited for the delirious shout of joy that wasn't coming.

"Guys, JCPenney just ordered *7,000 games*! What's wrong?"

"We can't fill the order," I said.

"Rob, you want to turn down one of the biggest department store chains in the country and the biggest order we've ever had?" Gary said. "*Really?*"

"Yep. Terry, you tell him,"

"Penney isn't Nordstrom," Terry explained. "With Nordstrom, every game will go on the shelf and when they're out of inventory, we'll know. We can just walk into any store and take a look."

"But it would be impossible for us to monitor every Penney store. If we ship to Penney's, the games could land in some massive warehouse.

And if they don't immediately ship them to their individual stores, we'll have a ton of Pictionary games out of circulation, getting moldy in that warehouse.

"And, should they decide not to pay us until *all* units have been sold, we'll be sitting waiting for our receivables and won't have the cash to order another print run. And even *worse,* if Penney can't sell the games and they decide to return them, even just a portion, we'll be screwed again," I said with a straight face.

"And finally, how is Rob supposed to do demos at every JCPenney in the county?" Terry added, smiling at me.

Gary nodded. "Seems I got a little ahead myself. I get it and you're right on all counts. I'll call and say thank you for your interest, but no."

While the JCPenney order was tempting on the surface, we would not sacrifice long-term success for short-term gain.

And it wouldn't be the last time.

IN THE RAMP-UP TO THE Christmas shopping season, the national bookstore chain Waldenbooks permitted their regional manager to buy games as a test for a national rollout. They asked me to "autograph a few" at a promotion in their store located in Bellevue Square Mall, the major shopping mall across Lake Washington in Bellevue.

Walden's heavily promoted the event. Their ads proclaimed: *"Meet the inventor of Pictionary!"* As far as we knew, no bookstore chain—regional or national—had ever ordered board games before, and certainly no national force like Waldenbooks had ever promoted the inventor of a game at a signing event.

I arrived at the mall and approached the table set aside for me to autograph. A big sign facing into the mall had my smiling face on it. *I don't look half bad,* I thought.

Before my butt even hit the chair, customers were lined up, clutching their precious games, eager to have my chicken scratch applied. I was a little taken aback that within ten minutes the first twelve on the floor were sold. The store manager sent an employee to fetch the remainder of the seventy-two games they'd purchased for my signing. As the full pallet was wheeled out, all decorum was abandoned. Customers were reaching over one another, elbowing people aside. I swear, it looked like a rugby scrum as they brawled to grab a Pictionary box and get in line to have it autographed.

Nobody wanted to get caught without a copy of the must-have game of the holiday season.

I smiled and signed, smiled and signed, and it couldn't be denied: Pictionary had become a force in Seattle. It was as if the game had developed its own personality and momentum, and I was an important part of the swift and wild ride, smiling and signing, smiling and signing. It was as puzzling as hell and super cool at the same time.

The pace didn't slow for any of us through the end of the year. We kept selling, promoting, and shipping as much and as fast as the three of us could.

As 1985 DREW TO A close, we'd sold an outstanding grand total of 8,600 games—a far cry from our original goal of 1,000!

No longer were Seattle-area consumers merely curious about Pictionary; they were demanding to have it. We were getting a glimpse of what Pictionary might become. Just seven months after we had launched in the very restaurant where I was a waiter, we were selling games so fast we could barely keep up. We were in awe, we were stunned, we were worn out, and we were excited beyond measure. And we were proud as hell of what we had accomplished.

NEW PLAYER

As we glided into January 1986 with the winds of the holiday season behind us, Pictionary was about to prove its worth against the biggest players in the industry.

January is traditionally a slow sales period for board games, but our seven-month-old game was defying the norm. Our sales were *increasing*. As we'd predicted, once people had the chance to play Pictionary over the holiday season, they'd hanker for shiny blue boxes of their own.

So, when the likes of Parker Brothers, Milton Bradley, and Selchow & Righter asked Seattle-area stores for their reorders of bestselling games like Risk, Clue, and even Trivial Pursuit, the answer caught them by surprise.

"Less than last year. By far, the most popular game in Seattle right now is a game created locally called Pictionary."

This got their attention.

PICTIONARY WAS HIGH IN DEMAND, and our accelerated growth meant we were headed toward nationwide distribution. Given our still-limited experience outside our local region, it was clear executing big sales from Seattle effectively would be difficult. We required some serious help.

The next step was to hire a national sales manager.

At a Seattle trade convention earlier that year, I had met an independent sales rep named John who was based on the East Coast. John shared his expertise generating big sales, rattling off his connections with top retailers, most of which I'd never heard of. John's slick delivery and in-your-face sales tactics impressed me. So, when it came time to look for our first national sales rep, I gave him a shout. The call was productive, and I thought he would do a good job for us.

Still, as soon as I hung up, there was something nagging at me that I just couldn't place my finger on. Something didn't feel right. And worse, I was feeling self-imposed pressure to hire someone *now*. I ignored my instincts, chalking up my wariness to a lack of familiarity with doing business on a national scale, and wholeheartedly recommended him.

My partners weren't on board at first, but I pressed. At my insistence, they agreed to hire John.

Predictably, it didn't take long for John to live up to Gary's and Terry's low expectations. He signed up a few small East Coast accounts but wasn't landing the chains and larger stores he'd promised. We wouldn't hear from him for days, and then every now and then, a small purchase order would trickle in. Hell, even I could have closed those orders.

It was clear I'd made a hasty and reckless decision. John had to go.

It proved to be an embarrassing lesson in the ramifications of not trusting my gut.

I CALLED KEITH: "DO YOU know a qualified candidate to be our national sales manager? We're done with slick sales guys who are all talk and no orders. We need an experienced and respected representative."

"You want to talk to Tom McGuire," he said. "He's a business associate of mine. Tom is the West Coast sales rep for Selchow & Righter, the toy company that puts out Trivial Pursuit and Scrabble. He's a bigwig in the industry and has been in the business for years. Tom knows everything, and everyone. He should be able to give you some names. Call him. He's based in Los Angeles."

I took Keith's advice and immediately called Tom for his.

"Send me a copy of the game," Tom said, "and let me think on it."

Three days later, at seven o'clock in the morning, my phone rang. It was Tom.

"I want the job," he said.

"So, you liked the game, huh?" I said, still a little sleepy.

"I played Pictionary with my family," he replied. "And the only other time in my thirty-year career that I've seen that kind of reaction was the first time I played Trivial Pursuit. I need to be involved."

I woke up out of my slumber when it dawned on me that *Tom* wanted the job. *But wait . . . maybe I'm still in a dream state because there's no way a major-league guy like McGuire would want to take a step down into our minor-league operation.*

"We need to meet," he said, driving home the reality.

I flew to Los Angeles and met with Tom at a nondescript restaurant near LAX. Tom was a good twenty-five years my senior with a kind face and a fatherly air about him. He also had a laid-back manner but a real sense of gravitas. Tom McGuire oozed class and professionalism.

For two hours, Tom versed me on the industry, the history of the games business, and how he had the means to take Pictionary to national prominence. It was like a father-and-son interaction as he patiently and thoroughly schooled me. While he talked, I got the same oh so familiar feeling I had when I first met Terry and Gary. Everything in me was saying that Tom was not merely the right guy for the job; he was the *only* guy for the job.

All the same, I didn't want to make the same mistake I'd made with John. I insisted that Gary and Terry meet him and form their own opinions.

Soon after meeting him they too were sure Tom was our guy.

For now, Tom would be our national sales manager of record. As he was still an employee of Selchow & Righter, he'd work with us on the side. We couldn't pay him anything—hell, we were still making just $500 a month—so he took a commission on all sales.

Tom McGuire was an incredible coup for Pictionary, catapulting the game, and us, into the big leagues and adding serious credibility to Angel Games, Inc. Having such an experienced colleague on our roster would prove instrumental in accelerating our growth and expansion.

Tom must have seen bigger dollar signs with us than S&R because he got right to work contacting his vast retail connections around the country. Overnight, some of the biggest single orders we'd ever received—96, 114, and 144—began pouring in. What took me weeks to accomplish with Nordstrom, Tom secured with one phone call.

The Pictionary train began to accelerate . . . faster and faster, climbing to top speed. The question was, could Gary, Terry, and I keep it on the rails?

LET'S TALK ABOUT
TOY FAIR

I n late January, just days after Tom unofficially joined the team, he called with some news.

"I signed you up," he said. "You're going to present Pictionary at the American International Toy Fair in New York City."

"The *what?*" this neophyte asked.

Tom chuckled. "It's the biggest toy show on the planet where all the major toy and game manufacturers debut new products, sell existing lines, and make connections."

"Okay, we can think about. When is it?" I asked.

"It begins February 8 and runs for about ten days," Tom replied.

"February 8? Tom, that's in less than two weeks! We won't be ready. Let's put it on the calendar to consider it for next year," I said.

Tom said more sternly now, "Guys, if you don't go to Toy Fair, I can't promise you there will be a next year for Pictionary. Toy Fair is where the most important decisions are made by retailers and the media about which toys and games will make it onto shelves that year. No matter how much we know Pictionary is a cut above the rest, if it doesn't have a presence at Toy Fair, it's like it doesn't exist."

"Mattel, Hasbro, Coleco, and Worlds of Wonder are there, competing for attention from the buyers not only between themselves, but between small, independent game companies like yours. Buyers from around the globe will be there, looking to get in on the next toy or game craze."

"Well, I guess one of us better start packing," I said, convinced. There was no way we were going to forfeit our chances by not attending.

Our budget didn't allow for all three of us to attend. It made the most sense for me to go.

I booked the cheapest hotel I could find. My room was so small that when I opened the door, it hit the end of the bed. I had to climb over my suitcase to get to the bathroom, which was so tiny, it felt just like my apartment back home, which was oddly comforting

I'd never been to New York, and I was awestruck. I was dizzied by the tall buildings, honking cabs, hot-dog stands on every corner, and people scurrying like mice in all directions as if perpetually running late or being chased.

At first, I felt small against the huge and overwhelming backdrop, like I didn't belong there somehow. I was out of place and way out of my element. As the cold February air kept slapping me in the face, it also knocked some sense into me. Hell, *yes*, I belonged there. *Pictionary* belonged there. I had the hottest game in Seattle, and now I was ready to share it with the world. Armed with the knowledge and confidence that Terry, Gary, and I had put in the necessary work, I was ready to take on the Big Apple.

Toy Fair was held at the Toy Center, the hub of the toy and game industry. It's where just about every toy and game you remember from your childhood had first been introduced to the world since World War I. By the 1980s, the Toy Center had expanded to a one-million-square-foot complex with two buildings on 23rd Street and 25th Street, at the intersection of Fifth Avenue and Broadway.

Tom made arrangements with his buddy, Seymour Butchen, for me to show Pictionary in his seventh-floor showroom. He was a small independent contractor who represented several different product lines. Seymour set me up at table slightly bigger than a TV tray, located at the back of his cramped and claustrophobic 12' square showroom. It was jam-packed with dozens of toys and games: plush animals, dolls, puzzles, and more lined the shelves. I noticed a raggedy doll in the corner, flopped to her side. It freaked me out a little, but I shook it off. I had to. It was game day. Literally.

With Pictionary's success in Seattle now expanding up and down the West Coast, and the fact that Tom promised I would meet key buyers, I imagined people would be climbing over each other to get a look at Pictionary. Instead, soon after the show opened, I was beginning to think I'd been deluding myself.

The Toy Fair experience was very different from strolling into a Nordstrom where the store managers were thrilled to see me. The buyers here couldn't care less about my "local-boy-makes-good" story. The few who did stop by didn't know diddly-squat about Pictionary— and even after playing with them, there was a constant refrain: "What is your nationwide marketing strategy and how are you going to move product off *our* shelves?"

I couldn't offer them my most effective sales weapon: demonstrations. I couldn't promise I'd come to all of their stores, one by one, and do demos.

When I informed buyers I didn't have a marketing strategy in place, they turned on their heels without placing an order.

I sat at my itsy-bitsy table, looking hopeful but feeling dejected, and selling nothing.

I was going a little stir crazy, being mostly alone in the showroom, and took to idly wondering where Seymour spent his time. It was one of the few times in the young life of Pictionary that I was bored.

And it was only day one of the ten-day show. Ugh.

Meanwhile, Tom was working his day job at the Selchow showroom upstairs. After all, he was still their West Coast sales guy. On a break, he came to check on me.

"Man, I'm not getting the hang of this, Tom," I said with a groan.

"Don't worry about it, kid," Tom said. "Trust me. I know what I'm doing." He winked and walked away.

The nerve, I thought, winking at my pitiful situation.

Ten minutes later, in walked the slickest, coolest cat I had ever seen: beautifully coifed, slicked-back silver hair and perfectly fitted suit. All I could think was, *I'm going to sell this Sinatra look-alike six games if it kills us.*

The guy looked left, then right, like he was casing the joint. Then he walked straight over to me, arm outstretched to shake my hand.

"Hey, Rob, right? Nice to meet ya," my visitor said with a New York accent so thick I'd only ever heard it before in movies. "I'm Kevin McNulty, an associate of Tom's. I have an order for you."

"An order?" I said, a little confused. Hardly anyone at Toy Fair had even seen the game, let alone expressed interest in ordering it.

He smiled. "I'm upstairs, selling Trivial Pursuit . . ."

"Okay . . . ?" I said, still not getting it.

"Tom said I should take some orders. I've been telling my biggest clients about Pictionary, telling them that in my professional opinion, it's the next big thing since Trivial Pursuit. I told them to get on the bandwagon and place their orders."

To my amazement, this complete stranger handed me an order form, and strolled out as smoothly as he had entered. He didn't even wait to see the look on my face as I looked at the order.

If he had waited, he would have witnessed my eyes bug out of my head when I saw the number: *285 games!* (Kevin clearly didn't get the memo that the games came in cartons of six, but who was I to argue?)

I plopped down in the chair to avoid fainting just as another man walked in. This guy was short, stocky, with a Marine buzz cut and the same confidence as McNulty.

"Hey, Rob. Dobby Dobson," he said. "I work the Southeast region for Selchow & Righter. I'm a friend of Tom McGuire. He told me to drop by."

Before I could reach out my hand to shake his, he handed me an order, turned, and walked out, just like Kevin had. I looked at Dobby's order: *288 games!*

An hour later, different guy, same thing. "Bill Napier. Tom sent me." *Bam! 258 games.*

An hour later, again, same thing. "Tom McGrath . . ." *Another 360!*

That day, six guys handed me orders totaling 1,205 games.

At the end of the day, I said to Tom, "You haven't been wearing yourself out giving game demos upstairs, have you?"

He grinned. "No, no—that's *your* forte," he said. "My secret weapon is my cadre of sales pros who know the game market and see where Pictionary's headed."

I looked at him, smiling and shaking my head in wonder. Hell, *I* didn't yet see the full picture of where Pictionary was headed.

Tom definitely had his way of doing things. But I sensed there was more to the story than a bunch of guys wanting to help out a kid out of the goodness of their hearts.

Tom gave me a look. "This is all off-books, Rob. Just me and my friends."

I shot him an "I don't get it?" look back.

"I've been working with my colleagues for a very long time. They are the most experienced sales group in the industry, each repping the most well-established brands for over twenty years. We're comfortable with each other, you know? Trust each other. We're like family. My sending them Pictionary meant the game had to be something pretty extraordinary. They took one look, agreed, and wanted in."

In what? I thought to myself.

Tom, sensing I wasn't tracking, put his fatherly arm around my shoulder, and said, "Come, Rob. Let's go meet the boys."

My new mentor walked me over to Phil's, a loud, bustling Irish pub where Tom's Selchow buddies regularly gathered to unwind after a long day at Toy Fair. Like Tom, these guys knew *everybody,* and *everybody* knew them. They'd witnessed products and trends come and go and come back again. This band of brothers was the "Who's Who" of toys and games, and I was about to enter their inner circle.

I can't say I wasn't more than a little intimidated as I followed Tom, but the guys immediately made me feel welcome as a bona fide member of the group. As we happily slammed back our cocktails, my new friends shared how they got started in the business and regaled me with success stories and failures with equal fervor. I could tell they liked the new kid on the block, sensing I had something very special on my hands.

And, they hoped, in their hands, too. It turned out they were in a pretty precarious situation.

Over the din and smoke of the crowded pub, Tom turned to me and quietly said, "These fine fellas here at this table? What you are seeing are the best game salesmen in all America." Lowering his voice a little more, he added, "But we're all at a stalemate in our careers. We're facing forced retirement when the sale goes through."

"What sale?" I asked, lowering my voice to meet Tom's.

"The Coleco buyout," Tom said. "They're purchasing Selchow & Righter. We're all looking at being fired or forced to retire. Coleco has their own sales force and will let us Selchow salesmen go the day after the sale goes through."

I learned that Coleco wanted to acquire the rights to Trivial Pursuit, which Selchow held. But Selchow wouldn't let go of their crown jewels, so Coleco purchased the company outright.

"What are you all going to do?" I asked Tom.

"Well, none of us are happy about it, obviously, but . . ." Tom said, smiling, "they're *very* excited about Pictionary. Your game could be a lifeline for them."

Tom had seen the writing on the Coleco wall. Aware of Pictionary's unlimited opportunity, he had begun laying tracks with a plan for himself, for his buddies, for us—and for Pictionary.

My eyes caught Kevin's; he winked and tipped his vodka glass toward me. I nodded, toasting him back.

They saw real potential in the game. And they had passion—the kind of passion that created loyalty you can't buy. A mutually dependent relationship was forming. These men were willing to roll the dice with Pictionary.

The next day, the guys kept piling on the orders. And the next day. And the next. At the end of each day, I'd tally the haul and call Terry and Gary who'd be waiting in anticipation for the phone to ring.

Gary wanted to know how the packaging was received. "Did retailers like the rectangular-shaped box?"

"They *love* it," I told him. "The novel shape and trifold board is a winner. And they love your modern, clean blue box. It's a real standout among a plethora of old-school designs."

Terry wanted to get down to brass tacks. "How the hell are we going to fill the orders?"

"I don't have a clue, Terry, but we'll figure it out. That's a production issue," I said, laughing.

When I arrived back in Seattle, I had orders for nearly twelve thousand games!

ON A PERSONAL NOTE, WHEN I arrived at Toy Fair '86, it had been just two weeks since the *Challenger* disaster on January 28 that killed all seven astronauts on board when it tragically exploded just seventy-three seconds after takeoff. I was still a little shaken by the event. Just a few months earlier, I had pinned a front-page newspaper article about Christa McAuliffe, the first schoolteacher in space, on my vision wall. I was in awe of her audacity and courage.

When the *Challenger* exploded, taking with it an ordinary citizen who had aspired to great things—someone I could relate to—I was crushed. Every day between the disaster and my trip to New York, I'd look over to the article about Christa as a reminder to live every day as my best day, with courage and audacity. Life is precious, and tomorrow is *not* guaranteed.

I was thinking of Christa again on my flight back to Seattle when I looked out the window and up at the vast sky. The Space Shuttle *Challenger* mission was McAuliffe's moonshot. And in that moment, Pictionary was mine.

My experience at Toy Fair was a turning point, and I was now on a new mission. A new set of goals and dreams were forming. My mindset shifted from taking one small step in front of the next, intuiting my way forward, not fully knowing where things were headed, to being ready to take one giant leap.

With the earlier milestones, I'd think, *Awesome—one task completed. On to the next!* Now, I was seeing how Pictionary could compete with any game on the market. It could sell *millions*. I could visualize introducing Pictionary to the world—and the fun and excitement on the faces of *millions* of people, rather than hundreds or even thousands.

Pictionary was the dream I'd been waiting for all my life. It was time to dream bigger. It was time to scale Pictionary to the stratosphere.

THE NEXT MONTH, TOM McGUIRE quit Selchow to come work with us full time, continuing to work on commission. We couldn't have afforded him otherwise.

Another major change involved the company name. At Tom's suggestion, we agreed to change it from "Angel Games, Inc." to "Seattle Games, Inc." As much as I loved having my name on the box, Angel Games didn't resonate with buyers, whereas Seattle Games would. It was best for the company. How's that for taking your ego out of a decision!

After Toy Fair, the other former Selchow guys—Bill, Dobby, Kevin, and Tom #2—plus an independent West Coast rep, a trusted friend of theirs, Frank Martin, became our de facto sales force. Pictionary orders were coming in, fast and furious.

To address the exploding demand, we had to manufacture more

games. *Lots* more ... and immediately. Terry ran the numbers. We could afford to double our last run of 10,000 units to 20,000 which would further reduce our per unit cost from $8.60 to $7.50—a significant and much-welcomed savings. This would solve the short-term problem of filling the orders from Toy Fair, while a bigger problem was looming. Producing 20,000 games at a time wasn't going to sate the public's ever-growing appetite for Pictionary. We had no way of financing more than 20,000 units given our cash flow. We were running a race in a Ferrari but were short on gas.

Terry placed the order.

Meanwhile, Tom was about to make our Ferrari seem more like a Matchbox car.

"Rob, 20,000 isn't going to cut it," Tom said without hesitating when I called to tell him the news. "Not even close. I'm confident advising you to produce 250,000 units. It's March, and we're already getting calls about holiday-season orders."

A quarter of a million games? Just a few months ago, we thought selling 1,000 games was an ambitious goal. Sure, we'd met that goal quickly, but it was hard for me to wrap my arms around producing 250,000 games! And that's when I remembered I was in "dream big" mindset.

I told Terry about my conversation with Tom, knowing that 250,000 units was more than ten times what we could afford. But it was possible that Tom was on target. So much for our desire to maintain control over each and every game sold. We calculated that we'd need an infusion of roughly *$2 million* to cover production, sales and marketing and building up our business operations to sustain current and projected levels of growth.

Our first thought was to go back to Uncle Jerome and Auntie Anne, our faithful financiers. After all, we now had even more proof that we were on the right track, not to mention the addition of the topflight industry veterans working with us.

We set up a meeting with Jerome to share the updates of our accelerated growth and financing required to meet the demand and fore-casts. Under any circumstances, $2 million was a gigantic ask—and something his conservative accountant would *never* condone. Hell, we knew it would probably give the guy a heart attack. This time, Jerome took his advice.

It wasn't a surprise. And we understood.

Without Jerome's investment, we were in a serious bind. Our financing options were still pretty much nonexistent. Our growth would be seriously hampered if we didn't come up with a viable financ-ing alternative.

We were clearly on the fast track to capture consumer hearts and wallets, but there was no guarantee they would keep us there. Other board games were also catching wind, and if we couldn't keep Pictionary on shelves, consumers would simply find an alternative. We couldn't let that happen.

Gary, Terry, and I tossed around ideas of how, and from whom, we could raise more capital. We were coming up empty and called Tom McGuire to see if he'd known of other fledgling game companies who had been in similar situations.

Without hesitation, Tom offered a solution: "Your best option, probably your *only* option, is to license."

Tom's clear and simple advice was not merely one of the many pivotal moments in the lightning-fast story of Pictionary; it would become one of the most monumental decisions we would ever make for the company—a decision that would alter the very trajectory of our lives.

"What, specifically, does licensing involve?" I asked.

"In its simplest terms," he said, "you're giving another company the right to manufacture, market, sell, and distribute Pictionary. In return, they pay you a royalty on each unit sold, a fixed percent of the net whole-sale price. They bear *all* the costs and, most importantly, they'll have the capacity to produce in the large quantities we need. Your financing and supply problems go away. You retain ownership of the IP. It'll allow you to operate under a business model that lets you move forward without the baggage involved in ramping up and managing all the moving parts of a large business. It frees you up to be nimble and take advantage of any opportunities that might come your way."

Licensing made perfect sense. It could propel Seattle Games, Inc., from a regional player to a national one, just like that. And at someone else's financial risk.

Terry, Gary, and I understood immediately that licensing Pictionary was the best and most logical option.

Now, we had to put Tom's advice into action.

WOW OR WHOA?

Terry put out a feeler to an old college buddy who worked at Worlds of Wonder, the Laser Tag and Teddy Ruxpin company. Terry sent him a game to see if they'd be interested in discussing a licensing deal.

We took mild offense to their letter confirming receipt, which read: "Just a quick note to tell you that we received your letter and the *Dictionary Game* this week."

Dictionary? Is it Worlds of Wonder or Blunder? We chalked up their misspelling to an overworked staff and hoped it didn't indicate a lack of attention to other important details.

A week later, we received an invitation to meet with Don Kingsborough, president and CEO of Worlds of Wonder. We were impressed and anxious to hear the CEO himself wanted to meet us.

Terry and I flew down to the WOW headquarters in Fremont, California. When we arrived, we were ushered into a cavernous office and directed to sit in what seemed liked little kid chairs. Facing us was a large, ornate wooden desk with an oversized plush, padded chair fit for a king. This was the kind of office I envisioned I'd be taking a meeting in at my very first sales call.

A side door to the office swung open, and a man clearly of massive self-importance entered the room through what I could have sworn was a puff of smoke. Mr. Kingsborough gave us an all-knowing look as he walked assertively toward his desk, eyes fixed on us all the way. He might have just come from a men's fashion magazine cover shoot. His shiny suit was so immaculately pressed it looked to be made of plastic. A silk handkerchief stylishly peeked from a breast pocket. His fingernails were perfectly manicured, and he sported pointy-toed leather shoes, polished to a reflective sheen.

He settled into his throne and surveyed us from behind his desk for a good thirty seconds of itchy silence. Finally, Kingsborough asked in a booming voice, "Do you want a game company . . . or do you want to make money?"

I thought it was the same thing. It seemed like a trick question.

If we had a game company to manage Pictionary sales, marketing, etc., and we did it right, the money would come. Seemed pretty straightforward.

"We want a game company," I said, looking at him square in the eye. I turned to Terry with a shrug.

Terry nodded his approval.

I turned back to Kingsborough, satisfied I'd gotten it right. "Yeah. We want a game company."

He made an almost imperceptible sound in the back of his throat, like: *Ooof—you blew that one, kid.*

Kingsborough the Omnipotent placed his hands flat on the desk, leaned toward us, and so quietly that we had to lean forward to hear him, said, "No. You don't. You want to *make money*. In business and in life, it's not what you make. It's what you keep. When you own a company, *you're* responsible for maintaining offices and hiring employees. There's research and development costs for continually developing new game concepts. You have a huge beast to feed. Year after year, never ends. Every expense you pay out is less profit you get to keep. If you boys have your own company, you ultimately don't get to keep as much of your money. With licensing, it's different."

"Different how?" Terry asked. The conversation was much more detailed than Tom's top-line explanation of licensing. We were processing the details of what Kingsborough said as fast as our minds would crank.

"As your licensee, we would handle all the heavy lifting." He counted off on his fingers as he listed the items: "Sales, manufacturing, distribution, and marketing efforts. You license with us, and all of these costs are borne by us. All of the risk becomes ours. We shoulder all of those responsibilities. We manage the brand for you."

He sat back in his chair, flashed a gleaming, toothy grin, and said, "And you boys get to collect the money. At the end of every quarter, we add up how many games we sold and cut you a check based on an agreed percentage of the net wholesale price. That's the licensing fee. It's yours. You don't put any money up, you don't carry any inventory, you don't call UPS or DHL or schlep to the post office."

"So, what do *we* do?" I inquired, now sitting a little straighter in my toy chair.

"For all I care, you can go home and eat bonbons in front of the TV while you watch *The Golden Girls* or *Family Ties* or whatever," he said, chortling. "Point is, you guys will be free to do whatever you want to do with your lives. Travel the world. Buy a mansion. A yacht. Start a new business. We handle everything, soup to nuts, headaches and all."

He had me in the palm of his pinky-finger-ringed hands. We wanted as much money as possible from Pictionary sales, and now the responsibility and hassle of running a game company didn't seem as attractive a business model as we'd initially thought. The picture Kingsborough painted was slick and clean, antiseptic even. And it alleviated all of the attendant problems of having to constantly produce the quantities needed to cover our explosive growth. And—the big and—we'd get our first royalty check in just a few short months.

"What I'm going to do is send my people up to Seattle, and they'll explain all the contract details." And just like that, he left on his magic carpet.

We boarded the plane for home, flew back on Cloud Nine, our minds on fire with the possibilities of the whole wonderful concept of licensing. I was already starting to spend the coming royalty money in my head. I'd bought hook, line, and sinker into what Kingsborough was casting our way.

A week later, we got a phone call. Worlds of Wonder was ready to make their official licensing proposal. We'd all meet in the offices of our attorney, Andy Bassetti.

We asked Tom what to expect a deal might look like, and he informed us that normal royalty rates ranged anywhere from 3 to 5 percent. But Pictionary was hardly a "normal" game. We were slaying the competition and had already proven Pictionary's landslide potential. In effect, we were proof of concept for Worlds of Wonder and had every expectation they would up the ante.

The day of the meeting at Andy's firm, the two WOW guys (*good cop / bad cop?* I wondered) sat across from Terry, Gary, Andy, and me. They slid a nicely bound, slick-looking proposal across the conference table. I opened it to the first page, pretending to read the content in order, but was really scanning for the royalty percentage.

And there it was. Instantly my mansion, my yacht, and my vacation to the Caribbean went *poof!* They were offering us a measly 3.5 percent.

And as if that insult wasn't bad enough, they also wanted total control of every aspect of the game.

"Our design staff feels the game could be enhanced significantly with a few graphics and rules changes," the proposal declared.

I glanced at Gary, wondering how he was taking the news that our baby was ugly. He was doing a magnificent job of containing himself. Not me. My blood was starting to simmer. It only got hotter when I read that they wanted first right of refusal on *everything* we invented in the future. They demanded TV rights—something we hadn't even thought of at this point in the nascent life of Pictionary.

They want to own us and *control us.* They didn't even offer any upfront money as a signing incentive. Just a $250,000 guarantee in royalty payments over time.

The Worlds of Wonder boys must've thought they'd been really clever and had pulled a fast one on the Seattle rubes. The unintended consequence of this lopsided proposal was it got us thinking of Pictionary as not just a game, but a *brand*. We were afforded a much bigger vision for our future beyond simply selling board games. And we wanted our due.

THE WONDER OF WORLDS OF Wonder was losing its sheen. We told them we'd discuss their proposal and repaired to another conference room. We huddled up. It was obvious we needed to push back, hard. The corporate beast was clearly trying to steamroll the little guy. I think they believed we, the starry-eyed pups, would be grateful for any crumb they tossed us. But their attempted coup backfired. It only proved to us we had something special. Something damn well worth protecting. And something worth fighting for.

To do that, we would have to keep a significant level of control over our licensees. We couldn't let them skate off with our product for a song (and off-key at that) in addition to doing with it as they pleased.

With this contract, who knows what would become of the game in their hands and, in turn, our royalties?

We walked back into the conference room and countered: "Seven percent and board game rights only. Furthermore, WOW won't be allowed to change *anything* regarding Pictionary, including design, packaging, and rules—not one single word without our written approval. And absolutely no right of first refusal on future games we might create."

Following the *Who the hell do you boys think you are?* look on their faces, they summarily rejected our counter, refused to go a nick higher than 3.5 percent, and nixed letting us retain control of the packaging. For two hours, we bumped heads, going back and forth, finally getting them to a 5 percent royalty but getting nowhere with the remaining, and equally important, points. Negotiations—or the lack thereof—came to an end.

A few days later, we officially rejected their offer.

THERE WAS A POWERFUL, UNDISPUTABLE takeaway from the WOW experience—one that would become an internal motto at Seattle Games, Inc.:

> *No one will love and respect Pictionary as much as we do.*
> *No one will care as much, or put in the attention to detail,*
> *or put forth the effort to keep Pictionary as perfect as it is.*

The WOW proposal made us see there'd always be some ego-driven marketing manager who'd try to put their personal stamp on the game by changing the graphics, the gameboard, the words—*anything*. There'd be some show-off number cruncher who wanted to impress the boss by saving a nickel here and a dime there, cutting corners to pad their bottom line at the expense of the game's quality. And there would be some sleazy/lazy salesman who wanted to give a steep discount to make his numbers for that month, diminishing the credibility of the Pictionary brand. All marketing, design, and salespeople have their own interests at heart, not Pictionary's. And definitely not Gary's, Terry's, and mine.

Star Trek had their prime directive, and we had ours: *Take care of Pictionary, and it will take care of us.*

We would treat Pictionary as if it were our very own child and trust that in doing so, financial success would come, accolades would come, and happiness would come. We would nurture it, take care of it, and protect it.

No one was going to harm a hair, or pencil, on its pretty little blue head.

DEAL OR NO DEAL

The WOW episode had the effect of turning boys into men. We had grown as businessmen and were determined to ply our newfound knowledge and experience.

Hasbro was the behemoth of the toy and game industry. With the purchase of Milton Bradley in 1984, Hasbro controlled 60 percent of the half-billion-dollar North American board game market. (At the time, the two company names were interchangeable and will remain so for the purposes of this book.) With the addition of Milton Bradley, Hasbro now owned leading brands like The Game of Life, Twister, Chutes and Ladders, Candyland, Simon, and countless others. When they expressed interest in acquiring the rights to Pictionary, we were pretty excited.

Needless to say, we sent them a game immediately. And this time, there was no calling our game "Dictionary." Hasbro was more professional and invited us to their corporate headquarters in East Long Meadow, Massachusetts.

Terry and I walked into the conference room and were greeted by the vice president of marketing, who stood grinning conspiratorially, holding something behind his back in his left hand, as if it were an engagement ring.

"Hey, guys; nice to meet you," he said, shaking our hands with his free one, then using it to guide us to the chairs in front of the conference table while he moved to the other side. He remained standing.

Just as we got comfortably seated, the VP whipped his left arm around and slapped a box down hard on the table, landing with a loud *whap!* Terry and I flew back in our chairs, startled by the theatrics. We caught our breaths, leaned forward, and looked at the . . . well, even today, I cannot aptly describe the *thing,* the atrocity, that was presented to us. At least it had "Pictionary" splashed across it. I thought it was Pictionary, anyway.

"Uh, what's that?" I said.

Smiling with exuberant pride, he proclaimed, "We redesigned your game! The whole nine yards. This is what we're going to do for you. We love this idea."

Good thing somebody did, because it had the ugliest piece-of-shit graphics I had ever seen. It made Gary's first design attempt look like a Rembrandt. The monstrosity was stark black and white and covered in psychedelic swirls. It was next to impossible to make sense of anything on this mystery box (we dubbed it "the eye chart"). The VP—still the happiest person in the room—lifted the top with the flare of a magician to reveal the gameboard, which was the same old four-fold square as other dull, unimaginative boards on the market. This scenario once again reinforced our prime directive. *Nobody will ever love Pictionary more than we do.*

Fresh off the WOW debacle, I was not only under wowed, but becoming hot under the collar. *Here we go again! Why does everyone want to change our game?*

"Look," I said, not bothering to hide my disdain, "Pictionary is selling just fine as is. That is why you are talking to us. I am fed up with people trying to tell us what's best for Pictionary. *We* know what's right. We intentionally designed Pictionary to be unique. To be different from all the cookie-cutter games out there."

I was about to continue when I felt Terry's hand under the table gently squeeze my knee. I stopped talking. "I think what Rob means to say is that Pictionary is not just another board game," Terry said in a tone much more measured than mine. "We have significant sales with our current packaging. We appreciate that you took the initiative to present something new, but the game is doing phenomenal numbers just the way it is. What's the saying? 'If it's not broke, don't fix it.'"

I had to hand it to Terry. He knew exactly when to step in and be the yin to my yang. I tended to speak off the cuff, wearing my emotions on my sleeve. When Terry felt I had their attention, he would gently interrupt my rant and deliver a more succinct, dispassionate version of our argument.

I never really knew when I'd start an impassioned plea—and neither did Terry, for that matter. While unplanned and completely organic, over the years together, our good cop/bad cop interplay would become our modus operandi.

And that day, our MO worked. The Hasbro VP now fully understood how deeply committed we were to not change a thing about Pictionary. Once we got past the eye chart, we had productive discussions. We had every reason to believe they would be a responsible licensee. They hadn't become the biggest player in the world by not knowing a thing or two about the category. It was not surprising that they laid out a strong sales and marketing plan. We were impressed.

A week later, the Hasbro team came to Seattle to discuss their official proposal. Right out of the box they offered us an 8 percent royalty— nearly double the Worlds of Wonder offer. At least Hasbro acknowledged all our hard work and Pictionary's future value. But that was as far as the good news went. The rest of their offer was practically a carbon copy of Worlds of Wonder's, less the first right of refusal. Hasbro expected control of all marketing and packaging decisions.

First step in our negotiations was to tell them their 8 percent royalty was too low. We countered with 10 percent.

On the other equally important issue, we insisted on retaining complete creative and packaging control; the agreement would be breached if they changed *anything* without our written approval. They'd be required to spend 3 percent of the wholesale price on marketing, advertising, and promotions. We would retain final approval of all plans to make sure they stayed on message.

Additionally, we wanted minimum annual sales guarantees. We couldn't have them lose focus and scale back on Pictionary in favor of the next big thing, or if our game no longer fit into their product mix.

"Pictionary is not just a game," Kingsborough had schooled us. "It's a *brand*."

Bottom line, Hasbro would only be licensing the rights to produce and sell the board game that *we designed*. They'd stick to their core competency: manufacturing, distribution, sales, and marketing. That was it. Nothing else.

We believed the executives heard us and were receptive to our requirements. They said they would discuss our points with their colleagues in corporate. One of them even said to our face that he didn't see any issues with our demands.

ONE WEEK LATER, A CERTIFIED package bearing the Hasbro logo arrived at Andy's office. Terry, Gary, and I were as excited as kids on Christmas morning to tear it open and review the contract together. We each had a copy and began a silent cursory scan through the document. Ten percent royalty . . . *check!* Minimum sales guarantees . . . *check!*

And then we got to the last page.

What? I leafed through the draft again and again, squinting, peering closer each time around, scanning across and down. *Where's the . . . ?*

I echoed the look on Terry's face with my voice. My very loud voice. "Where are the creative and packaging controls we demanded? We were quite explicit with our requirements—the same ones they said shouldn't be an issue!"

"Are there other pages?" Gary asked as he grabbed Terry's copy to see if his was missing something.

"No. There's nothing else," Andy confirmed.

Conspicuously absent were the guaranteed marketing spend, not to mention the promise that they wouldn't change Pictionary packaging and graphics without our express written consent. There was nothing about giving us oversight of marketing, and the deal would be only for the board game rights.*

We had to get to the bottom of this. Rather than going through the time and expense of having the lawyers hash it out, we approached it the same way we did with the owner of Fictionary. We picked up the phone, called Hasbro directly, and confronted the situation head on.

Terry and I went to sit near the speakerphone. Gary sat off to the side, nervously jiggling his leg. Andy stood close by in case we needed him.

The Hasbro executive picked up the phone right away. "Hey, guys. You received our offer, I assume. What do think? Fantastic, right? We're really looking forward to getting started as soon as you sign."

"We received the offer and we're nowhere near ready to sign," I said. "There are a few items missing. Where is the marketing spending guarantee and advertising allowance? Where's our quality control? All those things we agreed to?" I said in a calm voice while shooting daggers at the speakerphone.

After a couple of silent beats, the voice on the other end said, "Rob, we're Hasbro. You're going to have to trust us."

The arrogant tone of this guy's *"trust us"* did not sit well with me. What were all those hours of negotiating, smiling faces, and hearty handshakes about? What history did I have with these fools that I should trust them? I didn't trust anyone but the three guys in that room with me.

Andy wisely reached over and pressed the mute button to avoid the Hasbro exec hearing words we could never take back.

"What the hell does *'You're going to have to trust us'* even mean?" I asked aloud to no one in particular.

---

* It was clear in our negotiations that Hasbro saw no value in TV and merchandising, so they had no problem letting them go. But believe me, Gary, Terry, and I did.

"If they don't put it in writing," Andy conferred, "there is no way you can enforce their compliance."

Everybody nodded in agreement.

If we couldn't trust them to live up to their word now, how could we trust them moving forward?

Terry unmuted the call. "Listen, we're going to need those guarantees. In writing."

"Can't give them to you. Management won't sign off."

Terry punched it back on mute, as he, Gary, and I exchanged a shared look of resolve. No backing down, no matter what.

Terry hit unmute. "We need those guarantees. Or no deal."

"Sorry, can't do it."

"Then no deal." Terry clicked off.

Terry mumbled, in a voice trying to be steady and unflappable but undermined by the look of uncertainty on his face, "Let me get this straight: we just hung up on the biggest game company on the planet?"

"Yeah. And with a great royalty rate. And no Plan B," I said, as the ramifications of what had just transpired washed over me.

"Until we figure out a way to ramp up, someone can come along and knock us off with a competing product," Gary said. "Either we'll be out of business or our growth will be completely stymied."

"Guys, take a breath. This is just a negotiating tactic," Andy said. "They'll call back."

"Andy, *we hung up on them.*" I was overcome with the sick feeling that we'd just totally screwed ourselves.

"They'll call back," Andy repeated with faux confidence.

They didn't. We reached out a couple of times to try and keep negotiations moving forward. Hasbro wasn't budging. And neither were we.

Terry, Gary, and I were on the same page. We agreed that declining the offer was in our best interests—and what was best for Pictionary.

HERE I WAS, ALL OF twenty-seven, living on $500 a month in a shithole apartment and driving a beat-up ten-year-old car. I could have changed it all with one stroke of the pen. Instead, I turned down an offer that would've virtually guaranteed I'd be millionaire. Wasn't that the goal of licensing? To make and keep as money as possible? Did I just throw away the biggest potential payday of my life?

Despite this nauseated feeling in my stomach, in my heart of hearts, I was absolutely sure I'd made the right decision. I would not and could not compromise my integrity just to cut a deal—even if it meant going back to waiting tables.

The fact that Terry and Gary were in complete alignment with me on this, despite what they could have gained individually from a deal, made me appreciate our partnership even more. We had overcome so much together and were stronger than ever as a team and as friends. We had the same goals and vision for our future. It did *not* include this offer.

While the road ahead was uncertain, our unwavering determination was clear. We would take Pictionary as far as we could with the resources we had at our disposal.

MEANWHILE, AS ALL THIS WAS transpiring, Tom and his crew were working as hard as ever. Pictionary sales were rapidly increasing.

Filling those orders was another matter.

A JOINT VENTURE

Two weeks after we rejected Hasbro's offer, Tom called. He told us of a man he worked with named Joe Cornacchia. Joe was an independent print broker who worked on the Trivial Pursuit account for Selchow. He was responsible for coordinating the manufacturing of millions of TP units. He was *the* man to know in game manufacturing.

Like Tom and his sales crew, Joe became expendable after the Selchow buyout. Fortunately for us, he was scratching around for something new when Tom contacted him with the idea of licensing Pictionary.

Joe saw the potential in Pictionary, and we saw the potential in partnering with Joe. A few days later, Terry and I were on a plane to New York City.

Sarge's is an old-school New York-style deli, complete with padded maroon Naugahyde booth benches, dark-brown Formica-topped tables, and bright lighting. The hunger-inducing aroma of pastrami mixed with a light smoky haze and strong testosterone wafted through the air. Sarge's did not exactly exude the atmosphere of "high finance" I was expecting.

But this was where Joe had called the meeting, so that's where Terry and I, along with four others, stuffed ourselves into a booth built for four. Aside from Joe, we were shoulder to shoulder with Tom McGuire, Kevin McNulty, and Mel Long, a representative from

Western Publishing, our current manufacturer. We were so tightly packed in that none of us could lift a coffee mug without elbowing somebody on the right or left.

The conversation—if you could call it a conversation—was like radio static. Mel and Joe were chatting on the far side of the booth, alternately nodding or wagging fingers at each other. I figured they were negotiating some kind of an offer for us, but it was so loud in the deli, I couldn't hear what they were saying.

I glanced inquiringly at Terry sitting across from me and mouthed: *What's going on?*

He shrugged. *No idea.*

We sat semi-patiently, still and quiet.

After several more minutes, Joe shook hands with Mel and turned to Terry and me and said, "Western Publishing and I have come up with a plan to form a joint venture and would like to make you an offer to license Pictionary."

He had our full attention.

Joe proposed that Western would handle manufacturing and distribution, Tom would preside over the newly incorporated "The Games Gang"* to handle sales and marketing, and Joe himself would oversee the entire joint venture.

"We'll give you a fifteen-percent royalty rate," he added. "And we only want the board game rights for North America."

I looked at Terry with a euphoric expression. Terry met mine.

Joe continued, "Our advertising spend will be three percent. You will have final approval on all marketing plans. We'll guarantee 200,000 minimum game sales every year, or you get Pictionary back. We won't change anything about the packaging without your advance written

---

*   These would be the displaced salesman from Selchow who were already selling Pictionary. In addition, Frank Martin would handle the West Coast region. When The Games Gang revealed their logo, Gary wasn't impressed. He joked that the design of the "GG" looked like Gucci gone bad.

approval. And you will have the right to approve any changes to the wholesale price, less the normal cost of doing business."

Joe went quiet as the waitress set our food down. He looked around the table at each one of us until she left. Then he broke his silence.

"That's it. That's the offer," Joe said, as he picked up a steaming hot fry, dipped it in ketchup, and coolly took a bite. He didn't look up as he picked up the next fry, inviting us all to dig in. "You gotta try these. Best damn fries in all of New York City," he said, biting into the next.

Terry and I sat there for a moment to take it all in. *Was this really happening?* "We need a moment," Terry said.

I followed Terry outside into the bright New York sunshine. Having been burned by the last two negotiations, we were cautious, yet fully aware this might be our last chance at a licensing deal.

"Did I hear him right? Did Joe just agree to everything WOW and Hasbro refused to give us, and at a much higher royalty rate?"

Terry nodded. "Tom obviously told them about our previous unsuccessful negotiations."

"Joe has impressive credentials. He gets things done," I said. "And we already have experience with Western and the ex-Selchow guys. This sounds pretty hard to pass on. What do you think?"

"I like the idea of working with this group in a new venture that's in effect a start-up, like we are," Terry said.

"Except *this* start-up," I said, while making a hand motion in the space between us, "will get us a fat royalty and a familiar sales force that'll continue working for us, and *we* retain the rights to the rest of the world."

"And they . . ."

I knew exactly what Terry was going to say and finished his sentence for him: "*They* do all the heavy lifting—sales, distribution, manufacturing, and marketing."

He nodded. "It's why we held out. Any thoughts on the 200,000 minimum annual sales target? I think they can hit it. What about you?"

I sort of blanked out for a second. I was doing the math in my head on what I'd make from the royalty on the minimum guarantee. When I had the number, I was on the beach in Bali. I snapped back to reality. "Yeah. It feels like a good deal to me. Perfect, actually."

Terry and I went back inside and wedged ourselves back into the booth.

"We like your offer, Joe. Put it in writing, and we're in business,"* Terry announced to the group on our behalf. "Now, pass us some of those famous fries."

Kevin and Tom were also ecstatic. They now had their own game company rather than being out of a job. Everybody went home a winner.

We were thrilled to be dealing with a group of entrepreneurs who, like us, were hungry, creative, and independent from corporate constraints.

Tom became president of the newly formed Games Gang, Inc. He'd no longer be working for us at Seattle Games. However, Tom was still due his commission—on all future games sold, including games now sold through the joint venture. While under no obligation to do so, Tom graciously waived this stipulation, proving once again he was an honorable man.

Terry, Gary, and I signed the licensing contract with the joint venture (JV) on July 16, 1986, less than fourteen months after our *first* launch at Lake Union Café. We could now, officially, eat bonbons and watch TV, as Mr. WOW had suggested. I was missing *Days of Our Lives*, after all.

THE THREE OF US COULD have done what many founders do after they sign a lucrative deal like this: walk away from the business, collect the royalty checks, and do what they wish with the rest of their lives. Trav-

---

* Except for one small mistake: it didn't occur to us to put an expiration date on the contract or make it renewable at our discretion. The 200,000 guarantee seemed like a large enough number (given our 8,600) to let them continue with the license. The oversight would come back to bite us.

eling, lying on the beach, creating another game, or even becoming a serial entrepreneur were all attractive options.

We, however, were nowhere near ready to move on to the "next." Three reasons made us pause.

First, our financial futures were now tied to someone else's efforts. As much as we liked and trusted our licensees, we had to remain vigilant and make sure they did the job they were under contract to do. We would not let *them* ride off into the sunset with *our* financial lives in their hands. We had our contractual controls, and we would use them.

Take care of Pictionary, and it will take care of us.

Secondly, we still retained the ancillary rights to Pictionary, and there were multiple potential revenue streams to explore in areas other than board games: TV, merchandising, and promotions. Those opportunities were ours to exploit—and exploit them, we would.

And lastly, our agreement with the JV was for U.S. and Canada only. We still owned the IP worldwide. We had no clue about international business, not to mention no understanding of the cultural differences. We also had no concept of how enormous the international market truly was. But we'd kick our entrepreneurial spirit and drive into high gear and figure it out, as we had always done.

With so much at stake, we would absolutely stay involved. Instead of taking the fruits of our labor and kicking back, Terry, Gary, and I leaned in. We would work even harder and smarter to guide Pictionary to even greater heights.

We didn't own the world. Not yet.

A BOX OF PAPER

While we no longer controlled the rights to sell the board game, we maintained ownership over the fastest-growing board game in America.

Terry, Gary, and I reveled in this idea. Without the pressure of having to raise capital for manufacturing, we could focus our energy on seeking new and inventive ways to leverage the Pictionary brand. We were open and ready for opportunities to bring more joy to more people. And for more revenue to come our way.

There were personal benefits to licensing as well. It meant no more schlepping games to retailers, no more playing Pictionary in Harry's Bar on Capitol Hill to attract passers-by, and no more running from one in-store demonstration to another without a moment to catch my breath.

There was only one small problem. Actually, a big one.

I was flat broke.

Until our first royalty check arrived, my measly $500 monthly draw, even by mid-1980s standards, meant I'd was still relegated to bumping around Seattle in my beat-up Mercury.

Since I could remember, I'd been dreaming about the car I wanted to be my first *new* car. I was practically salivating over the thought of it, all shiny and black and sleek. Being an instant gratification kind of guy, it was painful to have to wait.

"What kind of car are you dreaming of, Rob?" Terry asked as I shared this with him over a couple of beers on a quiet summer evening.

"A Saab 900 S," I said without hesitation.

Terry looked at me inquisitively, as if my answer was the setup to a joke.

"It's Swedish," I said.

"I know what a Saab is, Rob," Terry said. "But it's not at all what I was expecting you to say. You're pining after a *Saab*? Not a Ferrari? A Lamborghini?"

"Oh please," I said. "Those are some pretty good-looking cars, sure, but they spend half their time in the shop. I want a solid, dependable car that spends its time on the *road*. Plus, I just think the Saab is a really beautiful car."

"Gee, and I thought *I* was the practical one!" Terry said as he took another sip of his Olympia beer. "How much would the Saab set you back?"

"Sixteen thousand," I said.

"Sixteen *whole* grand, Angel?" Terry said, laughing.

"Well, that's sixteen grand more than I have in the bank," I said with a little snark in my voice.

Terry chuckled and put his hand on my shoulder. "Rob, listen, I'll put the down payment for the Saab on my credit card. You can pay me back when you get your first royalty check. I think you're good for it, Mr. Pictionary."

I clinked my beer with Terry's. "Thanks, buddy. Means a lot."

The next day, Terry and I drove to the dealership to meet my new car. I spotted it immediately as we drove up to the lot.

"There she is, Terry," I said pointing to the car of my dreams.

The Saab was as beautiful in real life as I imagined it would be. I took my place in the driver's seat as Terry got into the passenger's. I slowly breathed in that unmistakable new-car smell.

"I can't believe it," I said as I gripped the steering wheel tightly, making sure it was all really happening. "Thank you, Terry," I added, smiling at my business partner who had, by now, also become one of my closest friends.

"Come on, Rob," Terry said, opening the passenger door. "Let's go take care of that down payment."

Terry put the two grand on his card, and minutes later, I was driving off the lot in the coolest car I'd ever driven, even if the Saab 900 S wasn't what most guys in their twenties would call a "cool" car. It might have been my sensible Spokane upbringing, but I'm no "Lambo guy." I've never been into flashy things. I have always been attracted to things with sophisticated beauty and lasting power.

My Saab was more than just a nice new car. It was the first tangible sign of my hard work, whereas until then, everything was still in the abstract. And when I gripped that steering wheel, I knew more than ever that my future was firmly in my hands.

A FEW MONTHS LATER, I was on my hands and knees scrubbing out an unidentifiable stain on my ratty carpet when there was a knock at the door. I yelled over my shoulder, "Come in!"

Terry entered, sat down on the floor beside me, and waved an envelope in my face. I looked up, noticing a hint of mischief in his eyes.

"I believe this is yours, Rob."

I wiped my hands with the rag, took the envelope, and sat back on my heels to open it. I could feel Terry's eyes on me as I slid out a slip of paper and unfolded it. It was a check made out to "Robert S. Angel" for . . . *what? $172,000?!*

"What the hell?" I gasped. "Is this some kind of a joke?"

"Nope. It's your first royalty check," Terry said with a huge grin.

"Are you *kidding* me?" I said, looking back at the check to make sure I had read it correctly. I had.

"*One hundred and seventy-two thousand dollars!*" I said to Terry, as if he wasn't aware.

My partner just sat there, on my ratty old stained carpet, smiling.

"Totally legit. Your share. All from game sales, buddy," Terry said as he stood up and held out his hand to pull me up, too.

One hundred and seventy-two thousand dollars, I said to myself, now choking back tears.

"You better not be pranking me. If this is a joke, you'd better tell me *right now!*"

I was laughing. I was crying. It was the craziest, most unbelievable thing that had ever happened to me. I couldn't stop staring at the check. But it wasn't the dollar figure I was looking at. I was looking at a whole new life for "Robert S. Angel."

"All this from a box of paper!" Terry quipped.*

"All this for a box of paper," I repeated, grabbing Terry for a big bear hug.

Terry had already seen his check and processed his newfound riches in his own way. He was delighted to no longer be climbing the corporate ladder. Only a few short months before, that seemed to be his path. For this, he was grateful.

Terry had another royalty payout number to show me.

"Look how much Jerome is getting," Terry said, handing me a royalty breakdown sheet.

My jaw dropped. My uncle had negotiated a substantial equity position for himself. Still, as much as he stood to make from his share of Pictionary, he earned every penny. He was the perfect silent partner. He invested the money and trusted us to do our jobs. Unquestionably, without him there's no way we would've progressed as fast as we had. Terry, Gary, and I never begrudged him his due.

Gary's life was also about change. The day he received his first royalty payment, he gave notice at the Alaska Airlines inflight magazine and joined us at Seattle Games, Inc. Gary's first purchase? A dog.

---

* The joke stuck. Over the next twenty years, every time we cashed a royalty check, sealed a super deal, or accomplished something extraordinary, we'd referred to Pictionary as "a box of paper."

"That was one of *my* original goals," I told him. We had a good laugh.

Terry and I were as relieved as Gary was happy to be coming aboard full time. We needed his creativity, energy and talent.

But, as much as I loved the guys coming over to my place, it was time for me to have some privacy. It was also important to find a more professional space for our growing company.

Terry, Gary, and I agreed the new home for Pictionary, Inc. (we changed our name from Seattle Games, Inc, to Pictionary, Inc. to give us broader worldwide recognition) would be one that felt like home. After being shown a number of cookie-cutter corporate spaces, we found the picture-perfect office space, right on Lake Union, above Triples, our favorite restaurant and watering hole. *How convenient for unwinding at the end of the workday.*

We loved the floor-to-ceiling windows overlooking the lake where we could watch the boats motor by. It was three times larger than my apartment, which meant there would be plenty of breathing room. Our new office was prototypically "Seattle": fresh, clean, and inspiring.

Gary set up his drafting station in a corner, along with all his numerous art supplies. Terry and I initially positioned our desks on opposite corners, but after a week, we missed the coziness of working close to each other like we had in my apartment. Plus, the neighbors didn't appreciate overhearing us shouting ideas back and forth. We scooted our desks together to face each other.

Our office culture formed naturally. A decade before the internet culture of casual Fridays became popular, Pictionary, Inc., was a "no jacket or tie required"—or to be honest, "no jacket or tie tolerated"—kind of workplace, every day of the week.

There was no company hierarchy; we were creators, marketers, and innovators. We didn't need fancy job titles to feel self-important.

The office joke was "First guy to arrive in the morning is 'president for the day.'" And he'd be in charge. But believe me, none of us rushed to be president. It was moot anyway since no major decisions were made without input from all three of us. We were a true democracy, moving together in the same direction. Egos were checked at the door.

We instinctively understood that in order for things to continue moving smoothly, none of us could have a thin skin. We could take it as well as we could dish it out.

And if one of us didn't show up at the office on a Monday, no big deal—we hoped he was extending a fun weekend. We had complete confidence that each of us was getting his work done. As far as a business was concerned, it was utopic.

That is, until the shit hit the fan.

My European
youth hostel
card. 1982

From left to right, Sean Curran, Terry, Gary, and myself. We're getting
our hands dirty, collating 500,000 cards in six days. May 1985

Our first production line consisted of 170 shoe boxes
from Nordstrom, 500,000 cards, and beer.

A sample of Gary's hand-drawn sketches of all 2,500 words that were included in The Official Pictionary Dictionary.

Working hard on my boat on Lake Union, with a brick cell phone, pencil, and frosty libation in hand.

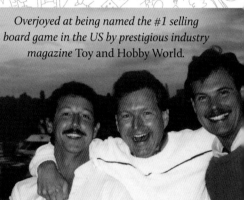

Overjoyed at being named the #1 selling board game in the US by prestigious industry magazine Toy and Hobby World.

Pictionary Junior launch in France. The word over my shoulder means "bull" in French. 1989

In the Lee Street apartment, a.k.a. the first Pictionary headquarters. I'm standing in front of my vision board. 1988

With Days of Our Lives *superstar Drake Hogestyn. 1990*

We had just received our first big order of 10,000 games. Production mishap: the sales sheets were put inside the boxes where no one could see them.

Hard at work on the Serif international contract in Malaga, Spain. 1987

The original members of the notorious Games Gang.

Host Alan Thicke interviewing myself and Terry for the *Pictionary* TV show in New Orleans. 1997

Showing off my drawing skills at the New York City national press launch. 1986

My first (and only!) magazine cover. 1989

*One of sixty-seven original
handwritten word list pages,
completed in my backyard. July 1984*

67 total pages

laundry	laugh	laughing gas ⓔ	lava
laxative	launch (N)	launch pad ⓔ	lawn
layer	lay	laurel (N V)	lawn mower
lazy Susan ⓔ	~~lead~~ (N)	law	leaf
leash	lead (N)	lawn bowling ⓔ	Leaning Tower P.
leather	leak (N)	lazy	left (N)
ledge	lean (N)	~~lazy~~ leader (N)	leg (N) (V)
leech (V)	leap (N)	leap year ⓔ	lei
leftover ⓘ	leapfrog (N)	least	leopard (a)
B. lemon (ade)	learn	ledger	letter (V)
lens	leave (N)	left-handed	lettuce
leotard	lecture (N)	legible	lever (N) (V)
letterhead	lend	length	liberty Bell
leverage (V)	level (N)	Leningrad	license plate
liberty	levitate	less	lifeboat
license (V)	lick	let	library card
lid	lie (N)	librarian	library
lifeguard ⓘ	lift (V)	lie detector	life boat (cr)
lighter	light (N)	life	life preserv.
lighthouse	limp (N)	life jacket ⓔ	life line ⓔ
lily pad ⓘ	lint (N)	lightning rod ⓔ	lightning (N
limb		~~light~~ light show ⓔ	light bulb ⓔ
Abraham Lincoln	2600-ish	like (N) (V)	line (N V) ⓔ
Charles Lindbergh	~~2560~~ words	limbo (N)	lineup
lineman		lime (V)	lining
lingerie	(2662)	linen	lint
li~~ft~~		linesman	lion

PICTIONARY™

Angel Games Inc.
(206) 281-7846

THE GAME OF QUICK DRAW

P.O. Box 19421
Seattle, WA 98109

Ed,

I know this whole thing is a little off the wall but after being
in the game business all of four months I have found that being
just a little strange and different is to ones advantage.
So bare with me and try not to fall asleep. Just check off all
that apply and drop it off in a mailbox, or better still, your
a big star have some one else do it.

--✓ The best game I have ever played. Send me a dozen for my
    friends and family.

--- The best game I have ever played. One is enough.

--- It's a great game but isn't as great as my favorite Trivial
    Pursuit.

--- A very very good game.

--- A very good game.

--- A good game.

--- Not bad.

--- Not good.

--- Bad.

--- Call me at home (___) ___-___, I'd like to be your best
    friend and get involved if I could.

--- Other.

Dear Robert,

Sorry it took me so long to play your
great game. Jeff Goldblum and Geena Davis finally
got me to play (Jeff started me on T.P. as well)
Thanks again for both games you sent

El Begley Jr.

*My first brush with celebrity: a personalized letter from
Ed Begley Jr. October 1985*

Almost getting trampled running with the bulls in Pamplona, Spain. I'm the guy laying on my back in the street. 2013

At the Pictionary launch party at Lake Union Café. Notice the upside-down box! June 1, 1985

At the National Association of Television Program Executives sales convention with Terry, Erik Estrada, and Rich Gill. 1998

This sticker, put on 15 million Pictionary boxes, reminded the consumer that we were the "Original Charades on Paper Game."

Visiting a small village school in Rwanda during the filming of the documentary Finding Hillywood. 2009

My beautiful, smiling lights of my life,
Ben and Sam. Ages 5 and 7.

DRAWING ATTENTION

The Games Gang set up their new offices in the same New York City building as Joe Cornacchia, on the corner of Lafayette and East Fourth Street in NoHo. They were a one-product company at this point. Their prosperity was as tied to Pictionary as ours. We were equally motivated to see Pictionary succeed.

Terry and I were flying to New York City regularly to keep tabs on our new colleagues, not only because we wanted to keep on top of how they managed our brand; we had a lot learn about the business. We couldn't do that from Seattle.

That fall, we faced our first serious competitive threat. A new game called Outburst had exploded onto the scene. It was receiving a ton of press and generating a lot of sales—too many for my liking.

Brian Hersch, the inventor, was traveling the world promoting his creation. At its current sales pace, I was worried it would race past Pictionary as we headed toward our first nationwide holiday season.

It was up to Tom and his team to put heavyweight numbers on the board to combat this looming threat, but something was bothering us. Since our office was no longer handling order fulfillment, and Tom wasn't communicating with us as regularly as we liked, we didn't know how many games The Games Gang actually sold, or what their growth strategy was. We didn't want to wait until the end of each quarter to receive the royalty statements from Western to find out how well, or not well, we were doing.

"Tom," I said, "it was reported in the press that Outburst has sold forty thousand games in Japan alone."

"I know, Rob," Tom said. "Don't worry."

"*You know? Don't worry?*" I said, my voice rising. "Tom, they've sold five *times* that many in the U.S.—two hundred thousand games, and in a short time span. This *should* worry me—and you!" *Why was Tom so cavalier?*

Terry agreed with me, but as was our practice, I was taking the more impassioned stance. The interloper was getting more attention than Pictionary. My ego was ruffled, and I was getting impatient with The Games Gang.

"I have a plan," Tom said.

"A *plan?* Here's a plan: Sell more!" I demanded. "We're losing battles to Hersch. I don't want to lose the war!"

The fear of not knowing what was happening was exasperated by Tom's lack of communication and transparency.

Tom motioned for us to sit down.

"What is this brilliant plan of yours, Tom? We're still learning the business, and we're relying on you to teach us," I said. "And as it stands, Terry and I are completely in the dark. Meanwhile, Outburst is eating our lunch."

Tom laid it all out for us.

"First, this other game isn't anywhere near as good as Pictionary," Tom said matter-of-factly. "And second, they're over shipping the market—classic rookie mistake for a new game. They're untested, completely unproven. They haven't been on shelves long enough to gauge consumer demand."

Tom leaned forward in his chair. "Here's what I know from years of experience, and what the upstart, Brian Hersch, is going to learn the hard way: retailers have a short memory. They tend to focus on unsold inventory gathering dust on their shelves in January, not what they sold during the year. They perceive this as a decline in demand and will be cautious about placing reorders. The *last* thing we want," Tom stressed, "are unsold units sitting on store shelves after the holiday season.

"Our strategy is designed to make sure that doesn't happen. We'll closely monitor sales and ship far fewer than the retailers are ordering. We will short the market so shelves will empty after the first of the year."

Calming down, I nodded my head in acquiescence.

"Okay, Tom," I said. "That makes perfect sense. Still, it is going to be one nerve-racking holiday season."

WHILE WE FOCUSED ON OUR sales strategy, Joe Cornacchia had been busy working on a major marketing coup.

"Put me on speaker, Rob," Joe said when he called a few days later from New York. "I've been working on something I think you're all going to want to hear about."

I put the call on speaker and waved the guys over to listen in.

"Okay, we're all here, Joe. What's the big news?" I asked, eager to hear what Joe had up his sleeve.

"You know Linda Pezzano, the PR guru who helped make Trivial Pursuit a massive success?"

"Yeah, I just read something about her in the paper," Gary said. "She's a brilliant marketer."

"Well, that brilliant marketer and her team have just agreed to work on Pictionary."

Engaging Pezzano and her experienced team, including Christopher Byrne, Judith Sussman, and Amy Jacobs, was a game changer. First, they'd established their credibility with Trivial Pursuit. Second, they had the eyes and ears of the national press. But what we appreciated most was that Linda proposed similar unconventional tactics to the ones we used when we launched Pictionary. With her larger, dedicated team, it could be done at a much grander scale.[*]

Engaging Pezzano would likely help propel Pictionary to new heights. The future looked bright.

That is, if Tom's sales strategy to "short the market" worked.

And boy, did it. The Games Gang's efforts resulted in sales of 350,000 games in 1986.

We had to pause and take that number in. Three hundred and fifty thousand games sold was mind boggling. It meant over $10 million in retail sales of our beautiful blue boxes.

The national industry year-end figures, according *Toy & Hobby World*, were just as dramatic. The top four best-selling games of 1986 were Scruples at 600,000; Wheel of Fortune at around 450,000; Pictionary at 350,000; and Outburst at around 250,000.[†]

Demand for Pictionary during the holiday season was much greater than the toy industry—or even Tom and The Games Gang—had projected. We had *under*shipped true demand by at least 250,000 units.

Orders and demand didn't slow down in the new year. In January 1987, everyone was still clamoring for Pictionary, consumers and retailers alike.

Remember Cabbage Patch Kids? Every little girl in America wanted one. But there were not enough on holidays shelves for everyone—which

---

[*]   In fact, once on board, Pezzano's team would organize Pictionary games in bars in big cities, drawing big crowds, just like we'd done in our early days in Seattle. But they would go even bigger, like playing Pictionary in Central Park. At a sailboat race in New York Harbor, Linda arranged for a spinnaker to have the word PICTIONARY emblazoned on it, catching the attention of thousands. And on a smaller, more intimate—yet still grand—scale, Linda would throw Pictionary parties at her home in New York City, inviting local celebrities and media to play. And like us, Pezzano's team would distribute PicPacks at large events like the Macy's Thanksgiving Day Parade in New York City. Christopher Byrne recently reminded me that they'd throw PicPacks to unassuming passengers when they'd get on an airplane, or even to toll-road operators as they were driving through. If there was a way to get Pictionary in the hands of more people, this incredible team would find it.

[†]   Outburst did indeed overship the market, and they suffered for it. While Outburst enjoyed long-term success overall, the game never again posed a serious threat to Pictionary. Brian went on to invent other successful games, including Taboo.

created long lines of frantic parents. Come the new year, nobody cared that the holidays were over. Parents rushed back to stores and bought Cabbage Patch Kids like it was Christmas Eve.

It was the same for Pictionary. Demand overriding supply made Pictionary the must-have game going into 1987.

As the creator and the public face of Pictionary, I was in demand, too. I was being interviewed by national newspapers like *The Washington Post* and *The Los Angeles Times* and appearing on TV and radio. Pictionary was gaining major national exposure, and it was hard to meet anyone who hadn't heard of the game.

I have to admit, when my dad mentioned that a friend told him he'd seen my name in the newspaper, or he bumped into friends that had seen his son on TV, it felt great to hear the love in my dad's voice when he'd say: "I'm proud of you, Robbie."

WITH PICTIONARY WELL ON ITS way to becoming a juggernaut, we hit our second International Toy Fair on February 5, 1987, with the wind behind us.

This year, Terry joined me at The Games Gang grand showroom, which looked and felt nothing like it had a year earlier in Seymore Butchen's little showroom, where I couldn't get arrested. We were now in a prime location in the main building of The Toy Center, not too far from board game giants Parker Bros. and our old friends, Hasbro.

Minutes after Toy Fair opened for business, The Games Gang had a line of buyers waiting out the door and down the hallway. In a shrewd maneuver, The Games Gang had not shipped *any* games between January 1 and Toy Fair. Shelves remained empty for five weeks, keeping retailers chomping at the bit and consumers hungry for Pictionary. Demand was at a fever pitch.

Toys "R" Us, Waldenbooks (their Pictionary test in Seattle had proven they could sell games), KB Toys, and Target were lined up. Everybody wanted onboard the Good Ship Pictionary. Terry and I lingered in the showroom, amazed at how The Games Gang sales force wrote up big orders one after the other. No sales pitch was needed; The Games Gang was just taking orders all day long.

Every now and again, they would point to us, "Hey, those guys over there invented the game." Terry and I would get some polite smiles, but buyers didn't really care. They just wanted their games and the profits that came with them.

At the end of the first day, Tom came bounding over to Terry and me. He had an exciting update for us.

"Guess who placed an order today?" he asked, trying to hide his own elation.

"Tell me!" I said, giddy with anticipation.

"Kmart."

"Yeah? How many, though?" I asked, being a smartass. "Eighty? Ninety thousand?"

"Fifty," Tom replied.

I fake rolled my eyes like: *Big deal.*

"A month," Tom added.

I almost shit my pants. *This was a Trivial Pursuit–level order.* If a board game sold half a million games in an entire *year*, it was considered a runaway success. Kmart alone had just ordered well over that amount.

DURING THE REST OF THE days of Toy Fair, Terry and I would occasionally leave The Games Gang showroom, wander the halls of the Toy Building, and try to drop into various other showrooms, curious what other game companies were selling. We had no idea it wasn't kosher for us to roam around like that. The big companies wouldn't let us in without the proper "Buyer"-designated badges. They had actual bouncers stationed at the entryways (okay, they were called "screeners.")

Nobody wanted their ideas seen and possibly stolen by competitors. It was a very secretive business. Everybody kept their products under wraps until the last possible moment—especially from those new kids on the block, the Pictionary guys, who were crushing it. It didn't dawn on us that we were perceived as "the competition" until after we were denied access to the showrooms.

By the end of Toy Fair, euphorically, we had too many orders to fill given Western's production schedule, so we had to put everyone on allocation. While it pained us, we even had to reduce Kmart's order so we wouldn't overship. The strategy had worked well for us, and we weren't ready to abandon it, at least not yet anyway.

THE DAY I RETURNED FROM Toy Fair, I met Gary for a drink. Terry and I had kept him up to date by phone from New York, of course, but I wanted to share the full flavor of what had transpired, in person. Gary and I had developed a strong, personal bond away from work. Since we'd all been busy preparing for Toy Fair, it had been a while since he and I had caught up.

We'd often grab dinner or drinks and talk for hours about the ups and downs of business, our lives, and the future. We talked of things that mattered to us and the things we wanted to matter more. Gary, being a spiritual guy, had a very human perspective on the world. He taught me a lot about life and, by example, showed me how to live it with style and grace. Simply put, Gary's friendship and support were immeasurable.

In many ways, he had become a lighthouse of stability as I navigated all the changes that were coming my way, propelling me into a life I'd never imagined.

ON TOP OF THE WORLD

The board-game business took on a dramatic transformation in 1987, becoming the hottest segment in the toy industry and arguably becoming part of the broader "entertainment" business. Until then, games were thought of as an activity for kids or the family, not a way for adults to spend time together. That changed with Trivial Pursuit—and the new trend was solidified with Pictionary.

The burgeoning popularity of board games was fostered by families who made a big deal of their family game nights as a way to strengthen the family unit, and college kids and adults played games together as a way to do the same for their social unit. So, while movies and TV shows like *Dirty Dancing* and *Family Ties,* and entertainers like Madonna and Michael Jackson, ruled mainstream media, Pictionary ruled game nights.

Pictionary sales had a big influence on the way retailers conducted business that year and in the future. Traditionally, 75 percent of all games were sold in the fourth quarter. While consumers continued to purchase games after the holiday season, it was for birthdays and special occasions. Now, because of strong *year-round* demand for Pictionary, retailers had to stock massive quantities *every month* to keep up. They had no complaints. It meant sales were more consistent out over the course of the year.

Buoyed by the mammoth success of Pictionary and industry trends, we felt the time was right to extend the licensing of Pictionary outside North America. Without really understanding the depth and breadth of the markets, we imagined that over time, we'd see a few decent royalty checks from international deals and thought of those sales as "gravy." The real "meal" was in the U.S.

We were completely unaware of what lay ahead.

Expanding the brand to western Europe would be our first step. Joe Cornacchia introduced us to John Pryke, owner of San Serif Print Promotions, Ltd., a UK company. Serif, as the company was more commonly known, were experts in licensing the international manufacturing, sales, and distribution rights for American toy and game companies wanting a presence in territories* around the world.

In turn, Pryke, as we called him, introduced us to his associate, Richard Gill, who would be our principal contact. Richard was running the games division for Serif, having come from a packaging background. He knew the ins and outs *and* the politics of the international game business. He was a cool and self-assured, easy to relate to, and laid-back kind of guy who knew his business. He was our contemporary, a kindred spirit of sorts. We took an immediate liking to Rich.

Pryke and Richard had connections with multiple organizations around the globe. Serif's role was to identify the sublicensee that best fit our objectives and needs. Once a relationship was established, they would oversee each sublicensee to make sure they lived up to the terms of the deal. In effect, Serif was the middleman acting on our behalf.

Pryke and Richard assured us Serif could plug Pictionary seamlessly into its pipeline of top-performing game companies throughout Europe. Most important, we needed them to navigate the myriad international rules, regulations, and laws at a time when we were only beginning to comprehend the intricacies of the U.S. market.

---

* I use the terms "territories" and "countries" interchangeably in the context of markets.

For this service, Serif would take a 5 percent commission. We'd still receive our 15 percent royalty, and they would charge the licensee an additional 5 percent to cover their fee. We'd receive the monthly accounting of games sold, broken down by country. Serif would collect the royalties in the local currency (German marks, French francs, English pounds, etc.[*]) and wire the money directly to our bank at the end of each quarter.

The terms for every sublicensee were the same as the U.S. joint venture. We'd retain all the same contractual controls over design, packaging, marketing plans, pricing, and so on. The one difference was performance guarantees; it would have been too difficult to predict a number for each individual territory.

When it came time to sign the deal, Terry and I flew to Malaga, Spain, during Serif's annual sales conference, where they had invited their licensors from around the world to introduce their products to Serif's team.

We read Serif's contract one last time before signing, and Terry caught a big-ass glaring error that would have been disastrous. There was no clause referencing an expiration date, something we regretfully hadn't caught before we signed the North American deal.

Having learned our lesson, we added a five-year term and a five-year extension with mutual consent. With that, Pictionary, Inc. had become an international company.

TERRY AND I HAD RETREATED to the swimming-pool bar for a champagne toast when we overheard a disconcerting conversation between three Serif salesmen sitting at a nearby table.

"So, we just got a new game to rep," said the only salesman I recognized from our presentation.

"Yeah. I heard. Frictionary, right? Or something like that," said a second sales guy.

---

[*] This was prior to the euro.

"I think it's called Dictionary," said a third. "We're repping a *dictionary*?"

"No, no—it's *Pictionary*. It's a board game," said the first.

I looked at Terry, and half in the bag, I whispered, "Man, we gotta stay on top of these guys."

"Yeah," Terry said, as pickled as me, slurring his words, "we'll hafta keep looking over their damn shoulders—make sure these guys are paying attention."

This eavesdropped conversation made it clear that we'd have to monitor our international partners just as closely as our North American ones; we would have to stay involved in every aspect of our product and brand. We would exercise our contractual controls to the fullest extent. The physical distances between us didn't matter.

There would be no letting up for us. Not for years to come.

DURING THOSE ENSUING YEARS, AT our own expense, Terry, Gary, and I would fly around the world to keep tabs on our licensees. It was our biggest expense and one of our most time-consuming jobs, but it was vital to the continued success of the Pictionary brand. We did this regardless that Serif was being compensated handsomely to monitor each country on our behalf. We felt strongly that our visits were crucial to aiding their sales efforts. We considered our international licensee visits an investment in our future earnings.

Going the extra thousands of miles proved its value right from the start. We found that when each new country came on line and began their marketing efforts, they weren't receiving any guidelines from Serif or affiliated countries on best practices for a successful launch or sales strategy. Basically, they were starting from scratch. And when they did hit on some exciting new creative strategy that spurred sales, they weren't sharing that valuable information with other countries. There were black holes all around

France, as an example, didn't know what worked in England. Nor did Italy know that Spain had created a killer promotion with a local hypermarket chain. In effect, they each lived in their own little bubble with no free flow of information.

We prioritized making sure each of our markets received that information so they could achieve maximum sales. Two of us would hop a plane and endure an exhausting flight to each and every country and do a dog-and-pony show for two days. We brought along promotion items from various countries and explained successful marketing campaigns and any other information they might find useful. We were quite methodical and deliberate in our approach, slowly walking them through everything.

We called these trips our "educational tours." We took long, exhausting flights six or seven times a year, but felt each trip was well worth it.

We could have saved ourselves a lot of time, energy and money by sending the materials by FedEx and following up with a phone call, but our mantra of "face-to-face interaction" was the key to *their* success. We took them into our confidence, we bonded with them, and we let them know we were always available: "Hey, call anytime if you have any questions."

We reasoned that if they felt good about the relationship and connected to our vision, they'd be more motivated to try hard to make us proud of their efforts and results. We became their new best friends. We likened our strategy to treating the teams like a parent does a child. We wanted them to feel loved, heard, supported and know they were a part of the process.

It worked. They appreciated that we treated them as partners, not just licensees. When they went on a sales call, Pictionary was first out of the bag. When a sales force needed to make their numbers for a year (without offering client discounts), they pushed Pictionary. With new marketing plans, they put a bit more effort into the execution. Our goal was accomplished: we stayed foremost in their minds.

Another important aspect of keeping Pictionary relevant was the word lists. Back when I created the original list, making it perfect was key. The word list remained my purview, and I curated it religiously.

Internationally, this edict would be no different. I was adamant that I would have final approval on every word that went into every game.

Around 80 percent of the words from the U.S. edition translated perfectly to other languages. *Box, house,* and *run,* for example, were internationally applicable. The other 20 percent did not, as they were specifically cultural to the U.S. These included celebrities, TV shows, slang, cities, and the like.

Reams of paper would arrive at the office. I'd review and compare every word on every page in the new language. The local marketing teams would propose new words to replace the U.S.-centric ones. In Sweden, for example, Nashville became Stockholm, and Ronald Reagan became Ingvar Carlsson (the prime minister), and so on.

I didn't always understand the local idioms and colloquialisms, so I'd make them explain why one should be allowed before I approved the substitution. For instance, Rich, being English, offered "look at them plates," which is cockney for "look at those feet." (I had no idea what this meant, but he assured me the English did.)

Including names of national celebrities was always dicey. I wanted them to think hard about why the celebrity they proposed was appropriate. Specifically, they needed some signature characteristic that made them identifiable—as well as "drawable."

Inevitably, a marketing team would get frustrated that this American guy didn't know some of country's most famous people or its history. How was I to know who the third cousin of the fourth king that was beheaded in 1417 on the banks of some river I'd never heard of was? But I wouldn't flinch; there would be no shortcuts or deviations.

As we expanded overseas, we experienced a few memorable episodes. On a tour through western Europe, Gary and I attended the launch of Pictionary in Sweden. The night before the event, the brand manager took us to the town's premier restaurant, famous for serving nineteen different types of herring. He was beside himself with glee. Pickled herring.

Herring *au gratin*. Herring with onions. Herring with spices. Herring with mustard. Thank God, there was no herring cake for dessert.*

The next day, when Gary and I walked into the hotel lobby for the launch, we were met with an easel supporting a huge poster with *PICTIONARY* emblazoned across the top. Beneath that was a sketch of a hot tub with two men and two topless women, smiling and having, uh . . . good clean fun.

I stopped and gaped at the poster.

Gary burst out laughing.

"What is *that* supposed to represent?" I asked our host.

"Group sex," he said, matter-of-factly.

"Group what—*sex?* Why? What—*are you kidding me?* We can't have 'group sex' in the game!"

The manager gave me a genuinely puzzled look. "Why not? It's perfectly normal here in Sweden. People love sex. People love Pictionary. Yes?"

"Yes, of course—but, um, no, I didn't approve this," I said, stunned, but also stifling a silent laugh as I examined the anatomically perfect female models.

Our host, a tad confused at my chagrin, told me it wasn't in the game and was used here only for marketing purposes.

Relieved, I politely asked that it not be used again.

DURING ONE OF MY FIRST trips in 1987 to meet with the marketing team in France, I was jetlagged and couldn't focus during our meeting. I put myself in one of my time-outs and took a walk to get some fresh air and collect my thoughts. As I passed a random toy store, there, prominently displayed in the window, was Pictionary. In *French*. I was awestruck. I stopped dead in my tracks staring for the longest time. It was the first time I'd seen my creation outside of America, and in Paris no less.

---

* This would become a ritual that played out in country after country. Marketing teams would take us to the most expensive restaurant in town because we were approved for their expense accounts. They got to go to places they'd never be able to afford on their own.

Gazing at the box, I choked up. I had to appreciate how far Pictionary had come. How far *I* had come. It was one of the few times I allowed myself a little pat on the back.

This was an aha moment. Pictionary was a big deal—not just any game, but the *real* deal. It was the moment I felt we had arrived.

Within twenty-four months, Pictionary would become the biggest-selling game in France.

I wasn't just accruing fond memories in Europe; I was making lifelong friends across the pond. Jennie Halsall, a marketing maverick contracted to handle the media launch of Pictionary in the UK, remains a close friend.*

YET, EVEN WITH THE FRIENDSHIPS I was developing, I couldn't protect Pictionary from battles looming on the British horizon. When we were granted the Pictionary trademark in the U.S. in 1985, we didn't think to register it in other countries, too—not that we could have afforded it. And the wait cost us.

When we tried to register our mark in the UK, we were too late. Someone had seen us in the showroom at the U.S. Toy Fair the year before and beat us to the punch in registering the name "Pictionary."

We hired London attorneys to argue our case and geared up for a long fight, vowing to do whatever was necessary to reclaim our rightful property. This was not only a matter of principle. What they did was outright theft. After weeks of intense preparation, a court date was set. On the appointed day, we arrived in force to face off against our enemy.

As we sat waiting for the trial to begin, one thing was missing: our adversary. Terry and I and our lawyers were getting fidgety. The judge sat with a solemn face, clearly not amused. After fifteen minutes, instead of arguing the case, our lawyers were arguing over where they were going to be having dinner that night.

---

* Jennie also represented Sir Elton John and the Eagles.

What the hell? The other side never showed up. We wanted to believe we had put the fear of God into them. But more likely, they knew they didn't have a leg to stand on.

The judge awarded us *our own* trademark. Score one for the good guys.

Although the battles wouldn't always be smooth sailing, we would never back down when it came to protecting what was rightfully ours.

A FEW MONTHS LATER IN our Seattle office, Terry sat at his desk with a spreadsheet in his hands. He looked at the paper, then out at the Monet-like beauty of Lake Union, then back at the paper. Finally, he looked at me and said, "Um, Rob, I think you'll want to see this."

I reached over the desk and took the paper out of Terry's hand. I studied it for a moment. It was the first royalty report from Europe.

"Terry! Are you kidding me?" I said with disbelief. "This is huge!"

It turns out, we weren't just making "gravy" with our International licensing partners; we were seeing our royalties per game almost double that of the U.S. It made sense. Pictionary's wholesale price in Europe was nearly twice that of North America. Plus, the currency exchange rate was on our side. While we'd originally looked at sales outside the U.S. as gravy, they were clearly the meat and potatoes too.

JUNIOR IS BORN

Midway through 1987, U.S. sales were accelerating. All indicators pointed toward a multi-million-unit payload by the end of the year. That summer, Tom McGuire called a meeting. "No resting on our laurels, guys—we need to extend the brand in the U.S."

"*Extend* the brand?" I asked. "Tom, sales are growing so quickly, we're just trying keep up. How can we consider adding more to our plate?"

"The game business is like the fashion business," Tom explained. "To sustain our growth, we have to keep the brand fresh by adding to and updating our offerings. Otherwise, consumers may get bored and move on."

"What do you recommend, Tom?" I asked, fully appreciating we were more than likely going to end up acquiescing.

"The 'Junior' category is heating up. Until now, there was no 'adult' game category. All games were considered to be children's or family games. With the advent of Trivial Pursuit, children are getting their own kid-specific versions of the adult games. The business is completely upside down. And that is welcome news as it opens an entirely new market."

PICTIONARY "JUNIOR" VERSION WOULD BE our first line extension. We were on a relatively tight development schedule; Tom was adamant we introduce Junior to the world at Toy Fair, which was only eight months away.

Gary, Terry, and I brainstormed multiple concepts. After a short while, it was clear we weren't on the right path. We invited Tom and the new The Games Gang game designer, Angelo Longo, to weigh in. Even though we had final approval, we were always open to new ideas and creative input.

And then one day it hit us—all at the same time. Gary explained the development process to everyone this way: "To create the new kids' game, we need to stop thinking like adults and start thinking like ten-year-olds!"

Duh. Since we were still pretty much kids at heart, switching to that mindset was effortless. In fact, it was easy and effective.

Gary's final design mockup was spot on. The game used crayons and two wipe-off boards, and all the other components were much simpler than the "senior" edition, as we called the original game internally. Even the packaging would be brighter and more colorful to reflect what kids find more appealing.

Unlike Pictionary Senior, the back of the box would display a picture of four kids laughing and smiling while playing the game. Gary's good friend, Cheryl Hill, volunteered her twelve-year-old niece, Courtney, to be one of the four models we'd feature. The kid was a natural.[*]

On the other hand, the word list, my purview, proved to be much trickier than I thought. Now a twenty-nine-year-old bachelor, I had no clue what words a ten-year-old would find inspiring or even comprehensible. I may have acted like a ten-year-old sometimes, but that would be of no use to me here.

I cobbled together a list of 720 words I thought might be in the kiddie

---

[*] Twenty years later at a Seafair party at my house, a young woman I didn't recognize approached me and introduced herself and her three young children. Much to my surprise, it was Courtney, all grown up. Small world.

ballpark, but I still found the Swedish word list a breeze compared to this task. I started with the simplest words from Senior, tossed in some after-school TV shows, cartoon characters, and popular images of the day like Garfield the cat, Kermit the Frog, Cookie Monster, and so forth, trying to adapt the game for a demographic I understood nothing about.

My next challenge was to find a kid to test the words. I knew only one ten-year-old, Emmy, the daughter of Sean's sister Molly. I called Molly and explained what I needed, and she invited me over to see what Emmy had to say about my word choices.

I gave the list to Emmy, handed her a pencil, and instructed her, "Just circle the words you don't understand."

She was up for the challenge and went right to work, studiously examining each one. I didn't know how long it would take, so Molly and I did the adult thing and went into the living room for a glass of wine to do some catching up.

We were barely into our conversation when Emmy shouted, "I'm done!"

Damn, I was hoping for a second glass.

Wow, was I surprised. There weren't many corrections. Either Emmy was a child prodigy, or my brain functioned more like a child than I thought. Probably a bit of both.

In the final analysis, maybe that's why Pictionary became so universally popular—it brought out the kid out in everyone.

Ah, but how Pictionary Junior would perform with a younger demographic remained to be seen.

THE GAME CRASHER

As the end of 1987 neared, Pictionary was continuing to take turf and claim board game supremacy across the U.S. And it was still just me, Terry, and Gary managing licensing, merchandising, and overseeing marketing efforts. So far, we had been able to keep the office running and business humming along, but we were stretched so thin that opportunities were at risk of slipping past us. It was time to hire help.

Bonnie London joined the team as our first office manager to help oversee day-to-day operations. Bonnie was around forty and was very organized, with a cheery disposition. Most importantly she was the calming force amid the daily chaos swirling around us. We thought of her as the "office mom." She did her best to keep up with the flurry of work, responding to mail, organizing our schedules, and answering the phone that seemed to endlessly ring off the hook.

Even with Bonnie on board, we still felt compelled to hire Tim Nelson[*] to help field and vet some of the countless promotional pitches that were pouring our way.

---

[*] And our later office managers, Kim Jones and Emily Griep.

In early 1988, we received the final sales tally for the previous year and were blown away. Completely and utterly blown away. I had to sit down.

In 1987, *three million* games had been sold across the U.S. and Canada.*

Pictionary was the number-one-selling board game in North America. By a mile.

To think that a game I created just two scant years earlier, sitting in a lawn chair, working on my word list, was now being played in *three million homes* across North America, humbled me. I was flabbergasted. This was some pretty cool shit.

I thought of the millions of people laughing and guessing wildly and yelling gleefully and making raucous fun of one another as they huddled together over this *simple game. My* simple game.

1987 had been a runaway success. There was no product on any shelves in January 1988, not only because we purposely shorted the market, but because the public was buying every game available.

This last detail brought us to a momentous, yet risky, decision.

Western Publishing, Joe, and Tom agreed that no retailer would be on allocation that year. All orders would be filled. To do this, they would have to open the manufacturing spigot and hope enough orders would come in to soak up production. Forget shorting the market; we would no longer estimate or try to predict demand. It was out of control.

This was a financially perilous decision for the joint venture. If demand subsided, even just a little, they could potentially be left holding millions of dollars of unsold inventory. This happened to

---

* Even with the huge orders gushing in, we never forgot the small retailers. These mom-and-pop stores had been instrumental in our initial success, and we made sure they got their orders filled, no matter what. A small retailer in California, The Game Keeper, got 288 games on December 23 and sold out in one hour. And a man and his wife in rural Nebraska drove two hours to the next town when they discovered their only local game store was sold out.

Trivial Pursuit, and everyone was keenly aware of the risk. Nevertheless, it was a gamble they were willing to take.

This decision was pivotal not only because we were able to take full advantage of the phenomenon that was Pictionary, but because if things went the way we hoped, it would increase our royalties dramatically.

It further proved we'd made the right decision to sign with the joint venture. Hasbro *never* would have done it.

MEANWHILE, PICTIONARY JUNIOR WAS AN instant hit with buyers at Toy Fair. We knew it the minute the annual toy convention opened.

The buyer for Toys "R" Us was tapping his foot in front of Mike Gasser's desk on the morning of day one, looking at his watch as he waited for the newest Games Gang partner to arrive. Mike hadn't been there the year before, so he wasn't sure what to expect when he saw the buyer waiting for him. Before Mike could even take out an order form, the TRU guy said rather forcefully: "We need one hundred thousand units! Eighty Senior and twenty Junior."

Mike, who stood six feet eight inches and weighed three hundred pounds, wasn't the type to get intimidated easily, let alone by a buyer, no matter how important he or she was. But the intensity and urgency of *this* buyer, not to mention that 20 percent of it included our brand-new, never-before-seen Pictionary Junior, made him think he was missing something.

"No problem," Mike said, keeping his cool, as if this huge order happened every day. "When do you need the games shipped?"

The buyer looked at Mike like he'd never taken an order before. "No, no—you don't understand," he said. "I need the hundred thousand delivered immediately and the same number delivered *every month for the rest of the year.*"

Mike lowered his pen and looked around, wondering if he was on *Candid Camera.* The Toys "R" Us buyer repeated his request, a little slower this time as Mike wrote up the order, a bit dazed.

The other Games Gang salesmen were getting massive orders, too.

Kevin took an order for 50,000 a month from KB Toys. McGrath had Kmart at 750,000 total units.

Toy Fair '88 was exhausting in sheer intensity for Pictionary. It was audacious, exhilarating, and utterly surreal. At the end of each day, Terry and I would catch our breath, take inventory mentally and physically, have dinner with the guys, and fall face down on our pillows at the hotel. The next day we'd wake up early, gobble down breakfast, meet the team at the showroom at 9:00 a.m. sharp, and then hit the lottery all over again.

Even though we were expecting—and betting on—healthy sales to continue, we were floored by the tsunami of orders that came in, dwarfing orders the year before.

Still, despite this undeniable success, there was trouble brewing down the hall, threatening Pictionary's dominance.

THE PREVIOUS FALL, A NEW TV game show created by Burt Reynolds and Bert Convey called *Win, Lose or Draw* had premiered. The show was supposedly derived from a sketching game Reynolds and Convey played in Bert's or Burt's living room with celebrity friends for years.

It sounded suspiciously like Pictionary to me.

Tom heard a rumor that Milton Bradley (MB) was going launch a board game version of *Win, Lose or Draw* at Toy Fair.

Backed by MB and hyped with the star power of Burt and Bert, the game would be a direct and well-funded assault to our dominance in the market.

Monday came, no announcement.

Maybe we dodged a very big bullet? I breathed a sigh of relief.

But the next morning, our fears were realized.

MB officially announced the launch of Win, Lose or Draw (WLD), the board game. They blasted the TV show and the companion board game with both barrels.

We called it "Black Tuesday."

"Damn!" Terry said. "Their show airing on TV every day is like a thirty-minute commercial for *their* version of *our* game."

"*That* game should be called 'Lie, Cheat, or Steal'!" I barked.

I inexplicably lost confidence in Pictionary's and our ability to vanquish this foe. Terry and Gary felt the same way. Given our sales and orders, it wasn't rational, but our collective emotions were running at warp speed.

MB was trying to beat us *with our own game!*

"Let's all calm down," Tom finally said, like the general getting a grip on his troops. "We have to think this through, not let them rattle us."

"Think it through?" I said bitterly. "Tom, they're out to wipe us off the map!"

"They could've licensed it from us," Terry said.

"Easier to steal it from us," I shot back.

Tom was trying his best to sound reassuring. "Look, guys, we're just going to have to stay the course. We have *the* superior product, and what we're doing is working. I've been in this business a long time. We can weather this storm. We just have to out-market, outsell, and outmaneuver them."

"Oh, sure, Tom. Just outdo a behemoth toy company. No problem," I said.

"Rob, you already *have* outdone them," Tom said, reminding us of the obvious. "That's why there is competition encroaching on our territory. Pictionary is number one for a reason. And remember, also-rans inevitably lose their breath just trying to get anywhere close to the first-mover. Advantage is ours. Don't look behind you; focus on staying the course, and most of all, keep the faith."

"Keep the faith," I muttered, looking down at my feet and shaking my head.

"Come on, guys, I'm starving. Let's go get some lunch," Tom said, as if Terry and I had an appetite for anything but contempt.

THE DOORS TO THE ELEVATOR opened to a familiar face. It was Richard Gill, our primary contact at Serif. A lot had changed in the year. Richard informed us that he had left Serif and moved to Barbados to run the international business for Horn Abbot Ltd., owners and creators of Trivial Pursuit. We asked our old friend to join us for lunch.

Since it was top of mind and in the pit of my stomach, I told Richard about MB showing up in our backyard with Win, Lose or Draw. Richard let out an empathetic sigh.

"Well, I hate to say I'm surprised, but," Rich said, "I've been in the business long enough to know that these game companies know how to play dirty. But hey, if it's any consolation, Pictionary is the talk of Toy Fair. I'm not worried about your ability to stay in the lead."

Richard had his own issue. He wasn't happy living so far away from his family in England. Even though Trivial Pursuit was his dream job, he was open to making a move.

Open to making a move, I thought. *Was Richard making overtures to join Pictionary?* I filed this in the back of my brain and took a big bite of my bland sandwich. It matched my mood.

What irritated me was that there was nothing we could do from a legal standpoint. Even though the WLD gameplay was similar to Pictionary, the name *Win, Lose or Draw*, was not. We had learned through our Fictionary experience with the U.S. Patent and Trademark Office that this would not be seen as a case of IP infringement by causing confusion in the marketplace. We couldn't sue MB.

So, we did what we did best. We got creative.

The fact remained, we were the first, the original, and certainly the *best* drawing game. We had to remind the public. But how?

"We'll say it right on the box," Gary suggested when we arrived back in Seattle. "Like a Good Housekeeping seal of our leadership position."

It was brilliant. We went into action and within days had a one-and-a-half-inch bright-yellow starburst sticker affixed to the top of our navy box loudly proclaiming Pictionary was "*The Original On Charades Paper Game!*" on every game produced from then on.

But a strange thing happened. The very existence of a successful rival inadvertently turned into a big long-term win for Pictionary. "Drawing games" become a major games segment, and with that rise came more buzz for Pictionary.

For example, the WLD TV show brought more consumer awareness that drawing games are fun. In fact, the fun of the game resonated more than the WLD brand as most people assumed *Win, Lose or Draw* was a TV show about Pictionary—but with a different name. And wouldn't you know it, they went out and bought Pictionary. *I guess there* was *some confusion in the marketplace*, I thought, smiling to myself.

In France, our licensee took advantage of the confusion. They shot a Pictionary commercial that they aired right before and after each WLD episode. We loved that ingenuity. Our sales went through the roof. Ironically, their show was a contributing factor to Pictionary becoming France's number-one-selling board game.

EVERYBODY WANTS
TO PLAY

Pictionary Junior was a huge success, with sales still increasing, so when Tom suggested launching a second edition of Pictionary Senior a year after Junior had been released, we balked—not at the idea, but at the timing.*

"We're doing great with the original game," I said. "Why rock the boat with a second edition that could cannibalize sales of the first?"

"Think of it as an update," Tom countered. "I say it's time."

I stuck to my guns. "I don't think the market is ready to abandon first edition. Pictionary has had a long shelf life because the play is flexible, Tom," I argued. It includes twenty-five-hundred words, which is more than enough variety before players start seeing words repeat."

Look who's teaching the teacher, I thought, smirking to myself.

Tom shot me a look. "Rob, players *are* starting to see words repeat—that's how often Pictionary is being played."

I wasn't convinced. *How could that be?* We thought there'd be years of play value with 2,500 words. So, I asked friends who loved the game if they agreed with Tom. The good news was they were playing the game

---

* We did add the words "first edition" to the original blue box with the next printing.

often. The bad news was that Tom was right. The words *were* repeating. Maybe I was a little too cautious and protective of our "first born."

"Okay, Tom," I said. "Let me speak to Terry and Gary and get their thoughts."

We quickly came to a consensus. Pictionary, Second Edition, was officially green lit.

I was back compiling a new master word list. And I won't lie, I was kind of jazzed.

I held firm to my original two criteria: I had to know the meaning of the word, and it had to conjure a picture in my mind. For the next two months, I threw myself into the task with reckless abandon.

I used some of the leftover words from my backyard list I'd complied years earlier but didn't limit myself to my tattered old *Webster's* this time. Instead, I looked for drawable words everywhere—on billboards, sides of buildings, street signs, on TV and while listening to the radio. Words were *everywhere*. I was inspired and obsessed with creating a dynamic, contemporary, and exciting list.

I dreamed of words in my sleep. Sometimes, I'd bolt upright at 3:00 a.m. and jot a word down on the pad of paper I always kept on my nightstand in case I had a brilliant idea. (Now I write them on my phone.) I consulted books of phrases and quotes and poured over *Roget's Thesaurus*. I even went to Elliott Bay Books, where a few years earlier, the buyer turned down Pictionary, and left with stacks of reference books on biology, history, and geography.

The English language adds new words all the time or gives old words new life and relevance. For example, "Apple" came out with its "personal computer" that had a "mouse" that rested on a "mouse pad," so you could "scroll" to find the "home page" and then "click" on it, and so on.

We decided to break with industry norm and produce a new full game, not an add-on pack of word cards to be sold separately. If consumers had more words, they'd need more paper and pencils too, which we were happy to sell them.*

DESPITE MY RESERVATIONS, CREATING THE list was getting me excited for the second edition launch. But in the midst of that endeavor, Western Publishing approached us with a proposal for a big packaging change.

"We are spending too much money on the structure and layout of the box," Western explained over the phone. "We want to use a plastic form to replace the cardboard box that holds die, markers, and cubes, as well as the cardboard platform that holds the pads of paper and pencils. We also want to print 496 game cards, a reduction from the current 500. The difference will be the four category cards that we now print separately.

As if this wasn't disconcerting enough, Western suggested replacing my beloved #2 blue pencils, *the ones they originally suggested,* with crappy little golf pencils.

"It's much more economical considering the volume of games we're moving," they said.

"No way!" I said to Gary and Terry when we got off the call and debated the proposal. "The game will look cheap and lose its upscale appeal. What's next—putting the components in a Ziploc bag?"

Surprisingly, Gary was all for Western's proposal.

"We did the original design on a budget, and now we have no constraints," Gary said. "Frankly, I think their ideas will make the game look sleeker, not cheaper. The packaging changes won't alter the game play. If it won't hurt sales, I say let's agree and let them do it."

Terry agreed. "This isn't the start of a slippery slope toward a total overhaul, Rob. We still hold absolute control over the design and can say no at any time in the future," Terry added. "Plus, as you know, Western Publishing has been a great partner since day one. I think it's time to

---

* While sales were brisk at first, Pictionary Second Edition didn't quite catch fire as we had hoped. Perhaps this edition *did* cannibalize the first.

show our appreciation and a little love. Let's work with them on this."

There was total logic in their reasoning, and I recalled Tom's rational response when I first rejected the idea of a second edition. I deferred to Terry and Gary, but with one exception.

"No golf pencils," I said adamantly. "I don't care what you say. It will cheapen the look of the game."

Western countered with using standard blue #2 pencils *without* erasers.

We agreed.

Unlike when Gary went off his rocker when Terry changed the type from salmon to white, we'd grown wiser and more pragmatic in our old age.

WE CONTINUED TO EXTEND THE Pictionary line. We took to heart what we had learned from Tom about refreshing the brand. Some updates were simple, and some were more detailed changes designed to introduce Pictionary to new markets and give consumers an entirely different way to play.

Over the ensuing years, we launched a total of nine separate and distinct versions, including the original senior edition.

The second kids' edition took on a new form. The game was called Play It with Clay and rather than draw, players would sculpt clay to convey their words. We loved this version and found ourselves playing it in the office all the time, though we always ended up flinging the clay at each other.

Soon after, we launched Travel Pictionary. It was an upscale design, coming in a hard plastic shell small enough to fit in a purse. While it was beautifully executed and hit all our design requirements, it garnered a tepid response. People preferred to take the full board game with them on trips. We also found people were buying a second full size copy and didn't see the need for the more compact travel-size version.

Then there was Bible Pictionary. Gary and his sister put the word list together for that one, the only time I agreed to turn over compiling a word list. Total sales limped in at 250,000 units over the first two years before sales disappeared entirely the third year. It was like everyone who wanted one had bought one. This was strictly a U.S. product. The rest of the world had no interest.

Party Pictionary included a large eighteen-inch square two-sided, wipe-off plastic easel with dry-erase markers that could be set up on a table. Teams squared off face to face across from each other. The packaging for this version was the anomaly; to show the difference between this version and the original, we decided to show people playing Party Pictionary on the back of the box. Gary, Terry, and I got in the act by "casting" ourselves as the models—three happy-go-lucky dudes playing the game with friends. Another decent seller, but like Travel Pictionary, it didn't take off.

WE WEREN'T THE ONLY ONES interested in leveraging the Pictionary brand. Never before had there been a board game with such broad appeal, reaching as wide a demographic as Pictionary. Scores of companies were eager to align their brand with the marketing and sales power of Pictionary's good name.

National brands were beating down our door, willing to pay us handsomely to be linked with Pictionary to promote *their* products. They bet big on Pictionary tie-ins, expecting them to have a positive impact on their sales. And they did.

Most of the tie-ins were mini versions of Pictionary, with the word list and graphics tailored to each company's specific brand and target consumer. We wanted the partners to feel special and have a sense of exclusivity.

We approached all proposals the way we did the game. We demanded final approval of the word lists and control of packaging and messaging. We were not interested in opportunities that would diminish the integrity of the Pictionary brand. While it was tempting, given how much money was being thrown our way, we refused to go down that road.

FIRST UP, KRAFT FOODS. KRAFT proposed producing *three million* mini Pictionary games with dinosaurs on them dubbed "Dinosaur Pictionary." The mini games would be placed on dedicated endcap displays in thousands of grocery stores across the nation. The promotion worked like this: Buy two Kraft products, like Velveeta and Kraft Mac & Cheese, and take home a free Dinosaur Pictionary mini game. I chuckled at the idea that Pictionary was just three years old and already a dinosaur!

The Kraft promotion was like having three million free PicPacks hit the market across the nation at the same time, only this time, we were getting paid. To boot, this deal, and the many deals that followed, accomplished the thing we knew spurred Pictionary sales. They were getting more pencils in the hands of millions and millions of people. Sample. Sample. Sample.

Pizza Hut ran a nationwide promotion to get any one of four limited editions of a mini Pictionary, each one with a different theme. For example, the Pizza Hut Pictionary Entertainment Edition included word lists with current popular movies like *Rain Man* and *Big*; hit TV shows like *Cheers* and *Golden Girls*; and song titles such as "Don't Worry, Be Happy" and "Desire"—probably a fun one to draw. The Sports edition included Seattle Seahawks, Magic Johnson, and Wayne Gretzky

This promotion resulted in 400,000 mini games delivered right into customers' homes, right along with their pepperoni pizza.

Post Alpha-Bits put a mini Pictionary Junior game inside millions of cereal boxes. I'd grown up eating Alpha-Bits and got all tingly to see my creation on such an iconic package as I walked through the cereal aisle in the grocery store. Kids could even spell out Pictionary words in their bowls. And as we hoped, kids clamored for the full edition of Pictionary Junior.

Lee Jeans did a promotion called the "Hip Pocket Edition." The promo read: "Buy a pair of jeans and get a mini game in your hip pocket."

The National Parks Service licensed a full-size game that included words like "Old Faithful" and "Mount Rushmore."

The Canadian government licensed a Pictionary edition with political words for their upcoming elections.

NASCAR did a full game; naturally, it sold really fast.

The Simpsons did a full game version with words like "Homer," "D'oh," and "Bart." And later, *Austin Powers* got into the act with a full cobranded version of Pictionary with terms like "one million dollars," "Goldmember," and "shag" included in the word list.

One of Terry's favorite partnerships was a creative European promotion for Bacardi Rum. Their ad agency figured out a clever way to put a mini game on the neck of their liquor bottle. Buy a bottle of rum, get the attached Pictionary game. It was pretty cool seeing this one in duty-free shops as we passed through airports throughout Europe.

THERE WAS ONE TIME THAT the decision to align Pictionary with a specific product caused a heated debate between Gary, Terry, and me. Salem pitched us this scheme: "Buy two packs of Salem cigarettes and get a mini Pictionary game, all neatly wrapped into one package."

While none of us smoked, Terry and I didn't see the harm. At the time, smoking didn't have quite the stigma it does now. You could even smoke on airplanes. And it was still legal for cigarette companies to advertise pretty much anywhere, and boy did they. It was hard *not* to see a cigarette ad on billboards, in magazines, or on TV.

Terry and I believed we could weather any negative reaction. But Gary was dead set against the deal on moral grounds.

"No amount of money is worth us being associated with smoking," he insisted.

"C'mon, Gary," I threw back, "half the people I know smoke."

"*All* the people I know like sex," Gary countered. "And you still nixed the naked hot tub scene in Sweden."

Okay, he had me there.

But because Terry and I shouted the loudest, as it were, the promotion was approved. I prepared the word list and sent it off to Salem for review.

When we didn't get a response, we assumed they didn't follow through.

The longer Terry and I thought about it, however, the more we knew Gary was right, so it was with some relief the promotion didn't come to fruition. As a nonsmoker, I was never in the cigarette aisle (they used to be sold in an aisle just like Alpha-Bits) and so, out of sight, out of mind.

Four months later, Terry opened the mail and was shocked to find a six-figure check from Salem.

"I guess Salem put the promotion in motion," Terry said, holding up the check.

It was a bittersweet moment. Sure, we'd deposit it, but Gary, our moral compass, was right all along. We never worked with a cigarette company again.

As THE PROMOS AND TIE-INS, big and small, kept pouring in, we pitched companies directly with our own ideas, building on the successes we were accumulating.

One day, Terry came to me with a pitch of his own. "I think we should do a Pictionary slot machine."

I rolled my eyes and continued with what I was doing.

"I'm serious," he said. "Wheel of Fortune has a slot machine, and it's hugely popular."

"Tell you what, Terry," I said. "Why don't you work on it, and if something looks promising, you let me know."

I was thinking *way* too inside the box on this one and figured it didn't have a ghost of a chance of getting off the ground. I didn't stand in Terry's way, but I didn't support his efforts, either.

Imagine my surprise a few months later when we were invited to the headquarters of Bally's, one of the biggest slot machine makers in the world, to discuss a deal for a Pictionary slot machine to launch in Vegas.[*]

Moral of this story: never bet against Terry Langston.

[*]   While Bally's came up with a clever design, a new manager came on board and nixed the project.

Over the years, there would be many avenues for Pictionary to be seen in strange and very popular settings. One of my favorite promotions took place during a college football game between archrivals Stanford and Cal Berkeley, known as "The Big Game." We all attended the game to see what they created and to be a part of the craziness.

As the halftime entertainment, the Cal Berkeley band, known for their theatrics and unconventional shows, came onto the field, scampering willy-nilly. The crowd didn't know what was going on until the members of the brand abruptly stopped in place and fell into formation, creating a "picture" with their bodies and instruments.

The announcer instructed the fans to guess what the band members had "drawn." It was deafening to hear the roar of the crowd shout out their guesses with each of the four "pictures" the band members formed. When the announcer said the word, 60,000 fans were laughing and screaming with delight.

Make that 60,003! Terry, Gary, and I guessed the pictures right along with everyone else!

Some of the most exciting promos came through film and television. One day our fax machine roared to life and started spitting out unsolicited contract pages from NBC/Paramount Pictures requesting our permission to work Pictionary into an episode of the hit TV show *Facts of Life*. The fax ended with a "sign here" on the dotted line. We couldn't scribble our names fast enough.[*]

The colossal hit show *Friends* featured Pictionary in one episode, with Monica drawing *Bye Bye Birdie* (very badly). Pictionary has also been played on *Will and Grace* and *The Big Bang Theory*. And Pictionary became a staple on *The Tonight Show Starring Jimmy Fallon*.

Gary Larson, the creator of *The Far Side* comic, drew *two* Pictionary cartoons. Scott Adam's *Dilbert* and Jim Davis's *Garfield* also got in on the act. Geico even did a commercial featuring a sloth.

---

[*] A few years later, our lives would intersect in a major way with Alan Thicke, who had written the *Facts of Life* theme song.

OUR AGREEMENT WITH THE JOINT venture included an annual guaranteed marketing spend of 3 percent of the net wholesale price. While Linda Pezzano was doing an incredible job creating buzz for Pictionary, we had no way of verifying how successful each promotion was specific to an increase in sales. Western Publishing pushed for quantifiable metrics. At the time, a television commercial was the best way to track and analyze the correlation between marketing spend and retail sales. The commercial would air, and retailers could point to immediate sales boosts, or no change. Western wanted to shoot a commercial to air nationally.

Pictionary sales had gone viral because of how we, then Pezzano, got games into people's hands. This type of word-of-mouth and buzz marketing was in the Pictionary DNA. Still, we agreed, albeit reluctantly, to shoot a commercial with the caveat that we'd exercise our contractual rights to approve the creative.

The ad agency pitched a few ideas. One of the first concepts they presented involved workers at Hoover Dam who were so engrossed playing a game of Pictionary, they weren't paying attention to the power generators. The lights went out throughout the entire city, causing a blackout, and playing Pictionary was to blame.

We thought the ad was clever, funny, and irreverent.

The Games Gang and Western were less enthusiastic. Even the ad agency said they didn't recommend going with this concept. (I suspected they showed this one before other concepts, hoping we'd see the increasing brilliance of their subsequent pitches.)

Even though everyone else pushed for a different creative, we exercised our right and approved the "dam" creative.

We should have listened to the experts.

The commercial aired over network TV during the fourth quarter holiday shopping season with a total broadcast cost of $2,000,000. Add to that the cost of production and, well, it was substantial. A substantial waste of money, that is.

As soon as it aired, the flack started.

People asked me: "Why do you have prisoners playing Pictionary?"

"Huh? What are you talking about?"

"The convicts, the ones in the prison jumpsuits."

"Those aren't prisoners! They're power company workers in jumpsuits with their names on the damn uniforms," I shot back quite defensively.

"Oh. So, what were *they* doing in jail?" they responded.

Shit. The commercial was a total flop. There was no evidence of incremental sales, not one little bit.

Okay, maybe we didn't know *everything*. The *game experts* should have left advertising up to the *media experts*.

ADVERTISING FLOPS NOTWITHSTANDING, ALL OUR hard work led to what can only be described as a wild and unimaginable 1988. By the end of that year, in the U.S. and Canada alone, we'd sold a staggering 11,000,000 games across our entire product range—and another 2,000,000 across the globe for total revenue of over $200,000,000. This translated to over *half a billion dollars* in retail sales worldwide.

Are you kidding me? It was hard to absorb the numbers and the enormity of it all.

Ironically, our nearest competitor was Win, Lose or Draw at a distant second with 3,000,000 units sold, ten million fewer than Pictionary.[*]

Pictionary was less than four years old and had become the number-one-selling board game *on the planet* and established itself as a cultural icon. According to *Toy and Hobby World,* the leading trade publication of the day, only the venerable Nintendo sold more units during those years. No other board game came close.

And we did it all with just *two* full-time employees. Our entire overhead, including salaries, office rent, and travel, was a mere $700,000.

Hey, Mr. Don "WOW" Kingsborough, you may have blown the

---

[*] Just two years later, Milton Bradley's Win, Lose or Draw lost the board game wars. The show was off the air, and the game was soon closed out around the world. The public had spoken.

licensing opportunity of a lifetime, but you got one thing right: "It's not what you make. It's what you keep."

And we kept *a lot*.

As the royalties kept pouring in, I recognized I was ill equipped to handle my financial success on my own. Here it was staring me in the face—and in my bank account—and I had no clear plan of action. It was crucial I figure out a strategy for managing my money so as not to one day find myself on the same path of so many other self-made millionaires: broke.

I had no intention of putting myself in a position of having to go back to working a "real job." I had worked too hard to let that happen. I couldn't count on lightning striking twice. My future was now, and I had to protect it.

I asked Uncle Jerome for his counsel.

"It's not for me to decide, Robbie; it's your decision," he advised. "Not your parents or a financial advisor, either. It's all on you."

He shared some advice that a financial advisor friend of mine in Seattle, Jim Richards, articulated quite succinctly a few years ago:

"First, determine what your intentions are for your life. What do you value? Do you want to be big man on campus and spend all your money buying Ferraris and expensive baubles for you, an entourage, or family? Do you want a life with no financial stress? Do you want to save most of it for retirement? Or somewhere in between? It's your choice. What is important to you? Don't let money dictate your lifestyle. That's undisciplined and a surefire way to go broke. Instead, let your intended lifestyle dictate how and where you will invest. Then find a financial advisor who will implement a strategy that honors *your* goals.

"And, one last thing: don't trust completely or blindly. Stay involved. It's your money, not theirs. Learn the basics of investing so you understand their investment strategies. Hold them accountable; you control the plan."

After all these years with Pictionary, I knew all about staying involved. No one would respect my money as much as I did.

In an instant, I knew what was most important to me: *freedom*. The freedom to make the choices I desired, not what others thought I should do or be. I wanted to be present in whatever moment I was in without worrying about my financial future—the immediate one, or most importantly, thirty years hence. I wanted to live life on my terms, no one else's. This meant I wouldn't be able to be speculative, risky or take flyers with my spending or investing, but that was okay. I refused to squander away my future.

PART III

END GAME

FAIR GAME FOR
COPYCATS

By 1989, we were no longer the young pup in the game category; we were top dog. And this made us the prime target for competition, inspiring all kinds of copycats.

There's an old adage: "Imitation is the sincerest form of flattery." When you are successful, your product is likely to inspire a slew of imitators. And boy, were we flattered. We couldn't stop any of these copycats from coming to market if their game was based on the premise of sketching and guessing words, a.k.a., a "drawing game." But there was no way we were going to let any knockoffs gain a foothold playing off our intellectual property, the name Pictionary.

We discovered several small companies wanted their fifteen minutes of fame and were introducing their own versions of a drawing game.

Three of them in the U.S. caught our eye in particular and warranted legal action, not because of game play but because of their names: Picture This, PicCharades, and PicDraw.

Even though they were produced by small, independent inventors, as we had once been, we had no qualms going after them. We could not let the precedence stand.

Andy sent cease-and-desist letters to all three, a prudent and easy first step to start the legal process of getting their products off store shelves. It didn't take long to receive their responses. In each case, the matter never went to trial. None of them wanted (or could afford) to mount a legal defense and agreed to stop production and sales.

Two of the company owners had a favor to ask. Both had significant portions of their net worth tied up in inventory. They would cease production but asked if we'd allow them to sell their remaining units to avoid bankruptcy. Terry, Gary, and I remembered starting out not so long ago and the financial risks we took. We sympathized with their predicament. It was an easy decision to honor their requests.

OVER THE YEARS, FIFTY-SEVEN BOARD games with a drawing theme would launch worldwide to directly compete with Pictionary. Yet, when all was said and done, not one, including Win, Lose or Draw, could supplant us as the premier game in the category. We were first to market and had the name recognition. Yes, the competition took a bite out of our sales, but in the long run, Pictionary maintained its commanding lead.

EVEN WITH THESE LEGAL ISSUES resolved, we still had a lot on our plates. Between the massive number of proposals for promotions and tie-ins coming in, and just staying on top of our existing markets, I was getting pulled in a lot of different directions. Too many. I felt disconnected and unfocused.

It wasn't just me. Terry and Gary were feeling it too. Adding to our time commitments and growing stress was our continuing practice of jumping on a plane when a new country came on line or a new marketing manager was installed in an existing one. We were already in twenty-four international markets including Spain, Italy, Finland, Australia, and Mexico and our travel schedule had not slowed down at all.

My friends were impressed that I got to "see the world." And while it may have sounded romantic, it was downright exhausting. We would land in Europe after an eleven-hour flight, or even fly as far away as New Zealand, go straight to the licensee's office, do our dog-and-pony show, and immediately go right back home, all in three to four days. There was no sightseeing. No cultural experiences. No souvenir shopping. And no clue what day or time it was.

Back home, it would take a few days to recover. We were thrown off our sleep schedules, and in turn, our moods were thrown off. And on a personal level, I was frustrated that all the travel was wreaking havoc with my personal life.

My relationship with Renee had really heated up. I wanted to spend more time with my now-girlfriend, but I was always elsewhere. Having a life outside Pictionary was starting to have some appeal.

Terry, Gary, and I were not only doing a disservice to ourselves, but to Pictionary. We were not taking full advantage of opportunities coming our way, and it became clear we could no longer manage international markets effectively from Seattle. We had expanded beyond our licensor deal with San Serif and had added a few smaller yet significant international licensing partners on our own.

It was time to hire someone to manage business development overseas. That person would need to be based in Europe, where the major source of our international income was generated. The candidates would have to be experienced, trustworthy, and able to work autonomously because we couldn't micromanage them. The candidates also had to fit in with the unique business culture of Pictionary, Inc.

That person was already in our sights. Rich Gill was based in Barbados, still managing international business for Trivial Pursuit. Since we'd run into him on "Black Tuesday," Terry had reached out to periodically over the years with questions involving international licensing and business strategy. Rich was always cool about helping us out.

Rich was a relationship guy with connections at virtually every game company in the world. He was highly respected for his industry know-how and understood the overseas business inside and out.

"Look, if Rich is available and open to an offer, I think we should reach out. It would be the best solution, in my opinion," Terry said as we floated around industry names for the position. "Obviously, he's got the chops, and we'd save a ton of time getting him up to speed. He could hit the ground running."

Gary and I fully concurred.

Rich was indeed interested, at least in having a conversation. Days later we flew him to Seattle to meet with us and get to know each other.

This would not be your normal interview. Rich was certainly qualified, but would he fit in with our company culture and dynamic? After years together, we knew each other's habits and quirks well. Cutting through that would be a real test of his mettle.

There's an old saying that if you hire someone into a small company, you should like them enough to want to eat dinner with them three nights a week. Working closely together would not only be a professional relationship but a personal one as well.

We all took Richard out for a get-to-know-each-other dinner at our local favorite restaurant, Anthony's Home Port. Over several bottles of great wine, well chosen by Rich, we were laughing and carrying on as if we had known each other for years. We talked of everything under the sun *except* Pictionary. He was a great fit.

The next day, we got down to the details. We explained the challenges we were facing internationally and the opportunities we were missing.

Rich laid his cards on the table. It was a little bit like when I "interviewed" Tom McGuire. His in-depth knowledge of the industry and the workings of the international markets was just as comprehensive. He was adept at navigating the myriad of licenses we already had in place and had specific ideas on where and how we could expand next. Plus, he knew all the players. He could indeed hit the ground running.

After a few hours, there was no question Rich was our guy. The only question was whether Rich felt the same way.

"I have a pretty good gig over at TP," Rich said as he got up to say goodbye. "And I hadn't been thinking about leaving until you guys called. I really need to think about it. But you should know that if I were to leave Trivial Pursuit, it would only be to join you at Pictionary."

Terry, Gary, and I shot a hopeful glance at one another.

That was all we needed to understand that if we made a convincing enough offer, we'd get our guy.

And we did. We offered Richard top dollar, plus hefty bonuses. He would be based in England closer to the territories (and to his family) and be our representative for all international licensees. Even though we weren't much for titles, the rest of the world was, so Richard was named "senior vice president of sales and marketing."

Rich came aboard, and it was as if he'd been part of the team from the start. We were no longer three. We were four: Rob, Terry, Gary, and Rich.

Not long after we hired Rich, he proved his value. He alerted us to a Pictionary knockoff in Spain called Dictiopinta (a not-so-clever transliteration of "Pictionary"). It wasn't hard to miss. The box was the same shape as Pictionary. The colors were almost identical. Same typeface. Same rules. They even used over 90 percent of our word list. The Spaniards were replicating Pictionary and marketing it as their own creation.

Spain was an exceptionally lucrative market for us. We had been the number-one-selling game there for two years now.

We put our UK legal team on the case.

Our attorneys immediately hit a roadblock, a.k.a. the Spanish legal system. The Spanish courts were notorious for siding heavily in favor of their citizens, no matter the merits of the case. It was an uphill battle.

It was crystal clear our rights were being violated, but the authorities couldn't care less. Months went by while the wheels of justice dragged on. They wouldn't even hear our case. Meanwhile, we grew increasingly agitated as Dictiopinta, because of its lower price point, continued to gain market share across Spain.

"Guys, I have a plan to stop Dictiopinta," Rich said.

"We are all ears, Rich," I said, eager to hear more.

He explained that the cure to the madness would not come by fighting a likely losing and protracted lawsuit; it would come by making Pictionary the steadfast winner in the Spanish court of public opinion.

Rich worked in tandem with Javier Conill, the incredibly talented managing director for Pictionary in Spain. With Rich's support and direction, Javier and his team conducted a full-court press on the territory. They placed ads in local newspapers, hitting consumers over the head with the message that Pictionary was the original and higher quality "charades on paper" game. They ramped up demonstrations and convinced retailers to promote *our* game, not the knockoff.

This inspired strategy paid off. Within a few years, Dictiopinta's sales plummeted, and the shoddy native doppelganger abandoned the market.

I have no doubt that without Rich's diligent work on this challenge, we would never have achieved these results. He was not only increasing our sales volume internationally, he was guarding the Pictionary brand with every bit as much integrity as Terry, Gary, and me.

Rich would continue to be a huge part of the success of Pictionary, and I'll always be grateful he joined the adventure.

SATURATION USA

While we were settling our international business, back in the U.S., we were facing new challengers. The market was getting increasingly crowded with an avalanche of new game concepts. The competition wasn't just coming from the drawing games; the board-game category was so hot that even the most off-the-wall ideas were starting to appear on store shelves.

Everybody was looking to be the next Pictionary. Practically any parlor game or activity people played in their childhood was put forward. There was the Garage Sale game, the Tattoo game, the Get-the-Whale-out-of-the-Fisherman's-Net game, the Teacup game, and on and on, ad nauseam. Whether the public would latch onto any of them for more than a season or two was another issue.

Some of the better games managed to gain a strong, lasting perch. Taboo, Scruples, and Scattergories were among those that would go the distance and live beyond the golden age of board games.

One of the best and most noteworthy was Balderdash, created and launched in 1984 by Canadians[*] Laura Robinson and Paul Toyne. Bal-

---

[*] It was a highly creative period for the board-game business, and coincidentally, three top-selling board games were created by Canadians. I was born in Vancouver, while Trivial Pursuit creators Chris Haney and Scott Abbott were from Quebec, as were Balderdash creators Laura Robinson and Paul Toyne.

derdash was a bluffing game based on our old nemesis and near-namesake, Fictionary. It was doing solid numbers in Canada and needed U.S. distribution.

Tom and Joe saw an opportunity. They were under no legal obligation to get our approval, but having learned that communicating with us was key, they came to us with the idea of licensing Balderdash in the United States. Our initial reaction wasn't a rousing yes. We weren't completely comfortable with the idea of The Games Gang shifting their focus to a competing brand.

Tom and Joe put forth a logical argument. "It's a strategic move that'll benefit Pictionary," Tom explained.

"Adding Balderdash to our roster gives us a new story to tell buyers," Joe added. "Having two popular games will open more doors and thus more sales opportunities for *both* products. Plus, unlike a lot of the crap that's hitting store shelves, Balderdash is a great game.

Tom said, "The more successful games in the marketplace like Pictionary and Balderdash, the more the entire industry benefits. Don't look at Balderdash as competition but as an additional way for the public to embrace the games category."

Tom's rationale made sense, so we agreed having Balderdash in the Games Gang stable was indeed advantageous to Pictionary. And we were right. Balderdash went on to become a bestseller in the U.S.

EVEN WITH OUR PHENOMENAL POPULARITY, sales were inevitably going to slow.

Penetration, competition, and people simply looking for the next "big thing" all took a toll on our overall sales.

An article in The *Los Angeles Times* reported: "Some board game icons are dipping in sales . . . the 'maturing market' syndrome for games like Pictionary and Trivial Pursuit."

Worlds of Wonder, probably to get back at us for turning them down, came out with a knockoff called *Get the Picture*. It didn't do well (drawing-game fatigue perhaps?), and although The *LA Times* reported that a WOW spokeswoman said, "the company intends to re-launch the game with more advertising support during the upcoming year," it never happened.

The New York Times chimed in with more dire news: "In the volatile toy industry, Worlds of Wonder, Atari, and Coleco all grew enamored of their best-selling products . . . hired huge cadres of managers and marketers, built new plants and went heavily into product development. But unlike such large toy companies as Hasbro or Mattel, which spread their risks and costs over a fairly ample stable of products, these companies relied on the continued growth of one or two faddish items to keep them afloat [and] found themselves drowning in red ink when their base products stopped providing enough sales to support their swollen operations."

I chuckled at The *New York Times* article. I certainly didn't want any company to fail; people's jobs were at stake. However, there was some satisfaction when I heard the news. Evidently, Donald Kingsborough didn't follow his own advice.

Despite the headlines and headwinds, 1989 was far from the end of the line for Pictionary. Our "box of paper" had become the newest member of the game-aisle staples club, alongside Monopoly, Risk, Clue, and Trivial Pursuit. Retailers kept all of us on the shelves, perpetually, knowing the public interest would remain evergreen.

MEANWHILE, IN EUROPE, SALES WERE still on the upswing, as Rich continued to bring onboard new territories. He was very adept at finding aggressive product managers by targeting the second and even third tier toy and game companies. They were hungrier because they did not have the breadth of products of the larger competitors. They were aggressive and willing to take risks to make Pictionary a success.

To support the sales efforts of our licensees in Europe, at our own expense, we hired Yellow Submarine, a company founded by the widely respected game-industry veteran Peter Rook. Rook and his team were tasked to handle European merchandising, promotions, and tie-ins. And just like in the U.S., Pictionary found itself associated with a wide variety of products.

Pictionary appeared on Fido Dog Food cans in Spain. Feed the dog, play Pictionary: Now you're both happy.

In England, an entire mini Pictionary game was designed as after-dinner mints. The game pieces were made of chocolate and if you guessed the picture correctly, you'd get to eat the chocolate.

Quaker did a European Sugar Puffs cereal promotion with Pictionary game play.

Evian packaged a mini game with *two million* bottles. People had to stay hydrated, after all.

But my all-time favorite was a champagne promotion in France. The vintner printed Pictionary's name on the label and sold it along with a free sample game.*

And finally, even for a board game, the old adage rang true: "sex sells!" Our evolving attitudes about European sensibilities allowed Durex to slip into the mix with "Buy six condoms and get a mini Pictionary game." The connection seemed obvious enough. People could play a hot and heavy game of Pictionary, then celebrate their victories (and comfort their losses?) with Durex condoms.

Terry, Gary, and I had a rather boisterous word-list session in the office. I'm sure the people in the office next door must have wondered what sort of debauchery was going on in our suite, hearing us gleefully yelling out provocative, and sometimes downright vulgar, words at each other.

Alas, Durex wanted to keep the words a little less risqué than we would have allowed (for the first time ever).

---

* I still have a bottle, but I'm not sure it's drinkable after all these years.

THAT YEAR, WE WERE APPROACHED by MCA Universal for a TV show based on Pictionary. Quantum Media, founded by Robert (Bob) Pittman, would produce the show. Before Quantum, Bob was the cofounder and creator of MTV, and later, CEO of MTV Networks.* Doing a show with Bob Pittman meant that we'd be working with the very best. We were thrilled.

The only twist was that it was slated to air on Nickelodeon, the kids' channel. But hey, we had learned our lesson with the damn Hoover Dam commercial, and this time we let the professionals do their job.

Terry, Gary, and I flew to Los Angeles for the taping of the *Pictionary!* pilot. Bob and his team took care to oversee every aspect of production, giving notes to the director, offering the cast and crew guidance and critiques to make the show the best it could be. We were in very good hands.

Pictionary! premiered on Nickelodeon on June 5, 1989, incorporating the cable channel's trademark green slime. The host, Brian Robbins, was an energetic young guy who was very popular on Nickelodeon. (Brian was also starring in ABC's *Head of the Class*.) The judge, a bald, mustachioed character called "Judge Mental," was played to perfection by actor and former professional arm wrestler Rick Zumwalt.

It had the feel and energy of playing an actual game, so we were not surprised when the show was picked for syndication.

While dozens of episodes aired over an eight-week run, the show didn't catch on with young viewers. Still, we saw a bump in sales for both Pictionary Junior and the senior edition. The experience whetted our appetite for TV, and this foray onto the small screen wouldn't be Pictionary's last.

IN THE MEANTIME, PICTIONARY WAS beginning to make cameo appearances on the *big* screen. Just a few weeks after Nickelodeon's *Pictionary!* premiered on TV, Renee and I went to see the new romantic comedy *When Harry Met Sally* starring Billy Crystal and Meg Ryan. Truth be

---

* Bob Pittman is now the CEO of iHeartMedia.

told, I probably would have preferred to see *Indiana Jones and the Last Crusade* instead. But here I was, being a good boyfriend, enjoying spending some rare leisure time with Renee . . . when about two-thirds of the way through the movie, I got the surprise of my life.

The scene opens with Meg Ryan's character, Sally, using a big fat black marker to sketch a circle on a white board . . . then eyes . . . some hair . . . a mouth . . . a body . . .

Oh my God! It's Pictionary! I can't believe Meg Ryan and Billy Crystal are playing my game.

I moved to the edge of my seat, laughing my ass off, even finding myself playing along. Renee moved up next to me, not quite believing what she was seeing either.

"It's a monkey! It's a monkey! Monkey see monkey do!" Bruno Kirby's character, Jess, blurted out.

"Baby fish mouth!" Jess yells out after a series of bad guesses. "Baby fish mouth!"

"Baby fish mouth!" Ha! That's hilarious! I couldn't stop laughing. *Do the people in this theater have any idea how freakin' cool this is?*

The rest of the movie was a blur.

As the credits rolled, I whispered to Renee, "I really hope that this romcom is a hit."

While the movie didn't mention Pictionary per se, it was clearly our game. And spotting Pictionary in a movie was a whole other level of milestone. Pictionary had reached pop-culture status.

TOM MCGUIRE[*], THE GAMES GANG, and San Serif proved that the news reports of our demise had been greatly exaggerated. By the close of 1989, Pictionary had maintained its status as the #1 board game on the planet with North American sales tipping three million across the range, coupled with another three million internationally.

---

[*] Tom McGuire died suddenly in January 1992 at age sixty-two. He was our mentor, friend, and guide, and we owe him an immense debt of gratitude.

To date, we'd sold an impressive 22,000,000 games across the globe.

My personal life was also reaching new heights. I had been busy building my dream house, complete with a nursery, on Mercer Island, on the shores of Lake Washington. As it neared completion, I was ready to ask Renee to move in with me. Thankfully, she said yes, paving the way for our future together.

1990 was off to a phenomenal start. Or so I thought.

BOARD VS. CONSOLE

s America moved into the 1990s, video games increased their hold on social interaction (or social *non*interaction). The essential elements of my childhood experience of riding bikes, playing baseball—and of course board games— were fading. Connections were missed, and creativity was falling by the wayside in exchange for the solitary pursuit of electric points won via machines against faceless avatars. Tastes were changing, family dynamics were shifting, and kids and teens were plugged in and tuning out.

Certainly, computer games had been around awhile, but now with enhanced graphics and playability, consumers' shift to video games was accelerating at a dizzying pace. Nintendo was the number-one console; Sega, PlayStation, and Xbox would soon enter the fray, creating a massive challenge to traditional board games. Super Mario and his brothers were now kids' best friends. An entire generation was becoming gamers.

We didn't want to be left behind. To cash in on the trend, we evolved with the times.

We approached Nintendo, based in our backyard in Redmond, Washington, to discuss a licensing agreement for a video game based on Pictionary to use on their console.

Nintendo expressed interest and enlisted LJN, a top-tier publisher, to manage the project. In turn, LJN hired Software Creations, a development team in the UK known for their out-of-the-box interactive video-game development. We contacted Software Connection to discuss their ideas.

The technology they proposed was an interactive drawing game that could be simultaneously accessed by multiple players. The concept was bold and cutting edge for the day. It also had yet to be perfected. But they convinced us the technology would work.

We bounced creative ideas back and forth for several weeks over the phone, fax machines, and early-stage video conferencing. Also in its infancy, the video imaging was slow, fuzzy, and herkie jerky, and what we could only sort of make out was raising creative concerns. For us to sign off, we had to see how it worked, in person.

Terry and I jumped on a plane to Manchester, England, for a face to face. We figured three days would be enough to hammer out the details. We arrived at the Creative Solutions offices after an eleven-hour flight and two-hour drive and got right to work.

The development team put their design schematics up on a big screen in their conference room. We divided into teams and started the playtest. Even though it was a prototype, once the graphics were up and moving, and crisp and clear, their concept was *now* easy to understand and more importantly, fun. And that was exactly what we expected.

What Creative Solutions designed was perfect—interactive and team based just like the board game. All it took was an in-person demonstration for us to sign off.

We had been there barely four hours, and our job was done. Terry looked at me and said, "Well, no point in hanging around. Let's go home."

No argument from me. We zipped back to Heathrow and caught the first flight back. Total time from takeoff from Seattle, landing in the UK, playtesting and approval, and back on the ground in Seattle, was twenty-eight hours, flat.

THE FINAL HURDLE WAS TO negotiate the contract with Nintendo for the video-game development. Nintendo and Pictionary were represented by the same Seattle law firm, Lane, Powell, Moss & Miller. Neither party was concerned about conflict of interest, but the attorneys were. Terry and I went to meet with the Nintendo brass at their corporate headquarters, in Redmond and were impressed to see that Howard Lincoln, president and CEO, believed this was a big enough deal to handle the situation personally.

We shook hands and adjourned to a nearby conference room. I walked over to a chair, absentmindedly fidgeting with my money clip.

As I was about to sit down, Howard said, "Well, what are we going to do here, gentlemen?"

Spur of moment, I said, "This is going to sound a little crazy . . ." and I held up my money clip.

Terry looked at me, ready to say, *"I think what Rob meant to say is . . ."*

"Let's decide it over a game of liar's poker,"* I said, looking around the table, still holding up my money clip, and gauging the response.

Howard broke into a big grin, reached into his pocket, and said, "I only have hundreds."

"Not a problem," I countered. I stripped a bill out of my clip and added my own grin.

Terry and the Nintendo executives were open mouthed watching us go at it.

"Winner keeps Lane Powell?" my adversary asked.

I nodded.

It was down to the president and CEO of biggest video game

---

* "Liar's poker is an American bar game that combines statistical reasoning with bluffing and is played with the eight digits of the serial number on U.S. dollar bills. The digits are ranked 0 to 9 with 0 being the lowest. Each player holds one bill, unseen by the other players. The objective is to guess how often a particular digit appears among all the bills held by all the players. Each bid must be higher in quantity than the previous bid. The game ends when the other player challenges a bid." "Liar's Poker," Wikipedia, December 2018. Of course, you can lie about what you hold in your hand.

company in the world and me, the creator of the biggest board game in the world. No better way to decide than two gamers playing a game.

Howard peeked at his bill, studied it, peered at me, and said, "I'll open."

"Give it your best shot, sir," I said, taking stock of my numbers. "Two twos," he said.

"Two threes," I countered immediately.

He didn't even look at his bill, just drilled me in the eyes, and said, "Four fours," hard and steady.

I held his gaze and said, "Five sixes," putting the slightest lazy inflection on it, as if I did this so often it was almost boring . . . like I win every time, so no big deal.

That shut him up. But would he call my bluff? (I only had four. I needed him to have one more to make my five.)

It went quiet in the room. Tension was thick as a World Series of Poker game.

He looked at me, trying to read a tell.

I had none. I'd played in enough bars in my day; I knew how to play. He swallowed; I had him.

A moment of silence. "Liar!" he chuckled and threw down his bill.

I showed my bill containing four sixes. Howard *did* have one, giving me the five I needed for the win.

Howard's eyes went wide. "Well . . . guess I'll have to go find me a new lawyer."

I laughed, offered him my hand, and said, "Nah. Let's tell Lane Powell they have the permission for both Pictionary *and* Nintendo to use their services. No conflict of interest."

Howard shook my hand. "Deal."

It was no coincidence that two game heavyweights found a resolution through play.

Unfortunately, the game mechanics were less simple to resolve.

The technology Creative Solutions had worked so hard to perfect never materialized. It was *too* cutting edge, and they couldn't get it to work as seamlessly as they hoped. The alternative game play option they proposed was still a lot of fun, but it didn't have the multiteam play aspect to it.

In deciding whether to launch or not, we felt the game was entertaining enough to release. We were comfortable attaching the Pictionary name to it. To be involved in the video-game market before other drawing games entered the space, we had to make a move. In this case, we accepted that good had to be good enough.

Ultimately, it wasn't. Sales were tepid at best.

FOUL PLAY

At the end of the first quarter of year four of our five-year deal with San Serif, Terry came over to my desk with some news. We'd been expecting a quarterly royalty payment of about $500,000, and it hadn't yet arrived.

"What's the holdup?" I asked

"Not sure. I've been hounding them for a week," he replied. "Serif says there was a glitch collecting from one of the bigger territories and they will get back to us when it's all sorted out."

We had always received our royalty payments on time, so there didn't seem to be much reason for concern. Besides, we'd been working with the San Serif team for four years and had become friends. We even vacationed together. We chalked up the missed payment to "gremlins."

But by the second month of runarounds, double-talk, and not returning Terry's messages, our frustration grew. We got on a call with Rich, who had also reached a boiling point.

"They should be talking to me, dammit!" he said over speakerphone. "They aren't returning my calls, either. I'm just going to show up at their office to see what's going on and get a straight answer."

"Rattle their cage, Rich," I added. "If they're lying to us, then this is full-out BS. Tell them we want our money, now!"

Rich had barely hung up when he was already in his car, driving over to the San Serif offices in Ipswich, UK, about three hours away from his home. He marched right in to get a full account of what was really going on.

The managing director tried to placate him, explaining that it was just a "misunderstanding." He apologized, shaking Rich's hand, assuring him that he was straightening it all out.

"I told them that half-a-million bucks is hardly a 'misunderstanding,'" Rich said when he called us from a pay phone before getting back on the road.

"Damn right, it's not. How'd he respond to *that*?" Terry asked.

"He said it'll all be sorted out by the next royalty payment," Rich said, not entirely convinced. "And we'll receive both quarterly payments at once."

Gary, who normally left the contract work to us, was also in the room when Rich called. Even he sounded alarmed. "This isn't the normal way they've operated. This feels different."

"Let's not panic just yet," Terry said tentatively. "Let's take them at their word. Our next royalty payment is due in less than four weeks."

We all agreed to give Serif one more accounting cycle to make it right.

But on the appointed day, there was no wire transfer. Two payments missed.

We had a problem—a *big* problem. We never had a partner steal from us. Or screw us.

Terry calculated that between both overdue payments, they owed us just shy of $1 million. To hell with friendship; we were going to get our money.

We demanded the Serif execs fly to Seattle and threatened legal action if they didn't come. They arrived a couple of days later, sheepishly walking into our office.

"Hey, Rob!" the managing director said, trying to hide the rattle in his voice. "It's been a while. It's good to see you!"

I didn't respond.

"So, as I'm sure Richard explained, we're really sorry for the hiccup, but . . ."

"'Hiccup?' It's not a 'hiccup'!" I said, before letting him finish. "You effectively stole a million dollars from us!"

"Guys, guys, I know. We should have come to you earlier and explained what's happened," he said, trying to calm the situation. "The long and short of it is, we've been having cash flow issues and used your royalties to keep our business afloat."

"Maybe had you come to us sooner, we could have worked with you to figure something out," Terry said.

I couldn't hold my tongue. "Instead, you bullshitted us for months! We trusted you, and you were lying to us all this time. No more. We want our money. *Now!*"

"We don't have it, Rob. And if you insist, we'll go under, and then nobody wins. We'll have to shut down, and all your sublicenses will be thrown in disarray. You'll have to manage each individual country yourselves. Do you have the resources to handle such an undertaking?"

The balls on this guy. His threat carried little weight. What Serif failed to realize was that we were now much more confident in our ability to manage all the licenses. With Rich on board, we could handle the task until we found new master licensing partner.

Terry, Gary, Richard, and I had a lively debate concerning what would be the best course of action to deal with this crap. We were *all* pissed off, but we had to be rational. In the end, negotiating a settlement was in our best interest.

Terry laid out the terms. Serif would pay what was owed over the next three quarters in equal instalments. If they did not pay, we would take them to court to force payment even if it meant them shutting down.

We didn't want to risk losing more money, so we broke the Serif contract, and all royalty payments would now come directly to us in Seattle.

Most of the sales and marketing plans were already in place for the fifteen countries Serif oversaw, and we felt confident we could manage the individual territories in the short term until we found a solution. Really, what choice did we have?

Over the next few months, we reached out to our contacts in the industry to see who might be interested in securing the international rights. Pictionary had earned a reputation as a solid worldwide brand and had three eager and qualified suitors. The clear winner was Kenner Park Tonka (KPT).

KPT was a multinational company and was well positioned to keep Pictionary's growth on track. They had a presence in many of our untapped markets, making it easier to expand globally without our having to take on several individual licenses. Unlike Serif, who was acting as middleman between Pictionary, Inc., and the licensees, KPT would be using their own sales and marketing teams directly in each territory.

We signed a lucrative ten-year deal with Kenner Park Tonka.

Not surprisingly, soon after, San Serif filed for bankruptcy. They never paid us a penny (or lira, deutschmark, or franc).

Screw them.

FROM THE START, WE KNEW we had made the right choice with KPT. By the end of 1991, just a few months into the KPT contract, six-year-old Pictionary was being sold in thirty-six countries and still expanding. Most of the major markets had been tapped but there were still numerous smaller ones to explore.

We added more territories in Central America and expanded in eastern Europe, including Poland and Hungry. Asia was on the horizon. Iceland was an astounding market for us. We racked up an incredible and almost unbelievable 32 percent household penetration, making it the hottest game for those cold Icelandic nights.

WE CELEBRATED OUR SUCCESSFUL NEW partnership with KPT over cocktails at the UK Toy Fair the following year with our friend Bob Wann, a Hasbro executive.

"It's been another incredible year for Pictionary," Bob said, raising his glass. "I have no doubt it's because of the hard work you guys at Pictionary, Inc., have done all these years and continue to do. You've kept Pictionary top of mind. And for goodness sakes, it's only the four of you!" Bob added. "It's truly remarkable and very impressive. Congratulations on your well-deserved success. Cheers!"*

"Thanks, Bob," I replied. "It's like we always say: 'We take care of Pictionary, and Pictionary takes care of us.'"

"That's key," Bob said. "Look, we see this all the time—new licensors sign on with us and walk away from the business before the ink is dry. No matter how hard we work on behalf of their games, nothing can replace the authentic support by the creators.

"So, before long, their game begins to fade. But not you, not Pictionary. The four of you hustling, day in and day out. You're dogged and relentless, and the result is that Pictionary has remained as popular as ever *and* is still growing."

"I'll drink to that!" I said, as we clinked our glasses. As I took a swig of my drink, Bob's words were still stirring: *Hustling day in and day out. Dogged. Relentless.*

Bob was right, but something inside me was starting to feel wrong. I didn't understand it, and I couldn't control it.

---

* Over the years, Bob's comments and sentiments were echoed by other top executives, including Alan Hassenfeld, then chairman and CEO of Hasbro; Norman Walker, then President of Hasbro UK; and many others. It wasn't creating Pictionary that garnered their respect; it was that after licensing, we stayed active and involved. It was sweet validation that our years of hard work and determination were appreciated, noticed and respected by these industry giants.

NOT ALL FUN
AND GAMES

I n early 1992, Renee and I were in love, engaged, and living in the house that Pictionary built. The partnership with KPT was working well, and Pictionary sales were going strong.

I should have felt on top of the world.

Yet I didn't, because something was wrong.

Inside me.

After years of flying by the seat of my pants, nonstop work, and having no downtime, I was starting to fray at the edges. I began feeling moody, sullen, and distant. Extreme anxiety would set in for long stretches of time, and I'd be unable to concentrate or get anything of substance accomplished. I didn't know where these feelings were stemming from, but they were there, taking over my every thought.

The first sign that something was amiss occurred a couple of years earlier. We came up with the idea of publishing a Pictionary Dictionary—like Pictionary, but in book form. Fun and easy, and we assumed, would be a big seller.

The concept was to a produce a paperback in two sections. The first would be the brief history of our journey creating the game. The second would be the "dictionary." Gary was to sketch all original 2,500

Pictionary words, five drawings to a page. At the bottom of the page would be a line where readers could write their guess as to what the drawing represented. The correct answers were on the next page so readers could see how well they guessed.

I thought it was a great idea and volunteered to take charge of writing our history section, hoping it might be just the thing to snap me out the funk that had been percolating.

It didn't.

I got the ball rolling, hiring a ghostwriter. By the time her manuscript arrived some weeks later, I was feeling so down I didn't even have the emotional energy to open it. The thick manila envelope sat on my desk, unopened.

"Hey, Rob. Where are you with the manuscript?" Terry asked one morning a couple of weeks later, standing at the door of my office. I bent over a box of folders and thumbed through them, pretending to look for something important.

"Relax, Terry," I said, pulling out a random folder, thick with papers, and slammed it on top of the unopened manuscript. "I have a lot of work on my plate. I'll get to it."

Terry nodded with half a smile, as if to say he only half believed me.

But I didn't get to it. And I didn't really care *if* I got to it.

I was too far inside my head, consumed with negative emotions that I didn't understand. These thoughts, not Pictionary, and certainly not the damn Pictionary Dictionary, fueled my days. I wasn't accomplishing anything or being productive in any way.

A few days passed, and I dragged my butt into work and was met with a red-in-the-face glare from Terry from behind his desk. He was so angry that I could almost feel the heat radiating off him. I didn't understand what was going on until I glanced down. I noticed the infamous thick manila envelope had been torn open and the manuscript was splayed out. Terry glared at me with contempt in his eyes and a red pen in his hand for a few seconds more, then peered down to circle something on a page in front of him.

Terry had me pegged. He'd grown tired of my inexcusable and unexplained procrastination and was editing the manuscript, finishing the project I'd promised to take on.

I was sure that by now Terry sensed something was off with me but was well beyond giving me my space.

It was the only time in our business or personal relationship I felt Terry's rage directed at me. And he was within his rights. I had thoroughly let him down. I had let Gary down. I had let Pictionary down.

I was letting myself down.

After the book incident, I somehow needed to force myself to push through whatever the hell was putting my relationships and business at risk. And at first, it was working, to some degree. But as time passed, as hard as I tried, it was losing a battle.

I had always been such a positive and happy person. And now I was the guy *I* didn't want to hang out with. The frustration of not even recognizing myself only added to my angst, and after a couple of years I was hitting bottom.

THE GAMES GANG ASKED GARY to choose a color for a Pictionary tie-in piece they were working on. Gary chose forest green—a color I wasn't a fan of. But instead of giving Gary my unemotional opinion of his color choice, I attacked his talent and abilities.

"You're losing your touch, Gary," I barked. "It's like you don't know shit about design anymore. Did you *ever?*"

In the moment, I was thinking: *You just attacked a man who is like a brother to you. Over a shade of green? What the hell are you doing?* Our culture had always been to argue for the benefit of Pictionary. Now, I was breaking the prime directive and making it personal. With that attitude, it was impossible for anyone to have a reasonable discussion with me.

No one, including Bonnie and Tim, had any idea what was going on in my head. How could they? I didn't even know. I did know that I was disconnected physically and emotionally from the business, and from them. I had lost my joy and passion for Pictionary, and at the time, for my partners. It was taking a toll on my relationship with Renee, too.

I was a wreck and withdrawing from everyone and everything I loved, respected, and cared about. The worst part was that I felt so alone.

Why doesn't anybody understand how unhappy I am? My internal struggle is making my life miserable. These are my family and friends. Can't they see that? Can't they see *me?*

I had lost all perspective.

From the outside looking in, everything was going my way, but on the inside, it was utter chaos. No amount of money or success could quell these feelings.

It had to stop. *I* had to stop.

I had to get help. I wanted to feel normal (whatever that was) again. I would do whatever it took.

After a particularly rough week of butting heads, I sat down with Terry, Gary, and Rich. I had become such a distraction that we came to a mutual agreement. They didn't understand what was going on but were genuinely concerned for me and saw I was in pain.

So, for the sake of my mental health, we agreed that I'd take a leave of absence.

"Go take care of yourself. Do whatever you have to do," Terry said on behalf of everyone. "We'll handle everything until you're ready to come back."

For the first time in a long time, I didn't argue.

With Renee's encouragement and support, I started seeing a therapist.

Her initial diagnosis was that I was suffering from clinical depression. A chemical imbalance was making it hard for me to see and think objectively. It was exacerbated by the pace of my life over the years: the nonstop work, no sleep, etc. It was all triggering the imbalance. Once it was brought under control, she said, I could at least start getting on the path to better mental health. The therapist recommended I go on antidepressants.

I railed against the notion. I was in too much pain for it to be a mere "imbalance." *My problems are real, not chemical,* I thought. *I need real help. I need more therapy. Not pills!*

But, after more therapy sessions, I wasn't making much progress. I still couldn't get out of my head. It was a closed loop of negativity and anxiety. So, albeit begrudgingly, I agreed to give medication a chance. At that point, I was willing to try anything.

I was more than surprised, and a bit relieved, to find the meds began to counteract the imbalance. The one I didn't believe even existed. They didn't "fix" me by making me happy and positive again. They did, however, allow me to see the world as it truly was, without all the negativity clouding my thoughts. I could now objectively process my life. There were still personal issues I needed to work through, but I could I see and feel that life wasn't as bad as I had made it out to be.

The antidepressants and continued therapy sessions helped me see the road ahead through a clearer and more optimistic lens.

AFTER SEVERAL MONTHS AWAY, I was feeling more like my old myself again and ready to go back to work. Slowly. I didn't feel the need to rush.

It felt good to feel productive. And, in time, I found my groove.

There are no words to describe how grateful I was that Terry, Gary, Rich, Bonnie, and Tim—and especially Renee—had my back during this utterly confusing time in my life.

They embraced me with open arms when I returned. There were no hard feeling or grudges. Just a simple *We're glad you're feeling better and back "home."*

I was humbled to my core. They accepted me, warts and all.[*]

---

[*] As I've gotten older, my bouts with anxiety and depression occur with less frequency and severity. I am not suggesting that medication was my only answer. I haven't been on meds for many years. I've been able to find my balance and peace through meditation, mindfulness, and being more sensitive to my triggers.

MISSING PIECE

As I slowly settled back into my routine at the office, Pictionary's frenetic sales and marketing pace were slowing down. The opportunities were not as plentiful as they once were. Pictionary had become a mature brand, and Terry, Gary, Rich, and I had become less entrepreneurial. Our roles were more managerial, focused on being stewards of the brand, moving it forward while remaining diligent in managing the business we already had in place.

Our continued involvement kept Pictionary's place at the top of the category, but the board-game industry itself continued to shrink as numerous video-game companies entered the market. The public's taste, and dollars, had drifted toward all things electronic. It was no longer just a few big companies like Nintendo that were chewing away at our sales; the video-game industry was rapidly expanding.

While Pictionary was reaching a plateau, on the home front, my family life was blossoming. Renee and I had gotten married, and in February 1994, our beautiful baby girl, Samantha Clare, was born.

My depression was at bay, and my world looked so much brighter than it had only a few years earlier.

AND THEN, IN THE BLINK of an eye, it didn't.

Late in 1994, Gary discovered a lesion on his leg. Our worst fears were realized when a diagnosis confirmed it was KS (Kaposi Sarcoma), an aggressive form of AIDS-related cancer.

Five years earlier, Gary had confided in me that he was HIV positive. As promised, I kept his secret, and we continued on with our lives until the inevitable time would come when Gary would have to confront the disease.

And here it was. Nothing could prepare us for this moment. But, as was his nature, Gary took the news with dignity. I felt it was almost like a relief to him. The not knowing when it would strike was eating at him as much as actually having HIV. Now, he could attack this horrible thing with all his might. And he did.

I took him to countless doctor's appointments. He ate well and took care of himself spiritually and physically, all in an effort to stem the progression of this deadly disease. Life-prolonging drugs like AZT were known to us. We tried to get our hands on some, but tragically they weren't readily available yet.

At work, Terry and Rich were equally supportive. We encouraged him to quit, but the distraction was good for him so he wouldn't dwell on the fate that was waiting just ahead to embrace him. He'd come to the office to give his input on creative projects, make us laugh, and, well, just be Gary.

He came over for dinner to Renee's and my house to see his favorite niece, Sam, and always make her laugh, too. That is what I miss most about not having him around. His lovely, endearing sense of humor, his love of life, and mostly, his laugh. He was such big part of my life. Above all else, Gary was my friend.

He and I continued to hang out as long as he was able. We'd go to dinner and split a great bottle of wine and chat about life and philosophy, and naturally, we'd laugh. Nothing could change his spirit. Not even AIDS.

Gary Paul Everson lost his courageous battle with AIDS on May 1, 1995. He was forty-four years old. I lost my friend, brother, and confidant. Pictionary lost its moral compass. And the world lost a beautiful, sweet, and loving human being.

I miss him terribly.

He is gone but will never be forgotten. Less than a year after his passing, Renee and I welcomed our second miracle, Benjamin Gary.

CAPTURE THE FLAG

Gary's passing put a spotlight on how short life can be and how precious it truly is. It drove home the importance of living each day as if it's your last. You never know when the journey will end, so Terry and I decided it was time to take complete control of Pictionary, Inc.

To that end, we approached Uncle Jerome and Auntie Anne with an offer to buy out their interest in the company. For years, they'd been the most supportive silent partners, trusting us to run the business as we saw fit. But now, it was time to pilot our own course.

Terry and I put together a generous proposal and flew to Palm Springs. Our timing was right; Jerome and Anne were ready to move on and cash out. Negotiations were swift and amicable. When my aunt, uncle, and I shook hands, the look of pride on their faces brought tears to my eyes. They believed in me from the start, going all the way back to my college loan.

Jerome was tearing up a little, too; I had lived up to every promise I made and was always a man of my word. As he was to me.

By now, Richard Gill was not only an employee; he'd become our dear friend and an indispensable member of the team. He was, in all aspects, our partner. It was time to make it official. As acknowledgment of the valuable role he played in the success of Pictionary, Terry and I gave him the opportunity to buy a portion of Jerome's shares. He had more than earned it.

Richard accepted, and we were honored to welcome him as our partner.

In 1996, SHORTLY AFTER THE buyout, the new president of Western Publishing decided to take the company back to its roots as a printing manufacturer. Being in the board-game business other than through manufacturing didn't fit his strategic plans. Western proposed selling their games division to Hasbro.

Although we had had difficult dealings with them the past, moving forward with Hasbro was really what was best. As the new licensee, they would have the ability to keep Pictionary at the top in North America.

The terms of our deal with the original joint venture (The Games Gang and Western Publishing) spelled out they could not assign or sell our licensing rights without our written approval. Seizing the opportunity to correct a mistake we'd made years earlier, we demanded a five-year term on the contract before we agreed. Hasbro wouldn't cede to our demand. It was *their* nonnegotiable.

We had a decision to make. Do we deny the transfer and hedge our bet that the next company, albeit a likely second-tier alternative, would agree to our terms? Or, do we forgo our stipulation and sign with Hasbro, the company most aligned with our business interests?

We went with the devil we knew. However, if we weren't going to get our expiration date, we were going to get our pound of flesh; we demanded significantly higher financial guarantees in the form of an increased minimum royalty per year.

This was *our* nonnegotiable.

Both sides saw it as a win-win. They'd get the game, and we'd get the cash. We agreed to the transfer.

It was poetic. We had spurned Hasbro's offer years before and they finally got the game they always wanted.

THINGS WERE CHANGING ELSEWHERE. WITH the transfer, The Games Gang was now working for Hasbro. This didn't sit well with any of them. The guys had no interest in going back to work for a large corporation. They took a buyout and went their separate ways.

Kevin McNulty and Mike Gasser started their own thriving game company called Endless Games. Tom McGrath retired to sunny Florida. Frank Martin continued managing his independent sales and rep company on the West Coast. And Joe Cornacchia continued to live larger than life, winning not one, but two, Kentucky Derbies.*

I will forever be indebted to The Games Gang. Each and every one of them had a hand in making Pictionary the huge success it was. Their dedication, drive, and sense of adventure all made for an astonishing and profitable ride for all of us.

---

* Bill Napier tragically passed away several years earlier.

PICTIONARY TV,
TAKE TWO

I n 1996, we were approached by Richard Kline of Kline and Friends to do another TV show. Kline had directed and produced many of the popular game shows that dominated daytime TV in the 1970s, '80s, and '90s, such as *Tic-Tac-Dough*, *Joker's Wild*, and, in an interesting twist of irony, *Win, Lose or Draw*.

Unlike the first TV show with Bob Pitman, Terry, Rich, and I threw ourselves into developing the pilot. We worked on storyboarding, establishing the look, feel, and the process for the game play. We debated whether to leverage some form of visual technology or use paper and marker like the original board game. Ultimately, we decided on the latter, going low tech. We felt markers on oversized sheets of paper would enable viewers to watch and mentally play along at home, feeling the energy of the contestant jumping around the stage as they sketched. It was as close as we could get to being in their living rooms.

Of course, we kept the team component. We had two teams of three players facing off. Each team included two celebrities and one "civilian" contestant. The civilian on the prevailing team would take home their winnings.

With the show developed, Alan Thicke,* well known for his beloved role as Jason Seaver, the father on the popular family TV show *Growing Pains*, came on board as host. The pilot received strong reviews and was picked up by Worldvision Enterprises, a leading distributor of first-run syndicated television shows, most notably *Judge Judy*.

We were a bit surprised by Hasbro's response, or lack thereof, to our getting a TV show on air. "That's nice," was all they said. They didn't see any real value in it—not even as a thirty-minute commercial for Pictionary. We couldn't get them involved to even place an ad around the show. It was very shortsighted on their part.

We had many of the most popular celebrities of the day on the show, like the cast of *Baywatch*, Mario Lopez of *Saved By the Bell* (now host of Access Hollywood), then standup comedians and future talk-show hosts Rosie O'Donnell and Bill Maher, and TV star Erik Estrada of *CHiPs*. In a full circle moment, I was beyond thrilled when Allison Sweeney from *Days of Our Lives* was on, and many more.

In a now-famous episode, Erik Estrada guessed the phrase "Tie a Yellow Ribbon 'Round the Ole Oak Tree" and was so excited, he threw up arms. The problem was, he accidently hit Bill Maher in the face when he did. Bill was briefly knocked out, though thankfully not seriously hurt. Bill took it with good humor. As he was helped off stage, he told his good friend Alan Thicke, "You owe me, buddy!"

We shot *Pictionary* at CBS Television City, Studio 33, in Los Angeles. We shared a sound stage with the venerable *The Price Is Right,* starring its long-time host, Bob Barker. Their production would shoot Tuesday, Wednesday, and Thursday, and then the crew would spend the day Friday breaking down their set and installing ours. We'd shoot every other weekend, five shows on Saturday and five more Sunday. Then, Monday morning, the crew would break down our set and reinstall *The Price Is Right.*

---

* Alan and I remained friends over the ensuing years until he sadly passed away in December 2016 while playing ice hockey with his son, Carter.

I WAS ASKED TO PARTICIPATE in a satellite media tour to promote the show and take questions from numerous TV stations around the country. As the one who represented Pictionary, Inc., in the media, I soon found myself sitting in a director's chair, earpiece in, the camera ready to roll, when something wonderful happened.

"What about Terry?" someone on the film crew asked.

I looked at Terry, expecting him to say no thanks. He had been conscious of his stutter and always begged off opportunities for camera time. But not this time; Terry caught me by surprise. He winked, implying he was "ready for his close-up."

You want to be on TV? I mouthed, smiling from ear-to-ear.

Terry smiled back, nodding. I couldn't have been happier seeing how far Terry had come and how much his confidence had grown.

"Hell, yes!" I said to the production team. "Mic him up!"

What a beautiful moment, the two of us together, sharing the spotlight that Terry so rightfully deserved. And you know what? Terry did himself proud. No stutter. Not once.

ON THE LAST DAY OF taping for the first season, I approached Richard Kline a bit hesitantly, and asked, "So, uh, what do you think about this idea . . ."

I paused.

Richard indicated to go ahead.

"How about if Terry and I appear on the last show, as two of the . . . celebrities?" I said.

Richard smiled and said, "That oughta be fun!"

I was partnered with Debra Wilson, one of the hosts from the popular *Mad TV* show, and Terry was with the talented actress Jennifer O'Neill.

We were having fun, goofing off and teasing each other before taping began. But as soon as the lights and cameras came on, the gloves came off. I wanted to win my contestant a lot of money, which meant I had to beat Terry. Besides, bragging rights were on the line.

I was up first to draw for my team. Nervously, I grabbed a marker and approached the board. I've pointed out before the irony of how I, the inventor of Pictionary, am not the best drawer. Actually, I stink. Cameras were rolling, and I began to draw the word "collar." My contestant and Debra were desperately trying to guess. I was doing a pitiful job, and they weren't even close. In the heat of the moment, I slyly touched my collar and gave them a little wink.

They both picked up on the highly illegal clue and yelled "Collar!"

I had forgotten that everything on TV lives on forever.

Terry saw me make the visual clue, jumped up, and at the top of his lungs, yelled, "He's cheating! He's cheating!"

Alan had to have seen it too but pretended he didn't hear him, likely thinking: *This is good TV!*

Either way, the game went on, and Terry sat there, face on fire, shaking his head in semi-mock disgust. He too badly wanted to win—the competitive spirit between us never dies.

Even with no further shenanigans, my team ended up winning the day, amassing the princely sum of $6,200 for my contestant.

We shot 170 original episodes of *Pictionary*, which aired during the 1997–98 season. As executive producers, Terry and Rich and I, along with Richard Kline, earned a Daytime Emmy nomination for Outstanding Audience Participation Show/Game Show.[*]

We were prepared with our acceptance speech to include "Thank you to the Academy. Amazing this all happened *from a box of paper!*" Alas, we didn't win and were unable to use our running joke. *Jeopardy* hogged the statue for the eighth year in a row.

---

[*] During production, we received an interesting letter from the Disney Company, demanding that we cease and desist from producing more Pictionary episodes and to stop airing the show altogether. Their claim was that we had stolen *their* intellectual property rights from the cancelled *Win, Lose or Draw*. Terry and I thought it was humorous (and some sort of universe kismet) that our game had existed in the market two years before WLD had even aired—and Disney was telling us to stop airing our show—long after their show had been taken off the air. We sent Disney a letter informing them we would be happy to have a judge and jury settle the issue, and for good measure, requested an autograph from Mickey Mouse. Disney declined to meet us in court and dropped their claim.

While our ratings were respectable, we did not get picked up for a second season. Nevertheless, this time, *Pictionary*, not *Win, Lose or Draw*, fueled our increased sales.

NEXT ROUND

eing around all the energy of the TV show got my creative juices flowing again, at warp speed. Terry and Richard focused on the day-to-day, while I focused on what I loved: creating something new. I loved the process with Pictionary and now felt I was ready to do it again. I was open to all possibilities and noticed opportunities everywhere I turned.

The next few years would culminate in three new inventions.

The first came to me when I kept stepping on my kids' toys. Whenever they opened a new toy, the pieces would inevitably be scattered everywhere, mostly underfoot. For instance, when Ben played with LEGO, the little bricks wound up all over the house, rendering them useless. There had to be a better solution to not only keep the play value alive, but the money value as well.

Terry told me he was having a similar issue with his kids' toys. I saw an opportunity.

I designed a bright-colored mesh bag system so kids could put all the pieces from whatever toys they were playing with *immediately* into their bags. This kept everything together and safely stored. The mesh allowed for the kids to see what was inside, and the large plastic "S" shaped hooks we included enabled the bags to be hung in the closet and out of the way.

We called it the "Red Squirrel EZ Toy Bag" and it came in three colors and five sizes. Terry and I even shot a TV commercial starring three of our kids!

Unfortunately, we only sold fifteen sets of the five hundred we produced.

While this product was an abject failure, I wasn't discouraged. If anything, I was more charged up than ever. The creative floodgates had opened, and I was open to the next idea to present itself.

It didn't take long.

I was playing golf with John Croley, a buddy of mine who was the vice president of marketing for the Seattle SuperSonics, the NBA team, when he mentioned how the bobble-head fad had run its course, and they were looking for a new novelty item for fans. I bookmarked this news in my head.

A few days later, I was at a sporting-goods store and noticed an M&Ms tube with a collapsing Disney Goofy push puppet toy on top of it. I bought a couple, and after Sam and Ben enjoyed their daily chocolate fix, I played around with Goofy. The more I played with it, the more it reminded me of a Gary Payton jump shot!

I pitched the idea to John, who loved it. Rich found a company in England to design and produce a prototype. And while I could visualize how it would work, it simply couldn't be designed to constantly go through the jump-shot motion without breaking. We tried again and again, investing $50,000 in the project, but it was taking too long. I couldn't convince John it was worth the risk of manufacturing, and eventually, he told me they'd moved on.

We abandoned creation number two. We had to accept it wasn't going to work. We let go of any ego attachment and moved on.

But hey, third time's a charm, right?

Terry and I were in our Seattle office while a marketing group pitched us their business idea. I had heard it all before and my mind began to wander. The words "Rorschach test" popped into my head, completely at random. *Why am I thinking of the inkblot test a psychologist developed a century ago?* I wondered. It was so out of context that I chuckled out loud. But my mind wouldn't let go, so I wrote *Rorschach test* on my notepad.

When I did, I immediately had a flashback to the beginning of Pictionary. *Had I found another aardvark? Had I just taken the first step to creating a new game?*

I began jotting down how a game based on inkblots might be played. The more I wrote, the clearer the idea formed in my head. I was in a flow state as the game laid out before me.

Knowing I was onto something, I kept writing until I was startled when Terry stood up to thank the marketing executive and lead him to the door.

I didn't get up, keeping the tip of my pen on the page so as not to interrupt my flow. I waved at the exec with my left hand, managing an awkward "Yeah, thanks," and kept writing.

"That was a boring meeting, even for me," Terry said. "But I noticed you were taking a lot of notes. Is there something you want to discuss?"

"Nope, not about the meeting anyway," I replied. "But there's something else I want to talk about." I presented my notepad to my partner. "Here's our new game," I said, smiling.

Terry sensed I wasn't joking and pulled his chair next to mine to see what I'd been working on. The moment felt just like our first meeting over lunch back in 1984 when Terry scribbled our Pictionary business plan on cocktail napkins.

Terry got the concept, immediately. "Rob, you're really onto something here! I can totally visualize this on store shelves."

"Yeah, Terry, I haven't been this fired up about a new game project since Pictionary," I replied. "I really want to get started fleshing this out."

The premise was simple—Pictionary simple. Players would look at an inkblot printed on a card and write down whatever images they saw. Then, they would read their answers aloud. If they could convince more than half the participants that the image was actually there, they'd score points. The person with the most points at the end of three rounds was the winner.

My first task was to create the inkblots. I experimented with numerous viscosities of ink and various paper weights and coatings until I found the perfect combination. I'd put a glob of ink on cardstock, fold it in half and see what developed when I opened it up.

Unlike when I was first creating the Pictionary word list alone in the backyard, the creation of inkblots was a family affair. Sam and Ben made a few, laughing and giggling that they got to make a mess in the family room. The kids making a mess wasn't the problem. Me being a bit of a klutz, I spilled the black ink on the red plush carpet, making *permanent* inkblots. Renee was none too pleased.

The name for the new board game would be "ThinkBlot." The game would include the best seventy-two of the hundreds of "blots" I'd created.

Once the prototype was completed, we decided to approach investors and produce the game ourselves. After all, who wouldn't want to invest with the creators of Pictionary?

Well, apparently, no one.

We were only able to secure ten percent of the $100,000 we were hoping to raise. Terry, Rich, and I went back to what we knew best: licensing.

Strike two.

IT WAS THE MID-1990s, AND game companies, hobbled by slowing sales, had become much more conservative with their purse strings. So, taking a risk on a game at prototype stage, even from the creator of Pictionary, wasn't a slam dunk. We couldn't get anyone to license the game in the U.S.

Never ones to take no for an answer, and in effect having to prove ourselves all over again, we approached Joel Sevelin, our Pictionary licensee in Sweden. Sure enough, he and his partner were willing to take the plunge. With a lot of hustle and confidence, they were able to take ThinkBlot to number one in Sweden in just two years. Based on that success, we launched ThinkBlot in an additional nine territories. We became the number-one new board game in most of them.

Meanwhile, back in the U.S., a new leadership team had taken over at Mattel, and Rich joined some of the new executives for dinner as the holiday season approached. A Mattel executive mentioned how one of the board games they were developing had fallen out, and they were on the lookout for a replacement.

Rich, ever on the ball and ready for the pitch, told the new team that their predecessors had passed on licensing ThinkBlot. Since then, the game had been licensed in Europe and was outperforming many existing board games. By the time dessert was served, Mattel was making plans to bring ThinkBlot to the U.S. They had clear proof of concept. If Hasbro had Pictionary, Mattel would have ThinkBlot.

Mattel gave the directive to their advertising agency to launch ThinkBlot in a big way. They cut a TV commercial that ran nationally and often. Given our last TV commercial experience, we tried to pull in the reins, firmly suggesting that Mattel link ThinkBlot to the creators of Pictionary, bring it to market slowly and organically, and let sales build as they had with Pictionary.

They didn't listen.

While sales of ThinkBlot were decent, the game never reached bestseller status here at home, despite our commitment and involvement. I believe it was because it was never given the chance to slowly find its audience. Mattel discontinued the game after three years. We took back the rights to ThinkBlot and still own them to this day.

SALES NOTWITHSTANDING, THERE WAS A personal victory in creating ThinkBlot. The most frequently asked question I was hounded with was, "What's your next game?"—which I interpreted as, *What have you done lately?*

At the time, Pictionary was the bestselling board game in the world, yet this question made me feel as if I wasn't a *real* game creator unless

I invented a second game. That likely wasn't their intention, but that's how I took it.

I started having moments where I didn't feel I'd earned my success and all I'd accomplished. I felt like I was a fake, and everyone *but me* was responsible for Pictionary's success.

You? Angel, you were just lucky, I'd think. *Sooner or later, they will all figure out you're a fraud.*

I would later learn I was dealing with what's called "imposter syndrome." It was rough for me in those moments when I didn't feel like I deserved a seat at the table of success. It was that old self-doubt crawling back into my psyche that I'd suffered with until I took my first step with Pictionary.

I know it sounds illogical, but what I perceived as slights messed with my head from time to time. Strangely, I didn't talk with my therapist about it, as if to keep it a secret. As I look back, I wonder how much this mindset played a role in my anxiety.

ThinkBlot proved I wasn't a one-hit wonder—not only to the inquiring minds, but also, and more importantly, to myself.

The fact that none of the products we created post-Pictionary were home runs didn't matter. It was energizing just taking another shot. To get started, to be open, to take that first small step all over again, made me feel alive, engaged, and happy.

I am, after all, an entrepreneur.

GAME OVER

As the year 2000 rolled in, I felt the new millennium beckoning me for a change.

Sixteen years had passed since I was a twenty-six-year-old single waiter with a big idea and pennies in my pocket. Now, I was a forty-two-year-old wildly successful entrepreneur, creator of the world's bestselling board game and an Emmy® Award–nominated executive producer of a national TV show. But now, the most important role in my life was being the married father of two young children, who meant more to me that anything.

Pictionary was like a child to me, too.

It was my brainchild, an omnipresent part of me. I raised it to become autonomous and live in the world on its own. But given my new priorities, I was ready to let go and let Pictionary fly the nest.

The timing was good. Our ten-year international license with Kenner Parker Tonka was coming to an end, and I had no desire to be locked in with them, or Pictionary for that matter, for another decade.

It was time to sell.

I woke up the next morning, confident in my decision. Before I could give myself the chance to change my mind, I asked Terry to meet me at the office, where I'd conference in Rich so I could share my news.

A few hours later, and while "technically" still morning, I brought a couple of cold beers over to the conference table as Terry took his seat just as Richard dialed in.

"So, to what do I owe the pleasure of this morning meeting, Rob?" Richard asked through the speaker in the center of the table. "Your email sounded like you have some big news to share. You doin' okay, buddy?"

"I'm good, Rich. In fact, I'm more than good. I'm great! I can't remember the last time I felt this great," I said, as I felt the weight of my decision loosening its grip.

"Well, that's good to hear, my friend," Terry said. "So, tell us Rob, why are you so chipper?"

"Well, I have come to a decision . . . a decision I won't make without your agreement, but then again, one I'm ready to scream the loudest for. I not only think it's what's best for Pictionary, it's also what's best for me," I said. "Terry, Rich, I want to . . . I want . . ." I knew I was making the right decision, but it was harder than I expected to say it out loud.

"You want . . . to sell Pictionary," Terry said, completing the sentence he could tell I wasn't able to utter myself.

"Yes, Terry, I want to sell Pictionary," I said, nodding my appreciation for his help. "Did you hear that, Rich?" I yelled into the speaker as if he couldn't hear me. I wanted to make it clear I had no misgivings. "I want to sell Pictionary!"

I began laughing hysterically, partly because I was yelling into a speaker phone for no reason, and partly out of relief. I'd said it. And I'd meant it. *I want to sell Pictionary.*

Terry was now laughing at me laughing at myself. *Ahh, I'll miss laughing like this with Terry.*

"Hey, I'm not sure what's going on over there, guys, but just so you know, I'm good to sell," Richard said. "But I'm also okay to keep going. Pictionary is still driving a ton of revenue internationally, and I'm in no rush to join some random internet sock-puppet startup. While I appreciate you including me in the discussion, you guys are the founders, and ultimately, it's your decision to make. I'll leave you guys to it and . . ."

"No need to leave the conversation, Rich," Terry interjected. "I'm onboard with the sale. In fact, Rob, I was hoping this was why you called the meeting. As much as I've loved just about every minute of working two feet away from you for the last sixteen years, it's time."

"Thanks, Terry," I said with a smile as we clinked bottles.

"I'm on this end holding up my own glass," Rich said, adding his own toast. "Cheers to selling the bestselling board game in the world!"

"Thanks, Rich. Hopefully we will have much more to toast about in person, soon."

And with that, the decision to sell Pictionary was made.

After Richard hung up and Terry left the office to go on one of his long runs, I remained to consider what had just transpired. I absent-mindedly began looking through old files when I came across a folder labeled simply "Gary" and opened it. It was filled with Gary's remarkable artwork. There were sketches of ideas for the Pictionary Junior gameboard, drawings of the original PicPacks, and a sheet of white copy paper filled edge to edge with tiny Pictionary-style doodles he'd drawn as samples.

"Hey Gary," I said, looking up, knowing he could hear me. "We've made the decision to let Pictionary go . . . but know that I'm never letting go of my memories of us creating Pictionary together."

I wiped away a tear, put the sheet of doodles back in the folder, tucked it under my arm, and walked out of the Pictionary, Inc. offices, letting the door close behind me.

BECAUSE OF HASBRO'S PURCHASE OF Western's game division several years earlier, the North American board-game rights belonged to them, for all intents and purposes, in perpetuity. This meant we had only the worldwide rights outside of North America to offer for sale. This included not only the board game, but everything related to the brand. It would mean a complete asset sale of the intellectual property.

We would be walking away.

Even without the North American rights, the value of Pictionary was still significant given current worldwide sales and status. Coupled with untapped market opportunities, acquiring the Pictionary brand would be very attractive.

There were only two potential suitors. The first, Hasbro, politely declined. With their recent acquisition of Pokémon, they felt they couldn't absorb both brands.

That left only one company: Mattel.

The fly in the ointment was that Mattel was just coming out of three years of dire financial straits created by the purchase of The Learning Company, an educational software firm. It hadn't performed to Mattel's expectations and, worse, had eroded the behemoth company's bottom line.

With our connection with Mattel through ThinkBlot, we put out feelers to gauge their interest. We were delighted to learn Mattel was *very* interested. They had long wanted to beef up their fledgling and underperforming international games division, and Pictionary was the perfect game to anchor their growth.

Terry, Rich, and I spent the next few months putting together a rock-solid proposal, one that was a universe away from the one Terry and I presented to Uncle Jerome and Auntie Anne sixteen years earlier in Vancouver.

Our plan showcased our impressive sales history, growth, and profitability. We provided three-year sales projections in each of the dozens of existing territories and demonstrated where the brand could grow under "new, dynamic ownership."

While confident in our pitch, we engaged Piper Jaffrey, a world-class mergers and acquisitions firm to provide the credibility we felt we needed at the table when asking Mattel for such a significant financial commitment. When the day finally arrived, Terry and I presented our well-rehearsed pitch to the Mattel negotiation team. We pandered to their ego.

"You're the premier toy and game company on the planet, smarter than Hasbro and everyone else in the business," I flattered. "Our licensees tried and failed three times to sell significant volume in the lucrative German market. It remains prime to be exploited. If anybody can turn that territory around, it's *you*. The profits will be astronomical!"

Sounded good anyway.

After several weeks of conducting due diligence, Mattel came back to us.

"Your business isn't worth what you're asking," they insisted. "Our finance department is strongly against the acquisition at your price."

Was Jerome's accountant working for them now? I wondered, sarcastically.

Even with our convincing pitch, Mattel's counteroffer was much lower than our "walk away" number. The company, still stinging from the Learning Company debacle, presented a number based on Pictionary's *current* revenue streams, merchandising, ancillary products—and put less weight on future *potential* earnings.

Unlike when we flatly turned down Hasbro's offer to license Pictionary in 1986, this time we had a Plan B. Sort of.

There were two smaller international companies interested in hearing from us. They would divide the worldwide rights between them. It wasn't a perfect scenario, but having this fallback emboldened us to stick to our guns.

"We have a great business, and to be honest, we are happy to retain ownership of our iconic brand," Terry said.

"We've got a great life, a profitable business, and other offers on the table. We feel no pressure to sell," I added for dramatic effect.

Our message was clear. If Mattel wanted Pictionary, pay our price. We projected an attitude somewhere between confident and cavalier, while making sure we didn't come across as arrogant or cocky.

We relayed our final number—one large enough to set us up financially for the rest of our lives.

Little did we know at the time that behind the scenes we had an ace in the hole—and it wasn't even our ace. Mattel's sales and marketing department desperately wanted Pictionary—and it created a battle with their finance team.

To make up the difference between our number and what the Mattel finance team deemed a suitable price, the sales and marketing department proposed allocating a portion of their future marketing budgets toward a four-year consultancy agreement with Terry, Rich, and me.

I really liked this concept. First, it meant they wanted Pictionary so much, they were willing to make a budget cut to have it in their stable. More importantly, while I was ready and able to leave Pictionary behind, knowing I would still be connected for four more years without any of the stress or risk that came with owning and running the business was very appealing.[*]

With these concessions, we agreed to the terms, and the deal was sealed . . .

Well, not quite.

Hasbro owned the North American rights and were paying the royalties to us. If Mattel owned the brand, those payments would now go directly to Hasbro. This posed a potential stumbling block. Mattel was worried about antitrust issues. If Uncle Sam saw that Hasbro, the largest toy company in the world, was paying the second largest a yearly royalty, it might raise a red flag, and the sale would be disallowed.

"We can't let this derail the deal of a lifetime," I pressed Terry and Rich. "I know Mattel considers Hasbro the Evil Empire and the thought of working with them is downright nauseating, but they want this as much as we do. We've come too far to be shut out."

Mark Sullivan, a big brain over at Mattel, came to the rescue. He suggested securing an insurance policy against any action by the government to block the deal. If the government did, Mattel would be reimbursed for their costs of acquisition.

---

[*] In those four years, Mattel called for our consultation just once. They needed clarification on a simple legal matter.

It was a brilliant solution, only Mattel wasn't willing to pay for the policy. Terry, Rich, and I weren't going to let the deal go because of this and said that *we* would pony up the $500,000 for the policy. It was a generous offer on our part, considering that if the government blocked the deal, we would not only lose out on the sale of Pictionary, but we'd be out half-a-million dollars to boot.

Mattel accepted.

In June 2001, just days after my forty-third birthday, all parties signed the contract to officially turn over ownership of Pictionary to Mattel.

And with a stroke of the pen, my beloved Pictionary and I parted ways.

It had been an astounding, surprising, lucrative, creative, and sometimes frustrating, but always entertaining, nineteen years together.

THAT NIGHT, TERRY, RICHARD, AND I went for a congratulatory dinner. Once again, Rich picked out the perfect wine for the occasion. After a few bottles, we got a little melancholy reminiscing about the amazing path we had all walked together, but took solace knowing we weren't saying goodbye to each other. Our bond had transcended business, and even Pictionary. We had become best of friends, and not even the sale would change that.

"What's next?" I asked to no one in particular.

"I am going to take a little time and be with my family before deciding," Terry said. "It's been a hell of a ride, and it will take time for me to process it all."

"You've earned it," I said. "For a guy who didn't like playing board games, you somehow managed to figure out how beat the industry at its own game."

"We *all* made it happen, Rob, in it together from the start," Terry said. "And here we are, still together at the end. And I know Gary is up there, smiling with us."

"And you, Rich? What's next?"

"I've always liked the challenge and energy of the toy and game business," Rich said. "I still get excited about new products and innovation. I think I'll look around and see what's out there."

"I love that about you, Rich," I said. "You're in perpetual motion, always looking for the next big thing. Hell, you've played a vital role in the success of *two* of the biggest selling board games of all time."

"Thanks, Rob. And you?" Rich asked.

"Yeah, Mr. Pictionary. What's next for you?" Terry added, tearing up a little.

"Well, I think I'm going to put myself in an extended time-out. Pictionary has afforded me the luxury of not having to decide right now what's next. I will just 'be' for a while and see where the journey takes me. For the immediate future, having the freedom to be there in the mornings to take my kids to school, teach Ben how to ride his bike, and play badminton with Sam, sounds just perfect."

Terry, Rich, and I kept talking, not wanting the night to end. But when the last drop of wine was poured, it was time to go. There were more tears and lots of hugs as we headed toward the door.

IT'S BEEN NEARLY TWENTY YEARS since that night. As I look back, I'm proud that Pictionary lives on in the hearts of millions. Knowing that I'm responsible for spreading so much joy and creating so many lasting memories for families and friends all over the world, is humbling and a true honor. So, it is with deep and abiding appreciation from the depths of my being that I thank you, dear reader, for coming along with me on my journey. I'm grateful to you for allowing me to share my story and pay tribute to Pictionary, the adventure of a lifetime.

AFTERWORD

For the first few weeks after the deal closed, I walked around in disbelief that I had actually sold Pictionary and it would no longer be part of my life.

I was a wet-behind-the-ears twenty-four-year-old waiter when I first sat down with a yellow legal pad and dared to dream that I could create something as magical as Pictionary. Then, nineteen years later, in the blink of an eye, I was forty-three. Talk about being disoriented. Selling Pictionary was like losing a limb. I'd survive, but I'd have to learn to rebalance myself without Pictionary there to support me.

The real kick for me is the journey Pictionary took me on—the ups and downs and the sheer adventure of it all. Creating a game that touched, and still touches, so many lives was ridiculously awe inspiring—and still is. Knowing this gives me a profound sense of gratitude.

As I closed that chapter of my life, I looked back in wonder at all that Gary, Terry, Rich, and I had accomplished. We'd come from different backgrounds and different dispositions, but it worked. We worked. We turned a silly late-night activity originally called "charades-on-paper" into a worldwide, superstar blockbuster.

I remembered the vow I'd made to myself that fateful day back in college, when I'd been put on academic probation and my father had been fired: that I would work hard to create the freedom to choose the life I desired. On my terms, no one else's. And I did.

It was paramount for me to be the most authentic version of myself and walk through any door that opened where I felt a sense of curiosity, connection, or interest. Those were the places I chose to invest my time, energy and money.

I may have retired from "working," but I did not retire from life.

I found myself at Burning Man. I love the openness and nonjudgmental attitudes. I've dived (or is it dove) with whale sharks and manta rays in support of WildAid, a wildlife conservation group. I've bungee jumped in Australia, I parachuted out of a perfectly good airplane in Mexico (with Ben). I've run with the bulls in Pamplona, Spain 25 times and have come dangerously close to getting trampled more than once. I've funded movies (not all successful) and a documentary about the Rwanda Film Festival I'm very proud of called *Finding Hillywood*. And, I make wine in Argentina that I love sharing with friends, old and new.

I have had many adventures and know there will be many more to come.

I think of myself as an explorer of the world.

But there's more to my life than just fun and games. Family, philanthropy and giving back by mentoring aspiring entrepreneurs, all nourish my soul and give me purpose. I particularly enjoy nudging those would-be-entrepreneurs to take that first step to "find their aardvark."

And finally, but certainly not last, I am blessed that my kids, Sam and Ben, are thriving, independent young adults who make me proud to be their dad every single day.

I'VE NOW EMBARKED ON MY next chapter. My third, I believe. It's a spiritual journey this time. I am striving every day to become heart-centered and be of service. I live a life full of gratitude, appreciation and as I did in my twenties, always go with the flow. I've never been happier, more present, or more content.

Once again, as I had done with Pictionary, I'm putting one foot in front of the other, not knowing where the path will take me. That's okay. I trust the universe to guide me once more. It's not the destination anyway, it's the journey.

So, here I go, headlong into this new chapter with an open mind, open arms, and an open heart. As it unfolds, I'll keep you posted!

WHAT IS FINDING
YOUR AARDVAK?

B efore Pictionary had a name or rules, I saw an opportunity to replicate the fun, connection, and joy of the game my roommates and I called "Charades on Paper." But, instead of getting started, I panicked. I got inside my head and was overwhelmed thinking of all the steps needed to realize my vision of having a board game sitting on a store shelf. Design, marketing, business plans, sales tactics—*Are you kidding me? You've never done anything like this before,* I told myself. I shut down.

The idea to create what became Pictionary never left my consciousness, as much as I tried to bury it. After two long years, I resolved it was time to get unstuck. While envisioning the big picture was too much for me to process at the time, taking a small step forward was accessible. I asked myself, *What is the simplest first task I can undertake?* The answer was: the word list.

There were no barriers to creating a word list; I had everything I needed at my disposal. I grabbed a pad of paper, a pen, and a dictionary which I opened to the letter "A" and wrote down the first Pictionary word: "Aardvark."

And with that first simple step, the entire world opened up to me. Eight letters un-stuck me and set me on my journey to making Pictionary a reality.

I *found my aardvark* and began the wildest journey of my life.

You may have ideas of your own that you believe can change the world. You may have flashes of inspiration wherever you go. And if you're like the many would-be-entrepreneurs who never put their ideas into action, the solution can be as simple as writing down one word.

There's beauty in big dreams and ambiguity and complicated plans. But *finding your aardvark* is about simplicity, about getting past your fears. *Finding your aardvark* is freedom from self-doubt, resistance, from never-ending to-do lists and unrealistic expectations.

Finding your aardvark is the key to not waiting for all the pieces to perfectly align before you get started. It's understanding that you have the tools right in front of you to make the first move. And when you take that step, you will see it lead to the next step, and the next, and so on. And eventually, you can relish the fact that you got started and gave yourself a fighting chance of success!

Step away from your business plan. Remove your vision board. Put down this book. And *do something.* Jump into the world. Open up to your big dream by taking action. Because when you do, you will *find your aardvark* and step firmly into your future.

GAME CHANGING
MOMENTS

OVER THE YEARS, PEOPLE HAVE graciously shared their favorite Pictionary stories with me. They are heartfelt, funny, poignant, and always appreciated. Here are some of my favorites:

Career in Pictures

I was in San Diego giving a talk on entrepreneurship at a great event called *Secret Knock* my buddy Greg Reid produces. During the lunch break, a tall, unassuming young man sheepishly handed me a folded note and walked away. The paper was covered with really clever doodles and characters. I was floored by what he had written inside.

The note revealed that when he had been in middle school, his parents, teachers, and counselors couldn't figure out why he wasn't learning. His loving parents grew frustrated when no interventions worked.

One day, his school counselor brought out Pictionary Junior. He immediately took to the drawing part of the game. In that moment, he realized he had a different way of learning. It was the first time he had really excelled at anything. After that, his confidence improved, as did his grades. He also started making friends by sketching caricatures of their faces.

After high school, he went on to become a regularly published cartoonist. His work has appeared numerous times in *The New Yorker* and *Mad Magazine*, among others.

I wanted to shake his hand. "I wonder what my life would have been like without Pictionary," he mused. "I'd probably be working at a truck stop or something equally as glamorous. Pictionary changed my life."

Fitting into the Picture

During dinner in a New York City restaurant, I got to chatting with the waitress. When she learned that I was the creator of Pictionary, she became emotional. In a shaky voice, she told me she had been a foster child who was an outcast among the three children in her foster family. All she wanted was to fit in and be accepted. The parents tried to improve the situation, but nothing they did altered the dynamic.

"Then one night," she said, as her eyes welled up, "we played Pictionary together. The other kids saw that I could draw pretty well and each one wanted me on their team. We all laughed and had fun for the first time as a family."

I handed her a napkin to wipe her tears. "Pictionary changed how the other kids looked at me; they finally accepted me. I finally felt like I had a home."

Precious Memories

At an event for aspiring entrepreneurs where I had just finished a speech, Nancy approached to tell me about her mother who had Alzheimer's. The only time her mother was lucid, she said, was when the family played Pictionary together. Playing seemed to trigger something in her mom's memory, and for those brief moments, she was able to stay focused and be present. These were the few times they were able to have fun together as a family just like they used to.

"I will carry those happy memories of us playing for many years to come," she said, tearfully, as she gave me a hug.

Drawn into Love

I was having dinner with my friend, Wendy, when her sister, Jerece, stopped by with her husband to say hello. As we were talking, Jerece told me she had met Buck twenty-six years ago playing a game of Pictionary. "We fell in love right then and there," she said, smiling ear to ear. "Now we have a family, with three happy, healthy children. And I owe it all to you and to Pictionary." I was floored that Pictionary had been the catalyst for the creation of an entire family!

A Picture of Holiday Unity

At a fundraising event, a well-dressed woman politely pulled me aside to tell me her story. "Growing up, my family life was disjointed and dysfunctional. Nobody ever really got along. The holidays were always a dreadful time until one Thanksgiving, my brother brought Pictionary. The entire family played together. Kids, parents, grandparents—we were all able to get along. Everything was forgotten and, in those moments, we were a happy, loving family." She gave me a beautiful smile and added, "I want to thank you for the positive holiday memories that wouldn't have existed without Pictionary."

Solidarity by Candlelight

A friend of mine named Dasha Guilliam, who is a successful artist in California, surprised me with this story. In the early 1990s, when she lived in Russia, every night from 7:00 p.m. to 9:00 p.m., the power was turned off in her apartment complex to conserve energy. It was dark and gloomy, but the neighbors from the entire floor would gather in the common area to talk and wait out the outage.

One night, a neighbor brought out an English version of Pictionary, and everyone played by candlelight. "As we had no paper, we drew on the wall. This is how I discovered my love of art and learned how to speak English!"

Redrawing Relationships

A man at a farmer's market in Carlsbad, California, told me that if it hadn't been for Pictionary, he would never have gotten married.

"Problem was, my future in-laws didn't approve of me. They didn't really know me and wouldn't take the time to try. It put a strain on my relationship with my fiancée." But then, during the holidays, he took his game of Pictionary to his future in-laws' house. They had a great time playing the game, laughing as they cultivated a relationship.

"I teamed up with my future father-in-law," he continued, "and the best thing happened. We won! And more importantly, we bonded. He saw I was a good guy and finally took the time to get to know me. He invited us back the following week to play again. I knew I would be okay as long as I brought my Pictionary game with me."

I chuckled and joked, "Good thing they didn't have their own copy."

ACKNOWLEDGMENTS

There are countless people who have contributed to my wonderful life, and to thank each individually would fill another book. So, to you all, I send my heartfelt gratitude for having a hand in making my life more rewarding than I ever dared dreamed. I'd specifically like to thank:

The talented writers who contributed to making this book a reality: Cliff Carl, Hilary Zaid, Lisa Pelto, M. Rutledge McCall, not to mention numerous friends.

A very special thank you to my friend and mentor, Melanie Notkin, who took all these voices and made them mine. You kept me on track when I went off the rails and captured the true spirit of my story. I am indebted to you for helping me make this book something I am proud of. I couldn't have done it without you.

To the team at Amplify Publishing, Naren Aryal, Nina Spahn, Ricky Frame, Lauren Kanne, and Erin Weston, for making my impossible deadline possible and for holding my hand so deftly to pull everything together, I am grateful. The book cover design *by Semnitz* is perfect. And thanks to photographer David Tenenbaum for making me look good.

To my partners in Pictionary, words cannot convey the love and respect I have for each of you. Your contributions to the game, and my life, are immeasurable. With deep and abiding gratitude, I offer a very special thank you for taking this incredible journey with me.

To Uncle Jerome and Auntie Anne for taking a chance on your nephew's wild idea.

To Terry Langston, the best partner I could possibly have envisioned. Together we changed the world. You showed me the meaning of courage, strength and discipline. You have had a profound influence on me, my friend. You've made me a better man.

To Rich Gill, I'm glad you took a chance on us, joined our little group, and became part of the family. I trusted you to take care of my baby, and you did, with loyalty and unwavering dedication. I am forever indebted to you and I cherish our friendship.

To Gary Everson, a light for us all. Your energy and zest for life live on in my heart . . . and in a shiny blue box of paper. I miss you, dear friend.

And to Sean Curran, the "fifth Beatle," for all your tireless help in the early days. For 45 years, our friendship has endured, and through it all, you are my brother.

To quality men, my mentors: Keith Corner, Tom McGuire, and Andy Bassetti.

And to everyone who is mentioned in this book, you played an integral part in bringing Pictionary to life. On behalf of myself, and millions of fans, I thank you from the bottom of my heart.

And to my beloved siblings, Leslie, Harvey, and Jackie, I treasure and adore you. You have always been there to support and encourage me, even when it wasn't easy. I am blessed without measure to call you my family. And to Mom and Dad, who always made me feel loved. I couldn't have asked for more.

Lastly, but certainly not least, to Sam and Ben. Being your dad is the best job I have ever had. Your compassion, heart, and the way you walk through this world, inspires me every day. I love the humans you have become. It makes me so proud when you call me Dad. I love you both.

With utmost respect and gratitude,
Rob

ABOUT THE AUTHOR

Rob Angel is the creator of Pictionary, the revolutionary, number one bestselling board game in the world. 38,000,000 Pictionary games had been sold in 60 countries by the time Rob sold the game to Mattel in 2001. Rob is an entrepreneur, explorer, investor, philanthropist, and sought-after speaker on a mission to help others create their own success and best lives by taking their first small step. From running with the bulls to swimming with sharks and parachuting out of airplanes, Rob seeks out adventure and aardvarks wherever he goes. He is the proud father of Sam and Ben.

 @therobangel
robangel.com